choosing survival

choosing

Strategies for a Jewish Future

survival

Bernard Susser

Charles S. Liebman

New York   Oxford   OXFORD UNIVERSITY PRESS   1999

Oxford University Press

Oxford   New York
Athens   Auckland   Bangkok   Bogotá   Buenos Aires   Calcutta
Cape Town   Chennai   Dar es Salaam   Delhi   Florence   Hong Kong   Istanbul
Karachi   Kuala Lumpur   Madrid   Melbourne   Mexico City   Mumbai
Nairobi   Paris   São Paulo   Singapore   Taipei   Tokyo   Toronto   Warsaw
and associated companies in
Berlin   Ibadan

Published by Oxford University Press, Inc.
198 Madison Avenue, New York, NY 10016

Oxford is a registered trademark of Oxford University Press

Library of Congress Cataloging-in-Publication Data
Susser, Bernard, 1942–
Choosing survival: strategies for a Jewish future /
Bernard Susser, Charles S. Liebman.
p.   cm.
Includes bibliographical references and index.
ISBN 0–19–512745–5
1. Jews—United States—Identity.
2. Jews—United States—Identity—Forecasting.
3. Judaism—United States.
4. Judaism—United States—Forecasting.
5. Jews—Israel—Identity.
6. Jews—Israel—Identity—Forecasting.
7. Judaism—Israel.
8. Judaism—Israel—Forecasting.
I. Liebman, Charles S.   II. Title.
E184.36.E85S87   1999
305.892'4073—dc21   98–29932

1 3 5 7 9 8 6 4 2
Printed in the United States of America
on acid-free paper

To Berel, Chaim, Danny, Howie, Jackie, Jay, and Lewis,
who understand even if they don't agree

and to
Talya and Ariella

contents

preface ────────────────────────────────

*T*his book began as an attempt by Susser to explore his own checkered relationship with the Jewish religious tradition. It was a difficult, often painful exploration that sought, in the very modern style, to exorcise devils by confronting them head on. But the going was slow and the results were disappointing. More and more he became convinced that it was a self-indulgent, overly personal project. The text suffered from the kind of luxuriating in oneself that is the hallmark of the contemporary "therapy culture."

The pivotal moment arrived when Susser's wife, after having read part of the text, played an invisible, sentimental violin to express her displeasure. Then and there he decided to give the project a rest for a full month. In that time, he reasoned, either the solution to the problem would suggest itself, or, if not, he would sadly return to the publisher and say, "Sorry, I can't do it."

As it happened, salvation arrived not in the form of an idea but in the person of Charles Liebman. While Susser is a political theorist by trade, Liebman's expertise lies squarely in the area the book was to explore. Indeed, in the background reading that Susser had done in preparation for the book, Liebman's work was quite central. Having been friends and colleagues for many years, they also found an effortlessness in communication between them. They had, in fact, carried on a dialogue on these very issues for many years—a dialogue that could be adverted to with only short cues and almost imperceptible hints. Liebman agreed to join the project.

The work that Susser had done previously was condensed and edited; it survives in his "Personal Prologue" and in the chapter on the ideology of affliction. Thereafter, the method of dual authorship was handled in the following way: After a brief discussion related to what should be included in the chapter to be written, Liebman would prepare an abbreviated draft. Susser would use both this and other materials to write the full-length chapter. This method worked remarkably well. When there were differences— and inevitably there were some—they were talked out until agreement could be reached.

Until quite recently Jewish identity was built around the image of Jews as the perennial victims, the unique objects of Gentile hostility—what we speak of as the "ideology of affliction." For much of Jewish history, the model fit rather well with the reality that Jews confronted. Their all-too-regular travails reinforced the sense that Jews had of their special status in the eyes of God.

This study asks what happens to Jews—in the United States and Israel— when such views are no longer credible. Some Jews, the study finds, persist in clinging to the adversity idea whatever the evidence may indicate. Others develop alternate forms of Jewish identity. In the United States the alternatives have been political liberalism on the one hand and the "privatization" of Judaism on the other. Neither of these, the authors contend, are successful in transmitting or maintaining a strong sense of Jewish identity.

In Israel, the ideology of affliction has been sustained by the unremitting security threats the country confronts. The image of Israel's being threatened, as of old, by a wicked world, created a deep-seated reluctance to trust the "enemy." Nevertheless, there has been a relative decline in the ideology of affliction—certainly in more educated and affluent circles. Yet, whatever threat to Jewish identity this decline posed, it has been offset by the fact that Jewishness is integral to the very fabric of Israeli culture. Sadly, however, it has led to trivialization of Jewishness.

Clearly, many features of Orthodoxy render it unacceptable to the vast majority of modern Jews. Still, if Jewishness is to survive and flourish as a distinct cultural identity, Jews need to learn from the Orthodox how to adopt a critical posture toward their surrounding culture. Like the Orthodox, modern Jews would do well to concentrate their efforts on developing the rich elements within the tradition, elements that are independent of the ideology of affliction and which encourage selective resistance to and critical evaluation of the regnant Western culture in which they find themselves.

This is not a standard academic work. Although there are many footnotes relating to the literature, this is first and foremost a reflective book that draws upon the accumulated experiences, professional learning, and (inevitably) the considered opinions of the authors. It will have succeeded if it serves to focus the often confused and polemical attitudes that dominate the Jewish Survival debate.

choosing survival

prologue

by Bernard Susser

Although it is doubtless a composite of many separate memories, the image is vivid and powerful. The rabbi/teacher is striding back and forth in front of the classroom. His forehead is furrowed in concentration and he is holding forth. He speaks a breathless, inelegant, ungrammatical Yiddish-English, and yet his sincerity and passion are unmistakable. He speaks as one who bears witness to a great truth, a truth he projects with all his powers to his rapt young listeners.

> The Phoenicians, the Assyrians, the Babylonians, the Hittites, the Philistines—where are they today? Gone! Not a living trace remains of their cultures, their faiths or their civilizations. They are of inter-est only to museums and scholars. They lacked the faith and resolve to sustain themselves and history passed its categorical judgement upon them and their civilizations.
>
> Of all the peoples that flourished in the ancient world, only the Jews remain. They and only they successfully withstood the ordeals of time. They triumphed over expulsion, exile, inquisitions, pogroms, fiendish oppression, even attempts at genocide. But Jewish survival is not pre-dominantly physical. Their prodigious achieve-ment is fully appreciated only when it is understood that the Jewish faith continues to be as alive and viable today as it was three thou-sand years ago. Thousands of generations have successfully trans-mitted the message to their offspring, often in the direst of conditions. When we fast on Yom Kippur or refrain from eating bread on Passover, we are part of an unbroken chain whose innumer-able individual links go back directly to Sinai. In the most heteroge-neous circumstances—from the deserts of the Middle East, to the great urban centers of America and Europe—the same Torah has been studied, the same *mitzvot* have been performed, the same faith has been affirmed. It is a record without historical parallel.

The rabbi intended two lessons to be learned from this historical homily. First, that the Jews are an eternal people whose very survival attests to the miraculous intervention of the Hand of God. Only the Divine Covenant to eternally preserve His chosen people can account for millennia of survival in the face of impossible historical odds. How else can this extraordinary historical odyssey be explained?

The second message was admonitory, a cautionary tale directed at the young who would soon face the seductions of the modern world. The decision to break the chain was neither an individual one nor to be casually made. A single broken link meant that the sacrifices of centuries would be repudiated and made to count for naught. A snapped link signified the abrupt end of one irreplaceable strand of the chain. What others had died to uphold, just so that it could be passed on to the likes of those sitting in this classroom, would be cast aside, their sacrifices dishonored. The tradition was a trust that each Jew received in order to pass on. Failing to discharge one's trust was nothing short of treason against Jewish history.

I heard this warning dozens of times in my youth. Its effect was intense because it was repeated both at home and in school. At home it took on a particularly charged and ominous quality because the agonies and grief were not abstractions out of history books. The Holocaust was the unspoken presence of my young years. Although my father managed to escape the European inferno just in time, many of his close family members and friends did not. My grandparents had perished. They were to follow my father to America but, as fate would have it, when the time came, their exit was blocked. Instead, they fled eastward to Poland where other family members took them in. They found their death in a Polish field together with hundreds of others, shot after digging their own graves. My father vehemently refused to satisfy my youthful curiosity about the details surrounding his parent's death—talking about "those years," as he called them, was unbearably painful for him. Once, however, when I was particularly persistent, he blurted out, "I don't know how they died, but I am certain that their last words were *Shma Yisrael* ("Hear, O Israel")."

There is a picture of my grandfather—virtually the only one we have—and it constitutes a kind of centerpiece of my young adulthood. My father's brother had come to visit from Israel, to which he had emigrated in the early thirties. The two long-separated brothers sat at the kitchen table of our Brooklyn apartment and spoke in hushed tones of "those years." I sat silently, too young at the age of sixteen to make any contribution to an adult conversation of this kind. They returned again and again to the subject of their father, to his dignified demeanor, to his robust physique, to his long red beard. "Die Kinder," my uncle said darkly, "will never know what he looked like." At this point my father stirred as a sudden memory flooded his thoughts. He reminded my uncle of a photo of their father that had appeared in the newspaper in the mid-thirties. In *Der Sturmer* no less. A group of Nazi thugs had seen this proud-looking Jew drinking the mineral water of a

German spa and photographed him. (Afterward he was beaten up and his beard pulled out with pliers.)

The next morning my father and uncle were off to the forty-second Street Library hoping to track the picture down. Although they went through the Nazi tabloid page by page, they could not find the photograph. The librarian to whom they turned said that there was also a weekend edition of *Der Sturmer* but it was available only in the Library of Congress. They left for Washington the next morning and returned the following day with the picture.

It shows my grandfather at about the age of fifty, with a mug in his hand standing in profile against a crowd of spa visitors. He wears a large, full-brimmed black hat of the kind that are common in ultra-Orthodox neighborhoods in New York and elsewhere. His beard is already gray. There is something imposing about his carriage—as a teenager, I could not dissociate this dignity from the chain linking him through the generations back to Sinai. Knowing the tragic fate that befell him only made this association more intense. I heard his *"Shma Yisrael"* as a direct call to me, his grandson, to accept and cherish the Jewish trust that I, as an adult, would one day receive. These achingly powerful thoughts rendered the photo's caption all the more monstrous. It read, in Gothic German letters: "Profiteering and Talmudic intrigues make the Jews wealthy. When they become ill through laziness and high living, they come to the German spas to drink the waters and regain their health."

I tell this tale as one who has "broken the chain." Certainly my father and grandfather would count my break with religious Judaism as a mutiny against the historical trust I should have accepted. They would, no doubt, point to the extensive Yeshiva education I had received, to the years when Talmudic study was my central vocation, to the deep awe at Jewish learning that persists even now. At one point in young adulthood, there was not very much that separated me from being ordained into the Rabbinate. This then was no ordinary chain-breaking. It was not, for example, comparable to the indifference and ignorance that underlies most of contemporary American Jewish assimilation. I needed to fight myself loose of ideas and practices that informed my identity down to its very roots. This was a conscious insurrection, treason aforethought.

I count the more than ten years it took for this transformation to take place neither as a heady liberation from obscurantism nor as a tragic loss of faith, the two modes in which tales of "a faith lost" are usually told. There was nothing exhilarating about it because forsaking the world of belief, of cohesive community, and of commanding moral compulsions was often a wrenching personal ordeal that I cannot, even now, remember without wincing. Neither is the "tragic loss of faith" genre appropriate because in place of one faith another commitment opened before me: dedication to the world of academia. I learned of its intellectual grandeur and slowly adapted myself to its modes of speech, dress, and behavior. I consciously repressed the Yeshiva style of argumentation that is so much more physical, impatient, unrestrained, and direct, and became reasonably adept at "passing" academically. Surviving my first academic cocktail party without major mishap was a formidable rite of passage.

Whatever the idiosyncratic mix of biographical, intellectual, and social factors that went into my change of life-course, they did not take place overnight. (Having undergone this painful process day by day, I am suspicious of those sudden conversions that are supposedly accomplished in a single moment of epiphany.) These difficult years matured into the recognition that one form of Jewish life—the traditional Orthodox—had become impossible for me to accept and follow. Years of cultural migration ensued. And they posed the question with which I have been wrestling ever since: Having broken the chain, is there any way of forging new kinds of Jewish links that can take the place of the Orthodox Judaism I abandoned? Can Jewishness be reconstructed to be more than ethnic nostalgia? Can it be suffused with life-giving meaning, even if it is not the meaning that moved my father and grandfather? Does the historical insurrection of modernity necessarily entail the slow extinction of Jewish civilization? After Orthodoxy, what?

The obvious answers to these questions were for me the wrong ones. Obvious answers divide into two basic categories. One has the rebel rejecting the Jewish context altogether—most commonly by searching for redemption in a pluralist cosmopolitan vision of humanity unfettered by tribal or national boundaries. The other has him or her latching on to the more "progressive" forms of Jewish belief and practice such as Conservative and Reform Judaism. Neither of these has had any real attraction for me. My Jewish roots were too deep to be replaced by undifferentiated universalism; they were too intense to accept the more relaxed attitudes characteristic of so many non-Orthodox Jews. What remained for me was a form of ambiguous, tension-filled Jewish identity best described as "post-Orthodoxy."

Post-Orthodoxy shows up nowhere in the many available surveys of Jewish states of belief. Indeed, I realize that there is even a humorous, almost spoofing quality that clings to the term. My generalizations about it are, therefore, necessarily impressionistic and speculative. Among the requisite characteristics of membership in the post-Orthodox category seem to be a substantial Jewish education, in other words, being reasonably conversant with the classical Jewish tradition. In addition, there is a powerful love-hate relation with Orthodoxy that colors one's attitudes toward other

Jewish alternatives. Third, the inability to accept simple secular alternatives to the religious life. Because the emotional and spiritual imprint of Orthodoxy are so very deep, the readily available forms of the secularism that dominates the West are found to be wanting. In short, post-Orthodoxy entails being stranded Jewishly: One is too skeptical to believe, yet too committed to leave.

For those who find themselves in this marooned category of Jewish identity, all manner of curious compromises are evolved. One friend dons tefillin (phylacteries) daily and prays devoutly although he observes inconsistently and believes even less. (He quips that in the argument between the believers and the atheists, the atheists are right—"but it's only on a technicality.") Another refuses to fast on Yom Kippur but complains that when he enters the shul (so that his children at least be "exposed") and hears the *Shaliach Tzibur* (the prayer leader) singing *"hinini he'ani me'ma'as,"* he is forced to beat a quick retreat lest the profound emotions of the past overwhelm him. Still another—a distinguished and highly polished academic—admits that when he sits alone and writes, he finds himself swaying back and forth and intoning the words he types in the yeshiva-style sing-song.

Post-Orthodoxy is, of course, a fictional category. There are no Jewish institutions that answer to this name. It is, as I suggested, the "home" of the Jewishly homeless. Even though the Orthodox world can still inspire the post-Orthodox, it obviously cannot provide a home for them. For the post-Orthodox, Conservative and Reform Judaism fail not so much because of their "enlightened" theological doctrines, which are sometimes rather congenial, but because of what appears from the Orthodox perspective to be a lesser form of religiosity. Conservative and Reform synagogues, as they appeared to me during those difficult years of transition, were assemblages of Jewishly lukewarm individuals whose decorous services were very far from the religious intensity I had known in the Yeshiva. The post-Orthodox often participate in Conservative and Reform services—in fact, their "synagogue skills" are often highly valued—but clearly this cannot be their home.

Usually it is in the secular world that they lead their day-to-day lives. This is also the world in which they raise their children. (And to their great dismay watch them grow up regarding Jewishness and Judaism in much the same way as any other modern secular person would.) Nevertheless, secularism too can be only a makeshift dwelling rather than a real home. For the indelible memories of religious passion intrude upon the scientific/naturalistic accounts that are the stuff of secular discourse. Although the post-Orthodox are particularly expert at puncturing the religious contentions of the Orthodox, they are, for all that, not entirely comfortable with their own arguments.

Because of their systematic marginality, the post-Orthodox have the remarkable quality of being proficient at virtually all forms of Jewishness. To be universally marginal is also to be universally adept. Not belonging in any one specific place means being available to them all—particularly when the search for a viable Jewish identity leads one to pursue every avenue that offers itself as "the way." Thus a post-Orthodox Jew can feel adept in a *shtiebl* (store-front synagogue) in Borough Park or B'nei Brak, in a *Shomer HaTzair* (radical socialist) kibbutz, in a Reform Temple in San Diego, in a bohemian-mystical Havura, on the UJA speaking circuit, in the night life of Tel Aviv, among Israeli politicians, and in WASPY, secular academic surroundings.

In many different senses, the author has lived in the vortex of contemporary Jewish life, experiencing a great many of its variants first-hand. Still, I do not wish to claim that such a multifaceted perspective provides a privileged point of view. (Modernism has dripped too much of its corrosive distrust into my mind to accept such self-serving positions.) Neither do I wish to arrogate the mantle of social science. I have conducted no new surveys nor do I present any startling new data.

What I hope, though, is that the confrontation between the contemporary Jewish scene and a troubled, atypical, post-Orthodox observer would at least issue in reasonably interesting ideas. This, then, is not a book written by an academic student of contemporary Jewish life. (My own academic interests lie elsewhere.) In taking on this project, I consciously took leave of the specialist's expertise and of the professional's authority. It is the book of a post-Orthodox Jew who has not found his place in the Jewish world—and not for the lack of effort.

Some twenty-five years ago, this Jewish restlessness brought me to Israel. Zionism and a Jewish state, I had hoped, would resolve the problem that the American Diaspora had left unanswered. Israel, after all, was a total Jewish civilization, and here, Jewishness could flourish even when religiosity was wanting.

This expectation was hardly unique. It was, in fact, central to the Zionist vision. Zionism, in virtually all of its forms, understood a sovereign Jewish state as *the* answer to the problem of Jewish identity in the modern world. The loss of spiritual direction and the ambivalence toward Jewish existence that created such anxiety in the Diaspora would no longer constitute a problem in comprehensively Jewish surroundings. An autonomous Jewish people living by its own lights in its own territory with its own language, national economy, and public culture was, in itself, the definitive resolution to the Jewish problem. This was the "normalization" that Zionism longed for so intensely. In such "normal" conditions Jewish self-understanding would cease to be a charged dilemma. What it was to be a Jew, like what it was to be a Frenchman, was nothing other than what Jews did in the Jewish state.

This has not been my experience. Having lived the greater part of my adult life in Israel, I remain unconvinced by this, Zionism's central contention. Despite a certain relaxation in the Jewish angst of the Diaspora, I soon came to the depressing conclusion that Israel does not solve the Jewish problem so much as pose it anew and in a profoundly acute form. The question of Jewish survival in Israel is not, therefore, the illogical issue it appears at first hearing.

Clearly then, my own pursuit of a meaningful Jewish alternative is never far from the book's surface. Much of the study that follows attempts to systematize and focus the wild-grown impressions that have been stored in great disorder as I confronted the Jewish options abounding in the modern world. Nevertheless, the confessional tone that has predominated to this point is dispensed with in the upcoming text; a more impersonal, analytical perspective takes over. But I want to alert my readers lest they mistake the relatively dispassionate register for a lack of passion. This book would not have been written but for an intense uneasiness about the future of Jews, Jewishness, and Judaism.

prologue
by Charles Liebman

My field of academic interest, unlike that of my co-author, is contemporary Jews and Judaism. For over thirty years I have explored questions in which I was vitally interested. In many cases I was passionately committed to a particular position. And yet I never felt that that commitment biased the manner in which I presented evidence or analyzed the issues. I was always confident in my ability to distance myself from my own point of view and was surprised by the inability of so many, including my fellow academics, to do so themselves. But I have never written on a topic in which I was unable to identify, at least hypothetically, with the various subjects and their differing points of view. I was always able to put myself in the place of whomever it was I was writing about.

I did this before I discovered that that was Max Weber's prescription for social science and, I would guess, humanistic research in general. If the researcher can understand his subject's point of view well enough to reconstruct the internal world in which he moves and thinks, he can ask himself how the subject would respond to problems or situations in which data is absent.

I have, to be sure, eschewed researching a few topics of Jewish concern because I was unable and had no interest in transposing myself into the roles of all the parties involved. But these were rare. Indeed, I often took perverse delight in the presentation of positions with which I was totally at variance. But I must admit that I find it increasingly difficult to do so. I am becoming increasingly cranky, probably a sign of age. The manuscript that follows, therefore, may be my last effort to undertake a fair and serious presentation of positions I find unpalatable. I hope I have succeeded. I will try to let the reader test me by offering some critical information about my own life and the value directions in which it has led me.

Two years after my first academic appointment I realized that what interested me was Jews and Judaism and not public administration and urban politics, the areas in which I wrote my dissertation and began my research and teaching. Since then I have written ten books and over seventy articles.

My belief that one can feel involved in an event or a controversy and yet disassociate one's own point of view from the analysis of that event or controversy is surely connected to a larger conviction: that reality exists independently of the observer and that morality exists independently of context. There is, in other words, absolute truth, which means there is absolute falsity, and there is absolute right and absolute good, which means there is absolute wrong and absolute evil. This may seem self-evident to the reader, if he or she does not find the moods of the contemporary intellectuals persuasive or is not overly engaged in the debates over post-modernism. But it is a matter that exercises academia, that lies at the heart of most of the current controversy in a good many areas of the social sciences and humanities, and, as we shall see, is really basic to much of the controversy over contemporary Judaism and Israel. I also believe that the successful resolution of this controversy is critical to the future of Judaism because there can be no religion or even community and nation without the sense of an independent moral power that renders the religion or the community worthwhile in more than a trivially subjective sense.

In 1969 my wife and children and I moved to Israel. We "made" aliya is the awkward terminology used by English-speaking Jews. As I have written elsewhere, I did not move to Israel because I thought that Jewish group survival in the United States was becoming untenable, nor did I believe that my own family had no Jewish future in the United States.

It is often difficult to understand the deeper underlying reasons for important decisions that change one's life. The decision to move to Israel was made by my wife and myself, which further complicates the analysis of causes. But to the best of my memory, the single most important reason for the decision was my feeling that Israel was a better place to give my children the kind of Jewish education I wanted them to have. I had no doubts, then or now, that the only adequate form of Jewish education, allowing for exceptions in a few areas of the United States, is the Orthodox Jewish day school. But I was afraid that the Orthodox Jewish day school in the United States offered inadequate exposure to the full gamut of Jewish culture, and it was this exposure that I sought for my children.

These feelings were a consequence of my own background. I was raised in a very traditional Conservative synagogue in Brooklyn, New York, where I lived until I was fourteen. The home in which I was raised was intensely Zionistic. Indeed, I was thirteen at the time the State of Israel was established, and my father was employed by the Zionist Organzation of America. At the age of fourteen and with my father's encouragement I attended high school in Israel for three years, and I retained warm memories of the rich Jewish education I received there. That was the kind of education I wanted for my children and this constituted the major factor in my desire to "make" aliya.

However, a more personal and emotional factor also stands out in my memory. In 1966 my wife and I decided to visit Israel and explore the possibilities of aliya. She had never been there, and I did not feel comfortable in deciding on aliya before she had some familiarity with the country. We chose to travel there the following year. I was holding plane tickets for late June when the Six-Day War erupted. I mention this as evidence that the question of our aliya was already on the table before June 1967.

But the war taught me, as it did others, how deeply we felt about Israel. I, of course, had no knowledge of how quick and decisive Israel's military victory would be. In fact, I was not at all sure that Israel would emerge victorious. And the "false" reports in the American media of the bombing of Tel Aviv led me to the conclusion that regardless of the outcome, the cost in human life would be enormous.

At that moment in my life, I was sitting in my office at Yeshiva University. I recall the intense feeling that if the Jews of Israel were to die, I wanted to die as well. I then realized that if my own sense of destiny was so closely linked to that of the Jews in Israel, I might as well be living there. I confess that the intensity of these emotions has, over time, dampened somewhat.

Since making aliya, I have been back and forth to the United States a few times each year. Often I have been back for extended periods. I have served as visiting professor for a semester or more in seven universities in the United States, mostly in departments of religion or of Jewish studies. At one point I was in the United States for three years. I have continued to read and write about American Jews. Consequently, I do not feel that I am more of an Israeli Jew than I am an American Jew. The flip side, of course, is that I feel equally distant from both Israeli and American Jewish society.

Religiously speaking, I have never felt more comfortable in my life than I did at the Jewish Theological Seminary where, on leave from Bar-Ilan University, I taught from 1976 to 1979. Gerson Cohen was then chancellor, but the fight over the ordination of women was just beginning and the religious atmosphere then was very different from what prevails today.

Despite my Conservative upbringing and my three years at JTS, I have lived the better part of my life within the Orthodox community. I am not Orthodox. I simply do not believe and have never believed that which an Orthodox Jew is called upon to believe—even though, I confess, I tried for a couple of years to do so. My wife and two of my three children are Orthodox, so it would be difficult for me to separate myself from the Orthodox community even if I should wish to do so. In Israel I find myself very sympathetic with the Conservative (Masorati) movement, and if there were a Conservative synagogue in my neighborhood I would surely join.

A few years ago, while at New York University on sabbatical, a department colleague, the medieval scholar Alfred Ivry, invited me to attend his Orthodox synagogue with him. I was surprised by the invitation since I did not think Ivry was Orthodox. I asked him whether he was. He paused for a moment and replied, "I'm not Orthodox, I'm philo-Orthodox." I loved that description and have adopted it as my own. I imagine there are quite a few philo-Orthodox among the constituents of today's modern Orthodox synagogues in the United States. That is less true in Israel, and that is another topic that will engage us in this book.

So, if the reader insists, against my better judgment, in assessing this book in light of my values, I hope I have provided the necessary background.

three ———— ## the ideology of affliction
Can Jews Survive the End of the Siege?

A Jew walks along the streets of Minsk (or was it
Pinsk?). A bird overhead relieves itself right on his
head. He looks up plaintively and says: *"Far de goyim
zingen zey"* (For the goyim they sing).

"*A* stiff-necked people," God called the Jews. They refused to bow to
the discipline He imposed upon them. They defied His word and
rebelled against His will. A stubborn waywardness subverted their calling
as the chosen people. They were fickle in their commitments, easily dis-
tracted from their responsibilities, and of frustratingly short memory.

In a bitter terminological twist, this same obduracy became, in pre-mod-
ern Christian civilization, the identifying mark of Jewish inconvertibility.
They were "stiff-necked" in being so unswervingly committed to their
anachronistic faith that they refused to accept Christian truths, manifest
and indisputable though they were. The tenacity of Jewish existence in the
face of impossible odds represented a grievous affront to the Church triumphant. The Jews were, in fact, that historically recalcitrant object whose
very continued existence witnessed the world's as yet unredeemed state.
Weighty theological consequences were drawn from this obstinacy. It was
said that the eventual conversion of the Jews would be the sign of the imminent Second Coming of Christ.

Whatever the arguments presented to them and however lethal the physical pressures directed against them, they refused to budge. Although victim-
ized, powerless, and at the mercy of others, Jews overwhelmingly chose
loyalty to their faith over the more expedient alternatives. At the point of an
unsheathed sword many cried "*Shma Yisrael*" and perished rather than abandon the faith of their fathers. They endured despite bloody pogroms, crusades, blood libels, mass expulsions, and the unspeakable horrors of the
Inquisition. Their historical resolve seemed to grow with the persecution
they suffered. The book of *Exodus* (I, 12) tells us of the Jewish slaves in
Egypt: "As they were persecuted, so they thrived." Wandering from land to
land, from one temporary haven to another, they brought with them (and
later often left with) little but their Jewish learning and their age-old faith.
(Botanists noted this remarkable fortitude by colloquially designating one of
the hardiest plants "the wandering Jew.") Even those Spanish Jews (the

"Marranos" or "swine," as Christians referred to them) who lacked the extraordinary courage to accept death rather than conversion, would often defy the edicts and continue to observe the Jewish commandments in secret.

In Jewish lore, this obstinacy and the fearful price of suffering it exacted are everywhere in evidence. In the words of perhaps the best known Yiddish folk song, "*Oif'n Pripichik*" (On the Oven), it is told of the *rabbi*, or teacher, who, in a warm and comfortable room, intones the Aleph-Bet, the Hebrew alphabet, to his very young students. He asks that they, his dear children, repeat the letters again and again and yet once again. But then in the second verse, he whispers to them plaintively: "When you, young children, come of age, you will understand, how many tears are soaked into these letters, how much weeping suffuses them." But then, as if to banish any thought of resignation or faltering, the wistful mood of this dark aside is rejected and followed directly by a spirited call to the students to repeat again and again and yet once again the sounds of the Aleph-Bet they are learning.

Another well-known Yiddish folk song, "*Eili Eili*" (My God, My God), cries out: "My God, my God why have you forsaken me? In blazing fires they burned us, everywhere they humiliated and scorned us, but they could never turn us away from You, my God, from Your holy Torah, and from your commandments." "Night and day," the second stanza resumes, "I think only of you my God. I observe with awe your Torah and commandments. Oh deliver me, deliver me from danger and from wicked decree as you did of old. Hear my prayer and my weeping, for only You God can rescue me." The lyrics end with a tragic cry that is inexpressibly defiant and resolute: "*Shma Yisrael Adonai Elohenu Adonai Echad!*" (Hear, O Israel, the Lord is Our God, the Lord is one!)

On the solemn and melancholy fast day of Tish'a B'av, Jews doff their shoes, sit on the floor like mourners, and, often to the trembling light of candles, recount tales of the abounding tragedies that have befallen the Jewish people throughout the centuries. But the gallery of martyred heroines and heroes is not paraded before the worshipers in order to rouse hatred toward the persecutors or even pity for their victims. This exercise in memory is essentially an exercise in steadfastness, in steeling the Jewish will. Every generation, the prayers imply, will have its trial. Our faith will be tested in ways that are various and devilishly inventive. In one age it will be the point of the sword, in another it will be the fleshpots of Egypt, in yet another it will be the seductions of wealth and power. We are to take our lessons from these heroic victims. They perished tragically, but in their martyrdoms they passed on to us, the surviving Jewish community, the charge of vindicating their sacrifice by clinging all the more tenaciously to the tenets of our faith. The persecutors are long gone, their civilizations often forgotten; but we, the eternal Jewish people, weep and persevere.

Hanukkah is the most fortunate of Jewish holidays. Although relatively minor, it has developed into one of the most widely celebrated of Jewish festivals. In America, it is the Jewish answer to Christmas; for Israelis, it celebrates Jewish military defiance of foreign adversaries. How different was its original intent and how ironic the transformations it has undergone!

Hanukkah is the holiday that celebrates Jewish separatism and exalts Judaism's anti-assimilationist core. In an important sense, Mattithias and the Maccabees were the *haredim* (ultra-Orthodox) of their day. They deplored the Hellenizing influences that were subverting the Jewish faith. The Jews, they warned, were becoming too much like their non-Jewish neighbors. They were studying Greek philosophy, dressing and living like Greeks, forsaking their Jewish identity for a cosmopolitan existence that was urbane rather than nationally rooted. Mattithias's ringing declaration— "He who is for God, follow me"—is the call of an embattled Jew. It demands that a choice be made between Judaism and the world of another culture, between steadfastness and assimilation. Being a Jew is not a casual commitment but a demanding, full-time occupation. Seductive though it may be, "synthesis," or the blending of Judaism with foreign cultures, is dangerous, perhaps even deadly. For hundreds of generations this was, with some notable exceptions, the accepted and conventional self-understanding of a beleaguered but enduring people.

But then, roughly 250 years ago, the great survivors began to succumb. Nothing like it had ever happened before. Vast defections from the tradition, often leading to outright assimilation, became the rule rather than the exception. No new tortures had been devised to break the Jewish will. If anything, Jewish physical security was improving overall. Neither had Jewish learning faltered. Some of the most brilliant traditional Jewish scholarship dates from this period.

Although there were some very important social and economic issues involved in the defection from tradition, our concern here is with the intellectual challenges that buffeted the Jewish tradition. What cracked the hitherto impenetrable walls of Jewishness was a suggestive cluster of ideas spoken of collectively as the Enlightenment and the attendant changes in the social and economic conditions of a limited stratum of Jews. After centuries of direct and brutal Christian assault on Jewish resolve, what succeeded in infiltrating the Jewish heart was an abstract philosophical doctrine only tangentially related to the Jews as a people and as a faith. Initially, the Enlightenment's effect on the Jews, particularly the great mass of Jews living in the Pale of Settlement (the area that today joins Poland, Lithuania, the Ukraine, and Russia), was negligible. Although the Jews would eventually become among the most enthusiastic proponents of "enlightenment," for them the "age of reason" would not arrive until considerably later. One might say that the Middle Ages lasted a century and half longer for these Jews than for many other European peoples.

But the ferment of change was implacable. Ideas infiltrated and left their imprint where crusades and pogroms had previously failed to gain entrance. Despite the profound opposition of rabbinic and lay authorities, the familiar world of Judaism was inundated by unheard-of heresies and by a shocking irreverence for tradition. Gradually, the intellectual disquiet that began in the larger urban centers of West and Central Europe migrated osmotically across the continent. By the late nineteenth century pitched battles between the progressives and traditionalists were fought throughout the entire European Jewish world. Even remote shtetls deep in the Pale of Settlement had their village *Maskil* ("enlightened one"), their share of secularists, socialists, anarchists, Zionists, and other black sheep of modernity.

The modernist spirit swept through the Jewish world leaving virtually nothing as it was. It awakened unprecedented political enthusiasms: dreams of social justice, of national independence, of a return to nature and poetry, even of a new secularly understood conception of Jewishness. In the short space of a few generations, the age-old hegemony of the rabbis and of the tradition was broadly challenged by overtly seditious ideas that had a compelling attraction for many of the young. The tales of Yeshiva students who hid a revolutionary pamphlet or a volume of poetry behind the large Talmudic tractate they were ostensibly studying can still be heard in the Yeshiva world today.

Even those who remained loyal to the status quo ante underwent wrenching changes. They needed to dig in their heels against the opposition, whereas previously their authority had been unchallenged. They were compelled to expressly formulate and defend their position; in the past there was no need to justify what was the only Jewish way of life. They were designated "Orthodox" when previously they had merely been Jews.

But Jews did not only join the bandwagon of secularism and modernization; in many important ways they led it. We only repeat a truism by saying that Marx, Freud, and Einstein form the central triad of modern consciousness. Probably not since tiny Athens gave us Socrates, Plato, and Aristotle in three successive generations has there been such a concentrated flowering of intellect deriving from so narrow a source. An outcast people comprising a negligible fraction of the European population stands at the crossroads of modern culture, defining its agenda and directing its course. And it must not be forgotten that each of these Jewish modernists was, in generational terms, barely removed from strict orthodoxy, in some cases even descended from distinguished rabbinical forebears.

From a people of martyrs for their separatist religious faith came the great prophets of secularism; from a people whose beliefs were unshakable came the most radical advocates of intellectual and moral relativism; from an organically consolidated people that remained steadfast in the face of unspeakable horrors came the most zealous advocates of universalism and assimilation. In the course of two and half centuries, Jewish life was quite literally turned inside-out. How curious that the credo of very many contemporary Jews is exactly opposite to what their forebears believed prior to the modernist deluge!

It is an irony that does not cease to fascinate: When pogroms and crusades carried out their tortures and murders, Jewish resolve never slackened, but when the allures of enlightenment were in the air, Jews tripped over each other to be first and loudest on the side of modernity. Jews fearlessly resisted brutal Christian assaults on their Jewish identity, but when they were given the opportunity, they renounced it voluntarily. If apostasy was repudiated with unparalleled courage, many embraced assimilation with hardly a second thought. Jews freely did to themselves what all their enemies could not.

How are we to account for this astounding reversal? What can explain the multitude of defections, the mass forsaking of tradition, the comprehensive reorientation of Jewish belief? Why, in short, did the Jews, history's greatest survivors, succumb to modernism so easily? Answering these questions is not simply an exercise in historical reconstruction. To understand the forces that lured Jews out of their protective isolation and thrust them headlong into the modern world is the necessary prelude to a study of Jewish survival. If we are to make sense of the Jewish future as seen from America and from Israel, this is the necessary starting point.

The simplest and oldest explanation is the "adversity thesis." Jews survived, so it is said, not despite their persecutions but because of them. It follows then that as persecution declines, we can expect a parallel decline in Jewish loyalties.

This argument was advanced more than 300 years ago by Baruch Spinoza, perhaps the first Jewish heretic of modern times.[1] There is nothing miraculous about Jewish survival, Spinoza asserted. Jewish survival and gentile antisemitism derive from the same source: the Jewish insistence on separatism. In Spinoza's own words:

> As to their continued existence for so many years when scattered and stateless, this is in no way surprising, since they have separated themselves from other nations to such a degree as to incur the hatred of all, and this not only through external rites alien to the

> rites of other nations but also through the mark of circumcision,
> which they religiously observe. That they are preserved largely
> through the hatred of other nations is demonstrated by historical
> fact . . . .[2]

Jews insulated themselves systematically from all other peoples by following practices (diet, language, rites, holidays, dress) that disciplined them toward difference. By segregating themselves from all others, they brought universal hatred upon themselves. This hatred did not imperil their national existence; on the contrary, it sustained it. First, because antisemitism kept Jews apart by blocking any exit from their pariah community, and, second, because persecution and humiliation stung a proud and ancient people into resistance and defiance. In the face of persecution, they found strength in their traditions and in each other. Jews survived because antisemitism defined them and preserved them as a people apart.

Spinoza wrote in the middle of the seventeenth century. There were then few indications that the shackles of subjugation were loosening or that Jewish loyalties were eroding. (His own defection from Rabbinic Judaism was part of no general movement or trend.) But, as if to corroborate Spinoza's thesis, when conditions did subsequently improve, Jewish resolve and cohesion relaxed. When, more than three centuries later in the closing years of the millennium, tolerance, even respect replaced adversity and persecution, the trickle of defections from Jewishness became a veritable torrent. Proponents of the adversity thesis conclude, therefore, that the fortunes of Jewish survival rise and fall with the tides of antisemitism.

Few would deny the power of this argument. It seems too well corroborated by the historical record to be rejected out of hand. It is, doubtless, the most favored explanation of those outside the committed Jewish world. From inside the Jewish ambit, however, important reservations need to be expressed. Committed Jews recoil from the ascription of Jewish perpetuity to gentile oppression rather than to Jewish belief and determination. There is something perverse and counterintuitive in contracting a remarkable intellectual and cultural tradition with three millennia of history to the status of an epiphenomenon. Not only does it trivialize the profound and original, it flies in the face of what Jews understood themselves to be doing in preserving and dying for their faith. It defies credibility to reduce a major cultural tradition to a defense mechanism or a social reflex akin to sheep huddling when the wolf approaches.

The adversity thesis, for all its shortcomings, has one virtue: It is a complete and self-enclosed explanation of Jewish survival and assimilation. The cause and the effect are symmetrical and unidirectional. It maintains, in the spirit of the old stimulus/response hypothesis, that the quality and power of Jewish commitment derive from the actions of others. If so, there is no point in pursuing the matter any further. Since Jews are what others make of them, there is no reason to enter into the logic and substance of Jewish thinking or to understand how the Jewish world understood what it was doing. Heine's play on words says it best: "*Wie es sich Christelt, so Judelt es sich*" ("As Christianity goes, so goes Judaism").

The alternative (or, more accurately, the complementary) explanation insists that the key to understanding Jewish attitudes lies in Jewish thinking itself. If commitment to Jewish survival weakens, the source must be sought in the internal push and pull of Jewish ideas. Even if it is obviously true that adversity has substantial effects on Jewish thinking, the specific way in which adversity is incorporated into and refracted through the Jewish prism must be understood in specifically Jewish terms.

Our question needs then to be reformulated: What is there in the mode and substance of Jewish thinking that creates so powerful an attraction to modernist ideas? Why did the prospect of "enlightenment" so inflame the Jewish imagination?

At the very simplest level, the Enlightenment did not involve the rejection of one's Jewish identity. As opposed to apostasy with its heavy overtones of betrayal and surrender, the program of enlightenment was presented as an authentically Jewish option, as an attempt to vindicate and reconstruct Jewish existence in a viable modern form. Its stated objective was to reform traditional Jewish life, not to abandon it. The Enlightenment could awaken such enthusiasm because it argued its case in terms that resonated deeply in the Jewish consciousness.

Initially, the message of the *Maskilim* ("enlightened ones") was not hostile to the core beliefs of the tradition. Their explicit aim was to broaden the Jewish perspective to include modern scholarship, belles lettres, and Western philosophy. They sought to open a window onto the closed Jewish world so as to expose it to the fresh social and intellectual breezes that were transforming the modern world. In all of this, they perceived themselves as rescuing Judaism from irrelevance and decrepitude. Only quite gradually did the "emancipatory" message become stridently antitraditional. Nevertheless, even at its most radical—when Jewishness was detached from Judaism entirely—the Enlightenment agenda understood itself as a legitimate and necessary step in the evolution of Jewish history.

This explains why the Enlightenment was able to avoid the contempt that rendered conversion unthinkable. It does not, however, help us with our original question: Why did the Jews respond so positively to the calls of modernization and enlightenment?

Many and varied reasons can be adduced; each adds another piece to a very complex mosaic. We make no claims to exhaustiveness. Moreover, in this highly intricate web of contributing causes, order and neatness are hard to come by. The best we can hope for is a provisional, and impressionistic account of the concerted pressures that transformed Jewish civilization from a stubbornly separatist religious enclave into one of the great catalysts of cosmopolitan modernity.

Jews were (and continue to be) an urban people par excellence. This placed them at the vortex of the modernist maelstrom. They experienced with particular intensity those forces that challenged custom and dissolved traditional loyalties. If the shtetl long resisted these pressures, in the end the intellectual disquiet that originated in the great urban centers was too powerful to resist. Jews harbored, besides, a deep respect for educational accomplishment. This rendered them especially vulnerable to the intellectual challenges that surrounded them. It was usually the allure of exciting new ideas rather than the enticements of wealth or power that prompted the original "emancipators" to shed their traditional identity, although it has been argued persuasively that in some areas economic changes, independent of ideology, played a significant role.[3] The Jewish middle and lower middle classes, striving for upward mobility, came into contact with those likely to be part of the prevailing currents of change. Social and economic success often drew in its wake exposure to modern thinking. As opposed to the poor, the uneducated, and the agrarian, these Jews found themselves at the hub of the modernist crisis.

Not only were they geographically and socially exposed to the inroads of modernity, Jews were also psychologically poised to sympathize with its message. There is something exceptionally beguiling to a persecuted minority about a vision of democratic equality and universal human fellowship. Rather than repudiating the Jewish tradition's moral earnestness, it claims to be redirecting these same energies into broader ethical channels. The invitation to join a universal human fellowship mitigates the sufferings of centuries by having the Jewish odyssey end in reconciliation and harmony. It allows concrete Jewish interests to be advanced and justified by appealing to a transcending moral ideal. How understandable then that no idea cluster, over the past 250 years, has had deeper or more lasting effects on the Jewish psyche.

Nor could the Enlightenment's emphasis on reasoning and inquiry fail to reverberate with comparable intellectual qualities in the Jewish tradition. For those already enticed by the promise of emancipation and equality, the familiar agenda of questioning, critical thinking, and progress through systematic analysis meshed with well-worn grooves of intellectual habit.

This helps to account for some of the susceptibility, the circumstantial vulnerability of the Jews to the lures of enlightenment. But what can explain the readiness to abandon their centuries-old identity so dramatically and so quickly? What transformed a virtually intact traditional Jewish world into one in which the number of traditionally observant Jews plummeted to perhaps 10 percent of their total number at the present time? To be sure, in the same space of time the Christian world also sustained major disaffections and disaffiliations, but not with the severity of those affecting the Jewish community. With the rapidity of a geometric progression, loyalty to the customary Jewish world of belief and practice contracted and then contracted more severely still. At the end of the twentieth century, books with titles such as *The End of the Jewish People?*,[4] *Saving Remnants*,[5] and *Will We Have Jewish Grandchildren?*[6] reflected the growing gloom and alarm that settled on the committed Jewish community. A major implosion had taken place; the Jewish world appeared to have caved in upon itself. It appeared to some that Jewishness could survive only as a fiercely independent closed system; even small holes in the highly pressurized form of Jewish existence spelled catastrophe.

All this is even more intriguing if we consider the unique difficulties that confronted Jews who wished to join the Enlightenment's "party of humanity." Although the ideas of the Enlightenment were subversive for all of European civilization, they presented the most radical and comprehensive challenge for those who came to them from the Jewish faith. Accepting the Enlightenment's program of universalism and equality demanded considerably greater departures from the Jewish status quo ante than it did from Christian antecedents. It was a secularized Christian world that the Jews were being asked to join. Christian civilization would henceforth be suitably declericalized in order to accommodate the universalist vision of humanity, but there would be little if any change in the language, diet, or dress of the majority. For Christians the transformation was mainly intellectual and religious; for the Jews it would need to be total. The Jewish minority and not the Christian majority would need to shed its cultural peculiarities in order to join the universal human fellowship.

There is another important sense in which the transformation demanded of the Jews was more daunting than the one that faced Christian society. Christianity always understood itself as a universalist religion. The Church was "catholic" in the original sense of the term: universal. Christianity claims to be the universal dispensation that replaces the nationally bounded idea of a "chosen people." The cosmopolitan aspirations of the Enlightenment, therefore, did not represent a departure from the basic contours of Christian thought. The belief in universal human rights, for example, did not involve a fundamental reorientation of Christian ideas. It represented the secularization of the prevailing conventional wisdom rather than its nullification.

For Jews within the confines of traditional Jewish society, however, the idea of belonging to a humanity that transcended national boundaries was problematic if not inadmissable. For as far back as Jewish historical memory extended, the Jews had been "a people dwelling apart," aspiring to be "a kingdom of priests and a holy people." Perhaps the most fundamental assumption of Jewish civilization was that the majority cultures that hosted them were not the domicile of truth. Although Jews were compelled to live alongside them, they were enjoined to remain separate and autonomous. As powerfully as all the barriers erected around them by their Gentile neighbors, the Jewish sense of a special moral calling and of a singular intellectual character blocked their assimilation into humanity at large. It was a basic article of the Jewish faith that this numerically insignificant and outcast people was the chosen bearer of God's word. To be sure, in the end of days humanity would recognize this truth and swarm repentantly to Zion; at that time, God's great design and the Jewish people's place within it would be revealed in all its glory. Until then, however, humanity was a suspect category, a source of danger, an obstacle to redemption. Relentless persecution only reenforced this conviction.

One of the greatest of Hasidic leaders, Schneur Zalman of Lyady, pondering the imminent Napoleonic invasion of Russia, remarked that if the French were victorious "riches will increase among the Jews . . . but they will be estranged from God." If, on the other hand, the Russian Tsar emerged triumphant, "the Jews will become impoverished but their hearts will be joined with God."[7] Two parallel lines are drawn: The one leads from suffering to devotion, the second from prosperity to religious degeneration.

How familiar is this motif in traditional Jewish discourse! Religiosity is at its purest and most ardent when it vindicates itself in trying circumstances. "Believing despite" ("*im kol zeh ani ma'amin*") is probably the most prevalent of historical Jewish postures. If there is a paradigmatic Jewish tale—from the Biblical Exodus onward—it is one of the embattled Jews suffering for their beliefs, resisting the pressures of a hostile world and prevailing nevertheless.

On the other hand, too much affluence or acceptance or serenity neutralizes the irritating grain that creates the religious pearl. Not surprisingly, the fleshpots of Egypt symbolize the destructive power of comfort and ease. One traditional Biblical commentator writes: "Torah and wealth flee from one another; they are as rivals to each other."[8] In a word, for religious commitment to truly flower, some form of adversity must be overcome.

Gentile hostility has been, overwhelmingly, the single most consistent—one might even say reliable—source of adversity in Jewish history. It has rarely failed to provide the calamities that necessitated ennobling sacrifice and heroism. So much so, indeed, that unremitting Gentile hostility has been both woven deeply into the fabric of Jewish folk wisdom and formalized in Jewish theology. It has, in a basic sense, insinuated itself into the very psychology of Jewish existence. The brute fact of persecution has become more than a simple historical datum; it has, over time, become an obsessive, tenacious, and pervasive mental fixture. It is not too much to say that ever since the destruction of the Second Temple and the Exile, Jewish consciousness has been built around it.

So dependable was this source of adversity that we find in Jewish religious and political discourse remarkably little interest in contemplating a world in which Gentile hostility has ceased, in which the siege had ended. What Jewish belief and practice would look like in an accommodating world where the only variable was Jewish self-discipline and religious resolve remains a virtually unbroached subject. Having passed beyond the status of a simple fact to become an integral element in the Jewish credo, the inevitability of Gentile oppression became reified, that is, transformed into a mental construct independent of its empirical referent.

One writer has commented that chroniclers of Jewish history have left the mistaken "impression that Jewish life in the Diaspora [was] uniformly and eternally plagued by the irrational, unpredictable, and all-encompassing evil of antisemitism."[9] It is certainly true that there were periods and places in which reasonably amicable relations between Jews and Gentiles prevailed. Still, historical memories often conspired to regard cordiality with suspicion, to believe, nevertheless, that it was tentative and exceptional. The internal image of Jewish life as insecure, of antisemitism as a permanent threat, and of violent onslaught as the residual condition, was so deeply entrenched in Jewish intuitions and perceptions that at least by the late medieval period it prevails even in periods of relative tranquility and prosperity.

Although the kind of lachrymose historiography[10] that portrays Jewish history as a series of unrelenting tragedies has been partially discredited, this does not mean that Jews themselves understood their condition in anything but embattled terms. That Jewish history should be stubbornly perceived as beleaguered and sorrowful even at times when this view was palpably incongruous with reality is, for our purposes, the relevant point. For example, Jewish life in Poland from the sixteenth to the eighteenth centuries may not have been as impoverished and afflicted as the stereotypes have it; there may have even been reasonably lengthy periods of security and prosperity. Still, Jewish leaders remained unswayed in their perceptions: They lived with a deep sense of insecurity and anxiousness.[11] What we are suggesting is that for them to have believed otherwise would have entailed a major revolution in Jewish theology, folk wisdom, and communal consciousness.

In the end the dominant attitude was, as the categorical rabbinic epigram puts it: "It is well known that Esau hates Jacob" (*"halakha hee k'yadua sh'Esav soneh L'Yaakov"*). Notably, when discussions of Jewish-Gentile rapprochement do take place, they almost invariably turn upon messianic deliverance. Messianic deliverance is, in fact, explicitly defined as such: the end to Jewish subjugation by the nations of the world (*shibud malkhuyot*).

Convinced of the permanence of oppression and of the illusory nature of historical reconciliations, Jewish civilization, from its most popular to its most abstruse, has insisted upon the immutability, indeed, the congenital quality of Gentile hostility. As no other element of Jewish existence, this sense of collective trauma, the feelings of anxiety and foreboding born of long and painful experience, have been faithfully passed on from generation to generation. Deeply encoded and primordial, forming a kind of collective id, they outlive the erosion of Jewish knowledge and the weakening of Jewish commitment. Even among the most assimilated, they appear to resist easy repudiation; they are perhaps the final Jewish remnants to persist when all else has been sloughed off. Many for whom Jewishness is nothing but a trivial vestige, draw the line when confronting the symbols (e.g., church and cross) of the historical oppressor. "It's not important if I'm a Jew," they seem to be saying, "but I know that I'm *not* a Christian." Many entirely marginal American Jews continue to carry within themselves this stubborn remnant: We have not forgotten persecution and we are not Christians.

This persistent sense of being a vulnerable, historically defenseless group lies behind many of the well-known paradoxes of American Jewish life. Although Jews are the most financially successful ethnic group in America (with perhaps twice the income of non-Jews), they voted, at least until the last generation, as if they were a underprivileged minority. Although the professionals report that there are virtually no areas of American life that are closed to Jews because of discrimination,[12] two-thirds of American Jews continue to believe otherwise.[13] When asked to predict how non-Jews will respond to questions measuring acceptance of Jews as equals in American society, Jews consistently and substantially overestimate Gentile aversion.[14] More piquant still: One-third of the contributors to the Jewish Federation in San Francisco expressed the belief that a Jew could not be elected to Congress from San Francisco—this at a time when (1985) all three members of Congress from the San Francisco area, the two state senators, and the mayor were Jews.[15]

Sometimes these sentiments surface in the most startling places. Erica Jong, queen of the picaresque-risqué novel, who led a generation of readers through some of the seamiest nonsectarian bedroom adventures in recent memory, devotes an essay to the subject: "How I Got to be a Jew."[16] The essay is vintage Jong: all frivolous razzle-dazzle and wise-cracking giddiness. But somehow, stuck between the leering banter and the lame one-liners, the following dead-earnest paragraph unaccountably appears:

> A Jew may wander from Egypt to Spain to Germany to America to Israel picking up different languages and hair and eye color, but nevertheless remains a Jew. And what is a Jew? A Jew is a person who is safe *nowhere* . . . . A Jew is a person who can convert to Christianity from now to Doomsday, and still be killed by Hitler if his or her mother was Jewish. This explains why Jews are likely to be obsessed with matters of identity. Our survival depends on it.[17]

There are many younger Jews in the sovereign Jewish state of Israel for whom the experience of antisemitism is theoretical and remote. Even among them the same curiously incongruous sense of being the victim of dark gentile designs erupts in the most unexpected contexts. Not far from the surface of even the most prosaic diplomatic friction between Israel and other states lurks the suspicion that all is not as meets the eye, that ancient enmities are being surreptitiously rehearsed. Perhaps a moment of reflection scatters these phantasms to the wind, but that these conditioned reflexes get past the gate-keepers of reason in the first instance says a great deal. When a referee in an international soccer or basketball game makes an ostensibly bad call against the Israeli team, some primordial string of this perennially wronged people is plucked and begins to resonate uncontrollably. In one such instance, a thoroughly secular, Westernized, sabra intellectual with whom one of the authors was watching a basketball game became so deeply agitated by the referee's call that out of some cavernous historical recollection and in the most pronounced Yiddish accent came the ultimate curse: "*Antezemitt!*" In our grandparents' generation they spoke lovingly of the "*pintele yid,*" that inexpressible center of Jewish identity they associated with love of learning and a certain fineness of the spirit— for many today, the knee-jerk memory of adversity is what it has come to.

The centrality of Gentile hostility in Jewish culture renders alternate interpretations of Jewish tradition, history, and practice difficult to sustain. And, in fact, no really adequate alternative to the view of Jewish existence as precarious, disempowered, and embattled has evolved—certainly not in the past millennium. There has been no enduring or widely accepted reading of Jewish existence in terms of Gentile acceptance. Nor, arguably, could there be such a reading that did not undermine integral parts of the Jewish emotional and intellectual constitution. What emerges for modern Jews is, therefore, a striking dissonance between the cultural assumptions of the tradition and the reality with which they are familiar. On the one hand, the tradition lacks the psychological and cognitive resources to incorporate and account for a positive, accommodating world. On the other hand, it is just such a world that Western, democratic, pluralist societies provide. Persecution as an idea has outlived persecution as a reality. And this discrepancy has created a major crisis of credibility that affects growing numbers of Jews. This is one major theme of our essay and we shall return to it on a number of occasions.

Does all of this mean that in the end Spinoza was right, that the Jews "are preserved largely through the hatred of other nations"? Our answer is a qualified No. It is not the fact of persecution per se that is critical but rather its having been Jewishly internalized and interpreted in a specific way. If Jewish resolve crumbles when the siege ends it is not so much because without adversity there is no solidarity; it is rather that having incorporated Gentile hostility deep into Jewish religious and popular perceptions there is great difficulty in reconstructing a plausible and relevant worldview when it is absent. The differences between Spinoza's view and the one we offer are, as we shall see, quite substantial.

What part do these perceptions of implacable Gentile hatred play in Jewish culture? How do they serve the Jewish religious theodicy? How do they function in the accounts that Jews give of their own remarkable survival? Some historical backtracking is clearly necessary.

Judaism, as the term is understood at present, is the creation of a rabbinic elite who, following the destruction of the Second Temple in year 70 C.E., became the undisputed arbiters of Jewish tradition. To be sure, Rabbinic Judaism had deep roots that reached far back into the Biblical period. But then again so did a variety of other radically differing interpretations of Jewish tradition that vied for ascendancy in the years preceding the destruction of the temple. The victory of Rabbinic Judaism over all its rivals determined the basic form that Judaism would take over the course of the following two millennia of Exile.

One essential element of rabbinic thought that triumphed so thoroughly that we can hardly imagine a different scenario was Judaism's character as an ethno-religion. Rather than a religion of individuals, or of humanity at large, or of smaller sub-national sects, the rabbis fused religious with ethno-national identity, creating thereby a community of faith that resists easy distinctions between religious belief and peoplehood.

Manifestly, Judaism is a system of religious beliefs: It provides an integrated program of doctrines, rites, and observances centering on the relationship between human beings and God. But it is very emphatically a religion of the communal variety, one that is concerned primarily with the bond between God and the Jewish people. Jewish history, from this perspective, reveals the working out of God's grand design. Humanity at large, although providing the context to the Jewish religious drama, is, therefore, of distinctly secondary concern. Although the patriarchs arise out of humanity at large to establish a separate Jewish existence, and although Jewish religious history culminates with the universal recognition of the God of Israel, from the moment of patriarchal separation until the moment of Messianic deliverance Jewish history is understood to be the leaven, the active ingredient in world history. What happens to the Jews, therefore, constitutes history's principle narrative—even for non-Jews.

Normative Judaism, to be very sure, is not racist. Non-Jews can convert and share both the Jewish condition and the Jewish destiny. Nevertheless, the axis about which Judaism revolves is a specific people descendent from the Patriarch Abraham, his son Isaac, and Isaac's son Jacob. Judaism is a birthright, not an acquired taste. Notably, in the Bible, the Jews are described in explicitly familial, kinship terms: They are the House of Jacob, the Children of Israel.

As an ethnic group, Jews take part in a myth of common ancestry and religious communality. In the traditional Jewish self-understanding, religiosity and ethnicity are indistinguishable. Judaism expresses and consolidates Jewish ethnic identity just as Jewish ethnicity is the context in which religiosity functions. As has so often been said by the rabbis, Jews and Judaism are related as body and soul.

Taking this analogy in a totally non-rabbinic direction we might say, however, that while the soul cannot, under any circumstances, survive without the body, the body can survive without the soul. More concretely: Whereas Jewish religiosity without ethnic identity has proven untenable (the program of classical Reform Judaism having failed), Jewish ethnicity separated from its religious qualities has proven to be remarkably hardy. Indeed, perhaps the most striking and unprecedented lesson of Jewish existence since the Enlightenment is just this: Jewish ethnicity can survive and prosper in the absence of, indeed in profound antagonism to, Jewish religion. Although Jews in earlier ages could not conceive of such a distinction, it has become entirely possible to cling to Jewish ethnicity while rejecting the religious component of Jewishness. Barring outright apostasy, Jewish ethnic/cultural bonds appear to be sufficiently enduring to maintain themselves for at least substantial periods of time. Whether they can do so indefinitely is an underlying question to which this book seeks to respond.

Questions such as these are, of course, characteristically modern. For Jews living between the destruction of the Second Temple and Exile until the Enlightenment and Emancipation, they would have been virtually unintelligible. What we speak of as a hyphenated ethno-religion was for them a seamless monolithic unity. Jews lived in their own communities, enjoying limited political autonomy and very broad cultural independence. But above all, they shared an intense sense of ethno-religious communality in which peoplehood and faith were scarcely distinguishable. It was precisely this unity—communal existence as a religious category—that sustained them in the face of intolerable realities. When confronting degradation at the hands of the gentile, discriminatory legislation, brutal pogroms, or large-scale massacres, religious faith aided them in making sense of what was a grotesquely illogical and unacceptable reality. It spoke to the question of theodicy when it was a pressing and unavoidable daily predicament. It provided the strength to rebuild after the attack, the comfort to resist despair, and the meaning to continue.

The hero of Isaac Bashevis Singer's *The Slave* is sold into slavery after a bloody massacre in which his wife and children are tortured and murdered in the seventeenth-century pogroms inflicted by Chmielnicki's Cossacks. Years later he returns to his village, dons Jewish garb, and resumes Jewish practices and learning. He finds solace in these observances. But he is nevertheless distraught. He cannot imagine that God is unjust but yet he feels cruelly treated. Certain that there is meaning but agonized by his inability to find it, he can lodge no more severe a grievance against God than the following: "I have no doubt that you are the Almighty and that whatever you do is best, but it is impossible for me to obey the commandment, Thou Shalt Love Thy God. No, I cannot, Father, not in this life."[18]

Just as their religious outlook granted them the strength to deal with adversity, so their faith reinforced the permanent fear of pogroms and expulsion in their minds. Adversity, so the tradition taught, was no passing burden; it was the unalterable Jewish destiny. Judaism both explained *and* predicted affliction as an integral part of the Divine plan. This adversity-centered paradigm permeates the Biblical narrative and has come to inform the traditional religious view of all of Jewish history. When the Jews sin, they are punished by God. God inflicts his punishment through the agency of the Gentiles. When the Jews repent and return to God, He releases them from their sufferings.

Few are the normative Jewish texts that fail to repeat this tale. Whether in Scripture, in prayer, in ethical exhortation, in rabbinic/halachic discourse, in the corpus of Jewish literature, this fundamental paradigm is variously expanded and elaborated upon. God loves the Jews; they are his chosen people. He gave to them, and only to them, His Torah and His Law. Only upon them did he place the holy obligations, the 613 commandments, that are the highest expression of His will. And because God loves the Jews, his special people, above all other people, He is especially strict and demanding with them lest they depart from His teachings. But the Jews are often not up to the high standards imposed upon them. They abandon His commandments and worship other gods. Forgetting their chosenness and singularity, they succumb to the ways of other peoples, aping their customs and adopting their values. They trample his courtyard in feigned piety, offering up bullocks and fat lambs, but their hearts are callous and obdurate. They fall prey to petty hatreds and avarice, they deceive one another, exploit the widow, the orphan, the stranger and covet what is not theirs. And for all of this, God's wrath is loosed upon them through the fury of the Gentile. In virtually every era, the Jews are struck with the force of this Divinely directed retribution, and, in the midst of their suffering, they are called upon to recognize their sinfulness and to seek forgiveness.

The opening chapters of the Book of Judges present a telling illustration of this paradigm. After the passing of Joshua, the Israelites

> did what is evil in Yahweh's eyes and served Baals. They deserted Yahweh, God of their ancestors, who brought them out of Egypt, and they followed other gods from those of the surrounding peoples . . . . Then Yahweh's anger grew hot against Israel. He handed them over to pillagers who plundered them; he delivered them to the enemies surrounding them and they were no longer able to resist their enemies.[19]

Hearing their groans under the burden of oppression, God relents and appoints judges to rescue the Israelites from their plunderers. But once again they refuse to listen, once again they abandon the path of their ancestors. "Yahweh's anger then blazed out against Israel." Not having listened to My voice, God says, the nations that Joshua left in Israel after he died will remain where they are. They will put Israel to the test: Will the Israelites cling to the paths of their ancestors or succumb to the temptations offered by their neighbors? If they resist the ways of sin and retain their purity, God will protect them. If, however, they fall under sway of their neighbors (the Biblical narrative relates that they, in fact, succumbed) then these very peoples that God has left among them will rise up to torment them.[20]

What is extraordinary about this account is that Gentile oppression, far from being a problem in the light of God's special relationship with the Jews, serves to confirm it. Gentile hostility demonstrates that Jews are privy to a special status in Divine creation. The baffling but consistent hatred of the Jew in all eras and cultures, their being singled out from among all peoples for torment and tribulation, the unparalleled magnitude of the crimes perpetrated against them, the palpable illogic in picking on this learned, upright, stubbornly committed people all serve to prove the centrality of Jewish history in the human odyssey and to verify, in Jewish eyes, how closely God's scrutiny follows them. The very fact that Jewish history abounds in extraordinary disasters justifies the conclusion that it is no ordinary history.

In persecuting God's chosen people, the Gentiles act out of unforgivable malice and enmity. They do not, of course, understand that in what they do they serve as instruments of God's grand design. Oddly, Gentiles appreciate the special status of Jews in God's eyes. It is, in fact, jealousy of this status as well as resentment of Jewish rectitude—by comparison to which they are convicted of their own deficiencies—that prompts them to lash out violently. In other words, the strange logic of Jewish chosenness plays itself out subliminally in the Gentile mind and provokes the punishing attack that is a wake-up call for repentance, and all this without conspicuous Divine intervention into the affairs of humankind.

This hidden religious drama, with the Jews cast as heroes playing at center stage, inverted the simple import of a problematic and melancholy tale. Ostensible victims were transformed into secret victors. Humiliation was transfigured into holiness and dignity. Inferior to Gentiles in power and position, Jews prove to be superior to them in their ordained destiny. Aggressive Gentiles venting their rage turn into unwitting pawns of Divine providence, while the Jews, passively bearing the blows, are cast as the true champions and movers of history. It was this turning of the tables that formed the heart of the Jewish theodicy: What appeared to be unutterably degrading and unjust was, in fact, the chronicle of Jewish redemption.

There can be little doubt that Jews found at least some emotional comfort in the remarkable turbulence and ingenious designs that surrounded their fate.[21] Still, were there no comforts apart from those available in this worldview, the burdens of Exile and suffering would have been perhaps too much, even for a Jew. Two assurances mitigated the Jewish condition. First, righteous Jews will enjoy their well-deserved reward in the world to come. In a heavenly world of truth, far removed from the mundane world of lies, justice will at last be done. The virtuous and innocent will be vindicated by God while their oppressors feel the full force of His wrath. Second, Messianic deliverance will arrive at the "end of days." At that time, Jews will be triumphantly returned to the Land of Israel, the entire world will recognize the unique mission of the people of Israel, and the God of Israel will be universally worshipped.

The conclusion is clear. Apart from its more obvious roles in ordering life cycles, providing ultimate values, and expressing spiritual needs, Jewish religiosity furnished a vindication of Jewish suffering and endowed communal travails with sublimated significance. By providing a silver lining to a very dark cloud, Judaism rendered Jewish misfortunes endurable; indeed, it construed the anguish of Jewish history as a source of pride and a harbinger of triumph.

A set of twin corollaries follow directly. First, were Jews to abandon their religious convictions, their oppression would be rendered meaningless. Worse, Jewish history would be reduced to a tragedy bereft of consolation, a mortifying tale of impotence and humiliation. Without the Jewish theodicy, degradation and injustice would be merely degradation and injustice. Clinging to their faith, therefore, went beyond metaphysical commitments: It was a pressing psycho-social necessity.

Second, were Gentile oppression to cease, Jewish ethno-religious civilization would need to undergo dramatic reformulations in order to retain its resilience and credibility. Much would need to be reconsidered. Jewish existence could no longer be interpreted as a interminable battle with a hostile world. Neither could Jewish singularity and the justifications for Jewish survival draw their moral and psychological energy from the fortress mentality of the besieged. Rather than Jews being defined in contrast to others, more self-referring categories would need to be worked out. The richness of Jewish culture in itself and not Gentile belligerence would need to legitimate the boundaries necessary for Jewish survival. The meaning of ideas such as chosenness and exile would be open for examination. Jewish isolation and insulation would need to be reassessed. Messianic visions would require new content.

That such theo-cultural revolutions could remain within the traditional fold is demonstrated by one of the early harbingers of Zionism, Rabbi Zvi Hirsch Kalischer (1795–1874). In contrast to the vast majority of traditional leaders and scholars of his era, Kalischer accepted the reality of the Emancipation.[22] It was no illusion or trick: The Gentiles were genuinely offering Jews civil liberties. Since it was obvious in Kalischer's mind that such an unprecedented development had to be the work of God, the Emancipation must signal a new stage in the Divine design for both Jewish and world history. If heretofore God had chastised the Jews through Gentile hostility, henceforth Redemption would be pursued in different ways. The new era demanded a new and active calling that had been closed to Jews in the era of oppression. They were to return to the Land of Israel, resettle it, and prepare for the era of Salvation. The realities of Emancipation entailed the responsibilities of Zionism.

But such attempts at the reformulation of Jewish tradition from within are very much the exception. For the most part, the traditional Jewish ethos remained hostile to such explicitly emancipatory themes and reaffirmed the permanent antagonism between Jew and Gentile. Where attempts to adapt to the new reality do take place is primarily in the nontraditional domain. Jewish socialism, Jewish nationalism, and the attempt to denationalize the Jewish faith (classical Reform Judaism) are very different strategies, each of which, in its own way, endeavors to adjust to a new set of historical givens. And yet, viewed retrospectively from the vantage point of a century and half or so, these attempts have either failed outright or, more often, have slowly reverted to the perceptual status quo ante, that is, to the view that Jewish existence is embattled, disempowered, and insecure.

It may well be that to read Jewish history is to develop at least a mild case of paranoia. After the Holocaust there is understandable resistance to the idea that the siege may be ending. The fears and sensitivities accumulated over the centuries have had so many painful reinforcements that they will not be easily swayed by a half-century of relative affluence and security—even if this new reality gives every sign of being essentially different from everything that preceded it.

But these stubborn fears—whatever their legitimate place in a healthy Jewish consciousness—are, at present, the source of a serious impasse. Since it is this other-directed, adversity-centered segment of the Jewish heritage that most powerfully resists attenuation, it often remains the core substance of Jewish identity—particularly among those most vulnerable to assimilatory pressures. Indeed, it becomes the surrogate for virtually all other Jewish content and prevents the creation of a culturally self-affirming and psychologically autonomous understanding of Jewish existence.

But if the memory of adversity is what remains to legitimate the boundaries with the non-Jewish world, if this is the proverbial dam holding back the assimilatory deluge, then one cannot help but wonder about both its principled justification and its practical viability. At the level of principle, the question virtually poses itself: Do such historical reflexes have it in their moral power to legitimate enclavic exclusivity, endogamy, and particularist institutions? At the practical level, on the other hand, the answer virtually formulates itself: Despite the palpably real sources of these sentiments, they are manifestly refuted by the reality in which they must function. In a welcoming and secure world, the penny will eventually drop.

Paradoxically, the adversity-centered worldview that once served to steel Jews to their tribulations and to ensure survival today endangers this very survival. It simulates Jewish substance when it is, in fact, lacking. It artificially resuscitates a moribund ethno-religious consciousness although it cannot tell those who are affected by this historical reflex why they ought to survive as Jews. Above all, it fails to encourage commitment or advance learning or enrich cultural life. If anything, it preempts just these developments.

Curiously, the view of Jewish existence as embattled is perhaps nowhere more prevalent than in those political communities where Jewish existence has become reasonably secure and promises to become only more so: the United States and Israel. It is this intriguing paradox to which the coming chapters will be devoted.

But before proceeding, we need to return to our initial question: Does all of this provide an adequate account of the dissolution of Jewish cohesion, of the rush toward disaffiliation? Can the crisis of credibility we have been describing account for the attraction that assimilation holds for so many Jews?

The thesis might be encapsulated as follows: Historically, Jewish perceptions of Gentile hostility served the deep psycho-social requirements of a physically insecure and emotionally battered people. These perceptions encouraged Jewish cohesion and fortified Jewish resolve. When, gradually, the supporting reality for these perceptions eroded, there were no credible alternatives to serve in their place. Faced with an incongruity between outlook and environment, many embraced both of these discrepant worlds in turn: They became fully integrated into the Western world professionally and socially, while simultaneously preserving typical Jewish apprehensions as latent residual categories. These categories acted to preserve them as Jews despite the weakness of their substantive Jewish commitments. Nevertheless, even the well-known mechanism of cognitive dissonance cannot endure indefinitely. In the end, with the adversity-centered worldview being discredited and sliding into practical irrelevance, there was a natural falling-away, a massive silent exit that now threatens Jewish survival as it has never been threatened before.

But this thesis is obviously wanting in at least one major regard. Jews lost their religion long before discrimination against them had ceased. In other words, intellectual Enlightenment preceded socio-political Emancipation. Hence, attributing Jewish disaffection to the psycho-social predicaments attending the decline of adversity would seem contrived and ahistorical. To adduce just a single illustration: Zionism, an exemplary product of Enlightenment thinking, assumed antisemitism as a given.

In truth, Enlightenment led in two different directions. Although it preceded Emancipation, it already contained within itself egalitarian and universalist messages that are the operative components of the emancipatory drive. If Gentile acceptance is potentially possible, a widely ramifying and deeply entrenched component of Jewish consciousness has been dislodged. By envisioning (long before it became a reality) a nonadversarial form of

Jewish existence in which Gentile acceptance was achieved without Divine intervention, Enlightenment thinkers subverted the unquestioned necessity for Jewish cohesion and solidarity.

The result might be described as a "loss of compression" within the Jewish community: What had been an air-tight, densely compacted closed system was now ruptured and unable to sustain its internal resilience and energy. At very least, Jewish creative energies could now flow outward—toward liberation from political subordination and harmony with the surrounding world—rather than inward—toward renewed religious dedication and communal integrality. The compulsive need for religious justifications of affliction, so critical in the pre-Enlightenment era, loses both in urgency and cogency. No longer are the tradition's protective powers indispensable. Severing the religious umbilical cord ceases to be outrageous or unthinkable.

Jewish socialists, for example, despite experiencing virulent antisemitism, were now capable of imagining a world that Jews could both affirm and be affirmed by, a world in which Jews and Gentiles could affirm each other because their particularist identities would slowly become inconsequential. Jewish exclusivity, from this point of view, was unnecessary, even mean-spirited. The traditional, adversity-centered circumlocutions were superfluous if not actually pitiable. Why give credence to a convoluted vision in which victims are portrayed as victors and affliction is recast as redemption when a simpler, more credible, tale of liberation can be told? In brief, theorizing a world in which Jews could flourish in security was the great fault line dividing premodern Jewish communal solidarity from the modern fracturing of Jewish loyalties.

But the Enlightenment also led in another direction. With the failure of the religious justifications for Jewish suffering, antisemitism became intolerable. If all the blood and tears were not part of a great tale of deliverance, enduring them was all the more agonizing.[23] It is no surprise, therefore, that severing the religious umbilical cord encouraged other Jews to search for more immediate solutions to the problem of Jewish affliction. In a word: In the aftermath of the Enlightenment, antisemitism emerges as a problem to be solved rather than as a divinely ordained fate to be endured. If Esau does not necessarily hate Jacob, if this hatred is attributable to specifiable causes (Jewish separatism, lack of sovereignty, economic jealousy, even Christian ignorance, etc.), if a different reality and different forms of Jewish life will create a different kind of Jewish fate, the tradition ceases to be the only way to vindicate Jewish existence. In these circumstances it becomes possible to replace the Jewish theodicy with a Jewish socio-cultural reformation.

The loss of religiosity offset by the preservation of Jewish ethnic loyalties generated a novel, sometimes promethean confrontation with antisemitism.

As a problem to be energetically resisted and overcome, antisemitism triggered a number of unprecedented visions of Jewish liberation. Zionism is probably the most celebrated of them. Paradoxically, then, it was precisely in those quarters in which traditional perspectives declined and religious Judaism modulated into ethnic Jewishness that activity on behalf of the Jewish people became most sustained and intense.

One further counterargument needs to be addressed, if only briefly and preliminarily. If the difficulties involved in retaining Jewish identity in a nonadversarial world lie at the root of mass disaffiliation, why do certain groups, most especially the Orthodox, thrive so remarkably both in the United States and Israel even though Gentile hostility is at a minimum? Two complementary rejoinders are called for. First, it must be said outright that cultural richness and religious intensity can, in principle, preserve social integration even in the absence of adversity. Second (and entirely compatible with the first), even ostensibly nonthreatening realities can be interpreted in terms that are consistent with an adversity-centered world view. Rather than struggle with alternate forms of self-understanding, the conventional wisdom can be endlessly recycled and refurbished. Confronted with an accommodating world but possessed of an ideology that can render the Jewish condition meaningful only in terms of oppression, some will construe oppression in highly creative ways, while others will insist that, despite appearances, oppression continues.

But this is to anticipate. We shall, in our ensuing discussion, return to these subjects in considerably greater detail.

american jews
Preserving the Old

I mages of Gentile hostility, as we noted, are pivotal to Jewish self-understanding. They underwrite the Jewish worldview and provide traditional concepts such as "the chosen people" and "messianic deliverance" with their most striking vindication. They also afford a comforting rationale for a history replete with tragedy as well as a promise of future redemption and glory.

But what if adversity and hostility visibly decline and the traditional images no longer seem appropriate? This chapter examines the efforts of American Jews to retain the old images despite the palpable decline of antisemitism in the latter part of the twentieth century. We shall focus on three such efforts. First, we take up the belief that antisemitism persists notwithstanding the surface appearance of decline. Second, we examine the intense engagement with the Holocaust that is said to demonstrate that Jews are never secure even among enlightened and progressive peoples. Jewish tragedies are always latent; if not here, then at least there. Finally, we study the passionate American Jewish concern for Israel's security.

"The Shoah [Holocaust], fear for Israel's survival, antisemitism," as one observer of American Jewish life summarizes it, are "the heartfelt issues for American Jews."[1] These concerns appear to run very deep and to affect even Jews who are not particularly traditional or institutionally committed. To paraphrase one unaffiliated Jew in his early forties who is anxious lest his children lose their sense of Jewish identity:

> I'll take the kids aside to talk. They'll grow up with a sense of Jewishness, a sense of some justifiable fear and pride. I'll tell them about antisemitism and the Holocaust and the vulnerability of the Jews. it is part of the survival indoctrination of children to know that they are particularly vulnerable because they are Jews.[2]

After exploring these traditional strategies for Jewish survival, we turn, in the next chapter, to examine the various efforts of American Jews to reconstruct the significance of Jewishness in nonadversarial terms.

Antisemitism

One of the most familiar Jewish texts provides a remarkably telling portrait of the course of American Jewish history. The Passover Haggadah tells of four sons and their relation to the Jewish tradition: a devoted son who wishes to carry on the ways of his forebears, an evil or (in the more politically correct version) contrary son who rejects the tradition with hostility and disdain, a simple-minded son who can do no more than pose the most rudimentary of questions, and, last, a son who remains speechless because he does not even begin to know what to ask.

Since the great wave of immigration from Russia and Eastern Europe to the United States at the turn of the century, four generations of Jews—parallel to the four sons of the Haggadah—have made America their home. The first generation did what it could to transfer the learning and ambience of the Jewish world they knew in East Europe to the swarming tenements of the New World. Although they were usually not very learned and often not Orthodox in the contemporary halachic sense of the word, (Orthodoxy being a reaction to liberalizing tendencies they had not experienced in Russia and Eastern Europe), they were, nevertheless, very committed Jews who held strong convictions on the nature of Jewish history and the ordeals of the Jewish condition.[3] Although the immigrant parents sometimes cut corners on Sabbath observance and Kashrut in response to the pressures of employment and expedience, they, nevertheless, established heders (schools for youngsters where traditional texts were taught), shuls (traditional synagogues), and other Jewish institutions to serve the needs of a thriving Jewish community.[4] Despite substantial hardships, they persisted in their deeply felt Jewish loyalties and attempted to transfer these loyalties to the new American generation that grew up in circumstances so different from their own.

But their sons and daughters had different ideas. The way their parents dressed, spoke, and comported themselves was often a source of acute embarrassment to them. What was taught in the heder had no relation to the rough and tumble world of "making it" into which they were thrust as soon as they were old enough. In fact, the behavior and mannerisms of the old Yiddish-speaking rabbis and teachers were so incompatible with their personal and social aspirations that the elders became the butt of malicious humor.[5] Religious ceremonies were observed under parental duress, with one eye on the prayer book and the other on the clock. These antiquated practices, they promised themselves, would not hinder them when they reached adulthood and could decide for themselves. Like so many other immigrant children, they understood that to become a real American required a sharp break with the conspicuously foreign practices of the past. Although a certain nostalgia toward things Jewish remained, it was more a sentimental fondness for the sights and smells of childhood than a substantial engagement with Jewish learning or practice.

When it was their turn to transmit their Jewishness to their own children, the world of the tenements was usually a thing of the past. They likely lived in middle- or lower-middle-class Jewish neighborhoods, had their small businesses to run, and felt that America had been good to them. They joined what they now called a synagogue or temple, a more decorous place of worship than the storefront shul they knew in their youth. The college-educated rabbi spoke English, men and women sat together, and what had been religiously obligatory observances now became ethno-cultural customs. Their children's Jewish education was, at best, limited to an after-hours Hebrew school where Bible stories and Jewish holidays were taught; but parents and children both knew that this schooling was extramural and of distinctly secondary importance.

These children—the third Jewish generation since the great wave of immigration—did not confront a dense Jewish reality that demanded an essential response. At best Jewishness was quaint and dispensable. Hence, they were neither particularly engaged nor especially rebellious. The folkloric world of *zaideh* (grandfather) and *bubba* (grandmother) no longer excited deep passions—neither negative nor positive. The energies of this generation went elsewhere: into university studies, professional achievements, and the creation of a successful, often suburban life. They could still perhaps formulate a rudimentary Jewish question or two, and perhaps the memories of youth could arouse an occasional twinge of nostalgia, but very little else remained.

Their children were likely born in affluent circumstances; in upper-income suburbs or in the more fashionable sections of town. As opposed to their parents, no memories remained of the old Jewish neighborhood with its calendar, rhythms, personality types, and typical concerns. Their neighbors and friends were often non-Jews. More than half would not be affiliated with any Jewish organization. A substantial percentage would marry non-Jews. Perhaps most important, precious little distinguished the routine of their daily lives from that of other middle-class professionals. Well-educated and cosmopolitan, Jewish questions often rang provincial and clannish in their ears. For lack of knowledge and interest, they were on the verge of extinction as Jews: They could not, nor did they care to, engage with "The Jewish Question" or, for that matter, with any other Jewish questions of a more prosaic character.

This same tale of growing disaffection and disintegration can also be related from a somewhat different perspective. Rather than tell it from the point of view of the immigrants and their movement from tradition to assimilation, it can be recounted from the viewpoint of the American society that absorbed them. At the turn of the century, Jewish immigrants came to a land that received them openly. And yet, it must be added that America was hardly free of its own local brands of antisemitism. To be sure, the garden-variety adversities from which Jews suffered in the United States cannot be compared to the horrors of the Old World, but antisemitism was, nevertheless, substantial and consistent.

Despite the relative respite from hardship, there was, therefore, no real imperative to alter the traditional adversity-centered Jewish worldview. Apart from local antisemitism, concern with the persecutions of Jews in Russia and Europe[6]—a series of major pogroms in Russia broke out in 1881, the Dreyfus Affair began a decade and a half later, and so on—reinforced the age-old conviction that affliction was still very much the norm. If America was seemingly different,[7] this only highlighted the abject condition of Jews generally—in precisely the sense that an exception demonstrates the validity of the rule.

With their close familial and communal ties to the beleaguered Jews of Eastern Europe, the early generations of immigrants had little difficulty in accommodating American exceptionalism to the traditional perspective of defenseless Jews in a world of hostile Gentiles. If any doubts remained, the rise of National Socialism in the late twenties and its accession to power in the early thirties put them to rest. That fascist parties with more or less antisemitic programs flourished in virtually all Western countries—from the United States and England to Croatia, Latvia, Spain, and Portugal—did nothing to mitigate these views. No paranoia was necessary for Jews to retain their classic notions of Gentile hostility. Indeed, so deeply rooted were these feelings of insecurity that at the close of World War II America's Jews anticipated, with considerable alarm, a serious outburst of anti-semitism—that, thankfully, never materialized.[8]

It was not, however, an entirely implausible anticipation. To begin with, American antisemitism was not all covert "gentlemen's agreements" or country-club snobbery; it had its virulent and violent strains as well. And it is important to recall (from the security of the closing years of the century) that Jews were affected by this bigotry deeply and variously. Although America retained its image as the "goldene medina," this was a comparative rather than an absolute evaluation.

A brief and highly impressionistic miscellany of this easily forgotten and very recent past is important before we proceed. Only by reliving the feelings Jews must have felt a mere fifty to sixty years ago do we begin to appreciate the dramatic nature of the changes that have ensued. As recently as the pre-World War II years, the obstacles placed before Jews in employment, education, and the professions were pernicious, conspicuous, and ample. In 1937, one in every ten employment ads appearing in a New York newspaper stipulated "Christians only." In 1940, close to half of those polled reported that it "would make a difference" to them if a potential employee was Jewish. Banks and insurance companies were largely closed to Jews. The Ivy

League universities severely limited the number of Jewish students by means of rigorously applied quotas. The same discriminatory policy was directed to potential Jewish faculty.[9]

It was the era of a major Ku Klux Klan revival, the nationwide membership of which numbered in the millions. Father Coughlin exploited the anguish and dislocations of the Depression to defame Jews on his revivalist radio programs. An "international Jewish cabal" was responsible for it all, he told his listeners. Doubtless, some of the ill-will toward Jews upon which Coughlin based his appeal was seeded by the millions of copies of *The Protocols of the Elders of Zion* disseminated by Henry Ford in the 1920s. In a 1940 poll, 63 percent of Americans believed that Jews had "objectionable traits"; only 30 percent reported that they would oppose an antisemitic campaign while up to 48 percent said that they would support or sympathize with one; in 1944 almost one in four said that the Jews "were a menace to America." It is chilling to recall that as late as 1948, Gerald L. K. Smith, the notorious Christian clergyman and hate-monger, ran for the American presidency on a platform that demanded the deportation of all Jews.[10]

This then is a different tale from that of our four sons. Whereas the engagement with things Jewish suffers a linear decline through the first four American Jewish generations, antisemitism remained a troublesome and intimidating presence through the end of the second, even the beginning of the third American Jewish generation. But then in the early fifties, a remarkable transformation begins, one that has no parallel or precedent in modern Jewish history. The antagonism toward Jews declines precipitously and in a decade or two they become popularly associated with favorable traits—more so, it appears, than any other ethnic group in America. Moreover, the obstacles barring them from the professions and prestigious educational institutions begin to crumble. Perhaps most significant, overt antisemitism loses its erstwhile legitimation—it becomes discredited, defensive, and outlandish.

In the late 1970s the Jews emerge as the single most successful ethnic group in the United States. Financially, professionally, educationally, politically, and even in terms of entrance into the glittering world of the American "aristocracy," Jews are in a most enviable position.[11] (Jewish success, it appears, is truly complete: One source cites evidence that Ashkenazi Jews also have the best sex life![12]) Indeed, they have so successfully entered the world exclusively occupied by the WASP establishment that many no longer relate to Jews as a distinctive ethnic group at all but rather as simply part of white America.

So profoundly has this sense of communal well-being percolated into Jewish consciousness that it is no longer necessary for Jews to change their names or conceal their ancestry. (Tens of thousands changed their names yearly in the prewar era.) Whereas their assimilating parents or grandparents related to their Jewish past with trepidation and anxiety, their children and grandchildren are easygoing and unperturbed. They see no particular reason to either abandon their ethno-religious identity or, for that matter, to embrace it. As one writer put it: "If Judaism was no bother, why bother?"[13] Paradoxically then, the unabashed prevalence of Greenbergs and Cohens in the high echelons of business, government, and education does not mean that we are witnessing a revival of Jewish identity. It signifies, on the contrary, that such marks of identification no longer matter very much one way or the other.

Growing accommodation to American society is strikingly reflected in Jewish residential patterns. Apart from some very salient pockets of Orthodox Jews (mainly in the greater New York area), the old-style Jewish neighborhood has gone the way of the horse and buggy. Important consequences follow: No longer is association with other Jews a natural, diurnal occurrence; it needs to be deliberately chosen and cultivated. The streets no longer educate to Jewish life (as shtetl residents liked to say); car pools to the Jewish Center are now necessary. Jewish surroundings need to be expressly created; they can no longer be taken for granted.

The disappearance of the Jewish neighborhood (roughly since the 1950s) has dealt a grievous blow to the kind of Jewish ethnic identity that managed to survive the decline of Judaism as a faith. Growing up in Jewish surroundings sustained Jewish identity even for those who were distant from religious observance. Their parents were often secular Yiddishists, Bundists, labor union enthusiasts, socialists, anarchists, perhaps even communists, but their bond to things Jewish was deep and abiding. Moving to the suburbs or to prestigious urban areas where Jews constituted only one strand of the polyethnic social fabric meant that this kind of ethnicity as a focus for Jewish identity was far more difficult to sustain. It was not only that the Jewish bakery, delicatessen, book store, and lodge were replaced by ethnically anonymous supermarkets and characterless shopping malls. The process was not simply one of Jewish assimilation into middle-class suburban America. The process worked in reverse as well. Foods, certain expressions and mannerisms, housing styles, even forms of child rearing that had once been distinctively Jewish were now shared by Gentiles, as Woody Allen's popularity can attest. This was both a cause and consequence of the fact that one's friends and associates were no longer likely to be Jewish. Non-Jews ceased being "the other" and began being comrades and colleagues. The local school was no longer overwhelmingly Jewish with all the social, psychological, and educational consequences that derive from such

ethnic concentration; the schools were a mirror to their supporting population, that is, so ethnically compounded that what remained was only the
American common denominator. Pluralism, in short, ceased being a doctrine taught in civics classes and became a lived reality.

Growing up in Jewish surroundings often meant not having real dealings
with non-Jews until one entered either the work force or the university. It
was quite common not to have been in the home of a non-Jew at least until
early adulthood. Under such circumstances, Jewishness was not a deliberately cultivated identity—that is, one choice made out of many alternatives—but a natural, almost inevitable state of affairs. As young people
growing up in homogeneous Jewish neighborhoods, it was hard for us to get
our minds around the idea that Jewishness was a contingent, numerically
negligible, geographically isolated phenomenon. Both of us, for example,
can recall our shock at hearing that Eisenhower had beaten Stevenson by a
landslide. Neither of us knew a single Eisenhower supporter.

Attempts to reconstruct a new form of Jewish life in suburbia had both
their heroic and their pathetic moments. The new surroundings, after all,
presented an entirely unprecedented challenge. How to inculcate Jewishness when it was invisible in the streets and only feebly present in the
home? In the absence of those natural forces that preserved Jewish loyalties
in the past, Jewishness became a professionalized, compartmentalized, and
localized experience. Religious professionals—rabbis and cantors—took
over the popular functions that were once performed by laymen but that
now, due to the lack of basic Jewish literacy, were beyond the ability of
most congregants. Large synagogues and community centers ("shul, school,
and pool" complexes) housed the Jewish activities that did not take place
elsewhere. The part-time Hebrew school—where Jewish children stepped
out of their real lives to be and act Jewish from four to eight hours a week—
educated to a Jewishness that was subverted by the message of the street
and the home.[14] To be sure, all this did not mean the expiration of ethnic
Jewish feelings. But without the sustenance of natural Jewish surroundings,
the future of Jewishness would have to rely on deliberate campaigns and
programs, on PR and contrivance, on the frank acknowledgment that particularist ethnic bonds competed with rival universalist values. And it was
universalist pluralism that was now "natural," that is, consistent with the
actual surroundings in which suburban Jews found themselves.

Still, had the major concentrations of Jews remained on the northeastern
seaboard or in the central cities of the Midwest, the inertia of the old
densely organized, cohesively kindred Jewish life patterns would have
retarded the absorption of Jews into the undifferentiated American mainstream. The masses of East European Jews had come to these old metropoli-

tan centers as a group, had established communal institutions as a group, and, hence, retained the compacted affiliations of a group. In moving to the "golden cities" of Los Angeles and Miami, however, Jews moved as unencumbered individuals. They did not take with them, nor did they seek to recreate, the tightly knit, obligating, and intrusive style of the East. What they sought was the more relaxed and disengaged life associated with the balmy climates and semitropical beaches of the South and West.[15] Not surprisingly, in these new surroundings, their identification with things Jewish attenuated, just as their immersion in the American mainstream became more and more unqualified.

But have these unprecedented transformations altered the underlying adversity-centered understanding of Jewish existence? On its face, there is every reason to believe they should have. After all, the incongruence between the traditional, beleaguered Jewish worldview and the affluent and auspicious reality prevailing in the last quarter of the century could not be greater.

Notwithstanding their abiding gratefulness to America for its largesse, and despite their unparalleled achievements in business, politics, the arts, and academia, a strikingly high number of American Jews, at least until the last decade, remained anxious and insecure. In a 1984 survey conducted for the American Jewish Committee,[16] the overwhelming majority (92%) agreed that American Jews must be vigilant in combatting any signs of antisemitism. In surveys conducted in 1983, 1984, and 1986, from two-thirds to more than three-quarters of those polled assented to the proposition that antisemitism in America may become a serious problem in the future. Consistent with earlier findings, a 1988 survey found that almost two-thirds (65%) disagreed with the contention that virtually all positions of influence are open to Jews today. An even greater majority (76%) rejected the view that antisemitism is not, currently, a serious problem for American Jews. In 1985 nearly two out of five (37%) Jewish respondents characterized American Gentiles as generally antisemitic. On a related issue, a clear majority (58%) agreed in 1988 that "when it comes to the crunch, few non-Jews will come to Israel's side in its struggle to survive." One is forced to conclude that at least half of all American Jews harbored anxieties about the genuineness of American Christian acceptance. Considering that those who allege Gentile hostility are found disproportionately among those who identified most earnestly as Jews, these findings become all the more telling.[17]

This curious persistence of anxiety and insecurity amid affluence and influence is not all of a piece. Two forms in which it occurs and two constituencies in which it prevails should be distinguished: first, a traditionalist minority that clings to an adversity-centered worldview, and, second, a residually traditional majority that, although more sanguine about the Jewish prospect in America, calls upon the imagery of adversity selectively and episodically. To paraphrase Abraham Lincoln: The traditional image of the antisemitic Gentile and the precarious Jew is accepted by some of the Jews all of the time and by most of the Jews some of the time.

The minority who hold this view all of the time, those who allege persistent, implacable Gentile hostility, are disproportionately old rather than young, recent immigrants rather than long-time American citizens, Orthodox and observant rather than secular or religiously progressive. They are more likely to be found among those who are thoroughly immersed in Jewish surroundings rather than among those whose Jewish contacts are infrequent and casual. Yet even among this minority group, numbers are declining and attitudes are changing.

It is interesting to follow the changes in rhetoric employed by traditional American Jews in their skirmishes with American liberals. In the past, the prevailing attitude was "A plague on all of your houses"; "Goyim" were all antisemites notwithstanding their protestations or ideological flourishes. ("Scratch a goy, find an antisemite" was a Yiddish commonplace heard on the Lower East Side and the heavily Jewish neighborhoods in Brooklyn.) Today, liberals may be castigated for their indifference to antisemitism, for their dangerous naivete about Arab intentions, for their dismissing the potential for antisemitism in certain quarters of Black and populist/right-wing America, but there is no automatic condemnation of Gentiles as antisemites.

Even among the ultra-Orthodox, in whose midst the traditional adversity-centered worldview probably remains dominant, changes are manifest. They too have absorbed some of the liberal tolerance at which America so excels and it has worked its way into the conduct of their public business— if not yet expressly into their formal teachings. It is now not unusual to confront—often in private conversation—more benign images of the Gentile and more complex and qualified interpretations of the "Jewish condition." Not too long ago, these groups shunned the public sphere both because they claimed not to be interested in what the Goyim were doing and, even more significantly, because they were convinced that any demand or protest on their part would only invite Gentile retaliation. ("Don't incite a Goy" was another standard Yiddish expression.)

Currently, these attitudes of silent submission and nervous insecurity are very much out of fashion. Recognizing that the American political system confers power on those who organize and lobby, the ultra-Orthodox have adopted a far more activist posture toward public life. They no longer perceive themselves as surrounded by enemies who are ready to pounce as soon as they raise their heads. There may be opponents, even authentic villains in the political arena, but it is no longer the immemorial encounter between defenseless Jews and depraved antisemites. They are only too ready to publicly criticize that which they find objectionable in American life—ironically, they agree with the Christian Right's criticisms of sexual permissiveness and the privatization of religion—and, if need be, they are willing to become visible and contentious in order to achieve their objectives. None of this would be possible without substantial changes in the traditional adversity-centered outlook.

This explanation is substantial but by no means complete. Although there has been something of a sea change in ultra-Orthodox conduct and in their operational codes relating to the public domain, they still inhabit a world dominated by oral and textual traditions that are, in this regard at least, largely unchanged for centuries. Not only do they confront these verbal and written texts frequently, they are beholden to live their lives in conformity with them. And these texts, as we contended in the previous chapter, present a theological, social, and psychological worldview in which Gentile adversity occupies a pivotal position. For the ultra-Orthodox, preserving the old means living in a world framed by such utterances. Rather than describe the quality of these texts abstractly, a number of specific illustrations will better convey their flavor and uniqueness.

The Bible relates the tale of Jacob's troubled relations with his twin brother Esau. After a separation of many years, they are set to meet. But Jacob is so fearful of Esau's hostility and so concerned for the safety of his family that he takes special security precautions lest Esau attack. Moreover, Jacob prostrates himself seven times as he approaches his brother. Yet, when the two meet, Esau embraces Jacob and kisses him warmly.

The Torah scroll—the rolled parchment from which the text of the Five Books of Moses is read in the synagogue— does not contain punctuation marks. Rather, the cadences, halts, and stresses with which the text should be read are signaled by cantillations (not actually present in the Torah scroll but in printed texts used by Torah readers to prepare for their chanting) that indicate how each word, indeed each syllable, is to be intoned in the public Torah reading. Over the word "kissed" referring to Esau's greeting, there is an extremely unusual cantillation mark. This rare cantillation has attracted a great deal of interpretive attention, not least from Rashi (Rabbi Shlomo Yitzchaki or Solomon son of Isaac, 1040–1105), perhaps the greatest of medieval commentators on the Bible and Talmud. (His commentary is so central that is published in all editions of the Bible meant for traditional Jewish use and is studied by virtually every traditional Jew.)

Rashi comments (citing as his source the much earlier and authoritative *Midrash Rabba*) that Jacob organized his family in serried ranks and stood at the head of the throng as they awaited Esau's approach so that if "the villain [*rasha*] has come to fight he will have to fight me first." Rashi asserts that Esau embraced Jacob only because his pity was aroused by all of the latter's prostrations. As to the very strange cantillation marks, Rashi observes that they come to provide an answer to the obvious question that anyone (any traditional Jew at least) reading the text will ponder: How is it that Esau kissed Jacob, "for it is the way of the world, as is known, that Esau hates Jacob"? Rashi's answer is forthright: The unusual cantillations signal the listener that although hatred between Esau and Jacob is indeed permanent, in this unusual case, Esau's sense of mercy was so moved that he kissed Jacob with all his heart.[18] There can be no mistaking Rashi's intent. Esau symbolizes the Gentile, Jacob the Jew; hatred between them, the momentary kiss notwithstanding, is inexorable and constant.

The Passover Haggadah provides a strikingly representative version of the adversity worldview told from the perspective of an exceptional and stunning victory. (Parenthetically, this adversity-centered narrative is *the* leitmotif of many Jewish festivals: It is, for example, the underlying story of the Purim and Hanukkah holidays. In each case, distress and fears of extinction are miraculously replaced by a turning of the tables on the Jews' enemies.) At the seder, the festive meal that inaugurates the holiday of Passover, the tale of oppression in Egypt is told with drama and color. (Being jubilant and celebratory in character, there is little attention given to the sinfulness of Israel that preceded bondage.) The focus is on oppression and slavery under the heavy hand of Egyptian domination. They caused us to suffer grievously, the Haggadah (the text read at the seder) says repeatedly. But we appealed to God out of the depths of our misery. He heard our call and, as the Savior of Israel had pledged to the Patriarchs, delivered us from bondage miraculously. Not only did he rescue us, he taught the Egyptians a painful lesson for having tormented God's chosen people. In both thankful and obsessive detail, the Haggadah recounts the Egyptian's downfall, spelling out the exact nature of each plague visited upon them and how fearful was God's wrath.

In the midst of this tale of affliction and redemption, the Haggadah's text alerts those who have gathered around the festive table that oppression of this kind is the rule rather than the exception:

> More than once have they risen against us to destroy us; in every generation they rise against us and seek our destruction. But the Holy One, blessed be He, saves us from their hands.

And, as if to hammer the message home pedagogically, the Haggadah concludes the narrative of Jewish emancipation from servitude with the following quite harrowing directive: "In every generation one must look upon himself as if he personally left Egypt." For it was "not only our forefathers whom the Holy One, blessed be He, redeemed; He redeemed us too, with them." Jews are commanded to internalize the reality of affliction; they must transpose themselves imaginatively to the archetypal instance of oppression and recognize that this (and, hopefully, Divine deliverance) is *the* Jewish fate.

As if all this were insufficient, the Haggadah lashes out fiercely against the enemies who periodically rise up to persecute the Jews. In so doing, voice is given to a subterranean, episodic, authentic but contingent Jewish emotion that is witness to the depth of injury that animates this adversity-battered people:

> Pour out your wrath upon the nations that know you not and upon the kingdoms that call not upon your name; for they have consumed Jacob and laid waste his habitation. Pour out your rage upon them and let your fury overtake them. Pursue them in anger and destroy them from under the heavens of God.

Although many progressive Jews urged the deletion of this paragraph, after the horrors of the Holocaust it has largely been retained.

Lest it be thought that the sense of vulnerability and siege are of recent origin, that it reflects Christendom's pressure on the Jews from the early Middle Ages up until the Holocaust, it must be added that much earlier Jewish texts express similar cautionary sentiments about Gentile intentions. Suffice it to say that the Talmud (composed and redacted in the first five centuries of the Common Era) warns Jews against going to non-Jewish barbers. With razor in hand, there is no telling that he won't slit the unsuspecting Jewish throat.[19] For the Orthodox, exposure to such authoritative texts cannot but leave their mark.

A final illustration focuses on a classic adage that likens the condition of Jews in a Gentile world to that of "a lamb among seventy wolves." Jews are, of course, the helpless lamb, the nations of the world (seventy according to the traditional Jewish account) the devouring wolves. At very best, the lamb can hope that the wolves will leave it in peace. The lamb is utterly defenseless, incapable of resisting the wolves if they should decide to attack. All it can do is to rely on Divine mercy.

An intriguing illustration of this mindset was highlighted in the response of Rabbi Eliezer Schach—one of the preeminent leaders of the Israeli ultra-Orthodox world—to an accusation made by Israeli Prime Minister Menachem Begin more than a decade ago that the then West German

Chancellor was an antisemite. Rabbi Schach was highly critical of Begin for his condemnation of the German leader. The underlying import of the criticism was as follows: Of course the Chancellor is an antisemite. Nothing unusual in that. Goyim are antisemites. Where Prime Minister Begin went wrong was in calling attention to such an obvious and dangerous fact. The only thing statements such as these accomplish is to incite the Goyim and further inflame their hatred. Accusations of antisemitism make as much sense as the lamb reminding the wolf of his voracious appetite.

Although such imagery persists—it is still quite standard in the storefront shuls of Brooklyn's densely Orthodox neighborhoods as well as in the Hasidic and Yeshiva worlds[20]—it would be difficult to describe the actual public posture of those who employ it as that of a lamb among the wolves. More and more, there is a striking discrepancy between discourse and deportment, between belief and behavior. It is hard to correlate their ardent political activism and aggressive posture toward their opponents with the image of a powerless and frightened people. The Orthodox would, doubtless, insist that they remain entirely faithful to the classical sources. We would suggest that these protestations need to be understood as symptomatic of a transitional period during which incongruities and internal tensions will necessarily induce dynamic evolution.

But the ability to accommodate novel realities to the traditional worldviews goes far beyond prosaic strategies such as outright denial or psychological compartmentalization. With creativity and imagination, the classical precepts can be deftly reformulated and the letter of the text preserved, even though its spirit is substantially altered. In effect, the old maxims that speak of a beleaguered and vulnerable people persist, but the nature of the threat posed by the Gentile world as well as the reasons for Jewish defensiveness are understood in strikingly innovative ways. Rather than Esau's hatred of Jacob being expressed through pogroms or inquisitions, today a more daunting and dangerous strategy has been devised. The older way was simply to annihilate the Jewish people physically—a strategy that has been tried many times and failed just as often. A saving remnant persisted despite the horrors and, recovering its confidence, set about the immemorial task of reconstruction.

The novel Gentile strategy says, If we can't beat them, have them join us. Drop all the barriers that insulated the Jews into their own small world, discontinue the persecution that steeled their resolve to survive nevertheless, subdue the antisemitic outbursts that stung them into defiance. Be accommodating, accepting, and respectful; have Jews freely enter the leading universities and corporations, welcome them as neighbors and friends, even marry your children to theirs. Relate to their Jewishness as casual and innocuous, and you will find that they will look upon it similarly. The secret is this: Pluralism is a one-way street; it is they rather than you who join the mainstream and abandon their uniqueness. Rape has failed to prevail upon this stubborn people; perhaps seduction will. What the Holocaust could not accomplish, assimilation can.

Admittedly, those who accept this starkly conspiratorial reformulation of Gentile intentions constitute a small and marginal minority. But introduce one small change and the perspective becomes entirely plausible: God tested the Jews in the past by unleashing Gentile fury upon them to see if they would remain steadfast; today He repeats the test in a new way. It is no longer trial by ordeal but trial by embrace. The silk glove rather than the mailed fist. In place of the *auto da fe* or the blood libel there is the multicultural cocktail party and the narcissistic self-congratulation attendant upon having been accepted into the world of the Gentile.

Make no mistake, they argue: For all of the comfort and esteem that Jews enjoy, the American dream is no less of a test. Indeed, it may be the most formidable challenge that Jews have ever faced. And what better proof of the life and death struggle that America's Jews face than the massive defections that have decimated the Jewish people in the last half-century? Probably never before have the Jews self-destructed so rapidly or so cheerfully. Liberal pluralism, they continue, is a far more effective weapon against Jewish survival than oppression ever was. Once again the Jews are surrounded by hostile forces, made all the more perilous for their masquerading as allies. Once again they confront extinction. And once again they are called upon to reject the counsel of surrender. In short, the tale of a beset and beleaguered Jewish people continues unabated.

Christian ecumenism and good will are especial danger points. Whether connivingly in order to lure Jews into their religious net or sincerely in order to atone for past sins, Christians have, for the most part, repudiated church-sponsored antisemitism and offered a welcoming smile to their Jewish friends. They vaunt their liberal credentials; indeed the priest and minister are eager to foster interfaith activities with the rabbi. But there is an unstated premise to all of this: Meet us halfway, meet us in the American mainstream. It is because we all shop at the mall, play golf on the same course, and send our kids to the same colleges that this dialogue is so easy. We can set aside our differences because they are, in the end, so paltry. This, for much of Orthodoxy, is the severe modern ordeal with which God tests his people.

There is at times a near-apocalyptic state of mind that attends this vision of a people besieged. The Jewish people has been doubly decimated in our time. One in every three Jews perished in the Holocaust and a half-century later one in every two American Jews marries "out." Can it be doubted that all around us the Jewish world disintegrates apace? Does this not reflect the

Hand of God? The ultimate test? Is it not clear that we, the Jews who have remained loyal to God's Word, will be the only Jews remaining in a generation or two? Now more than ever it is our sacred duty to resist the inroads of a culturally hostile world. And can there be any doubt that ours is the way of God? It is, after all, manifest that the further one moves toward ultra-Orthodoxy, the greater the communal cohesiveness, the deeper and more exclusive the commitment to Torah, the fewer that are lost to temptations of the non-Jewish world.

Nothing heightens this sense of siege and separation more than public differences of dress and comportment. Walking the streets of Boston or the Loop or Rodeo Drive (to say nothing of a corporate board room or an Ivy League campus) wearing traditional garb or even a small *kipah* (skullcap) still makes for double-takes among many passers-by. Even if these looks are no longer threatening, they still foster a sense of isolation and self-consciousness. They nourish the sources of communal inwardness and make community members comfortable only when in the company of those who are similarly ill-at-ease in the non-Jewish world. They encourage the moralistic equivalent of a fortress mentality: We, the Jewishly steadfast, form a communal redoubt dedicated to purity, learning, earnestness, and chastity. It is our charge to resist the encircling armies of dissolution, vulgarity, frivolousness, and abomination.

Indeed, the ultra-Orthodox do not cease impressing upon the members of their community how critical their unique dress and distinct comportment are and how important the consequent feelings of "a people that dwells apart" are for Jewish continuity. Perhaps no interpretive comment is so often repeated in the ultra-Orthodox world as the *Midrash*'s (an interpretive gloss on the Bible from the early Talmudic era) observation that the Jews were delivered from Egyptian bondage because they did not change their names and their language or forsake their code of ritual purity.[21] One need only imagine the sense of foreignness and discomfiture that traditional Jews feel when walking the streets during the tumult of the Christmas season to appreciate how easy it is to cling to the old mental habits of isolation and adversity. Indeed, among many Orthodox and especially ultra-Orthodox Jews the custom remains not to study Torah on Christmas Eve, "*nittel nacht*," as it is called. The collective memory of violent drunken attacks on the Jewish quarter of town rendered Torah study and the total absorption it entails a dangerous occupation. At such perilous moments vigilance is of the essence.

Add to all this the residential patterns and total support systems necessary for Orthodox observance and the picture approaches completeness. Orthodox but especially ultra-Orthodox Jews who remained in the older and poorer Jewish neighborhoods find themselves in proximity to crime-ridden, slum areas. This is certainly true of their large concentrations in the

Williamsburg, Crown Heights, and Borough Park sections of Brooklyn. Their view of the "outside world" is, therefore, mediated through especially menacing human realities marked by violence, dissolution, family breakdown, and communal devastation—realities with which they rub shoulders constantly. Comparisons between their "benighted" neighbors and their own sense of probity and earnestness cannot help but reinforce their sense of isolation. When, as in the Crown Heights turmoil of recent years, intercommunal tensions explode into tragic violence, the vision of an inhospitable and belligerent reality (reminiscent of the Jewish shtetl encircled by hostile Gentiles) receives its ultimate vindication.

Lest the reader be misled by our exclusive emphasis on the Orthodox world, it is important to make clear that these feelings of isolation and vulnerability are found among other sections of the American Jewish community as well. We specifically chose the Orthodox to illustrate the continuing resilience of the "ideology of affliction" because they are so uniquely and intensely in its grip. They are its paradigmatic representatives but hardly its sole proponents. Proceeding from the Orthodox epicenter in ever-weakening circles, the "ideology of affliction" extends outward to cover a surprisingly large portion of American Jewry.

And yet Jews who are closer to the American mainstream tend to express their sense of precariousness differently from the Orthodox. For them, it is not the menace of assimilation or the anxieties of cultural isolation that are the contemporary incarnations of adversity. Their understanding of "affliction" centers on the Holocaust and on Israel's embattled position in the Middle East. It is to these subjects that we presently turn.

The Holocaust

Above all else it is the image of the Holocaust that sustains and embodies the American Jewish sense of vulnerability. One very wide-ranging and instructive study that conducted scores of interviews with American Jews— from the marginally Jewish to the strongly committed—reports that perceptions of antisemitism inevitably return to the destruction of Europe's Jews:

> What surfaces over and over again in these and similar speculations on Jewish vulnerability is the image of the Holocaust, it *could* happen here . . . . [Respondents] discount the statistics and surveys and insist instead on their own intuition of the ineradicability of antisemitism. Antisemitism, they are convinced, has not declined; only standards of politeness have changed . . . . To complicate matters,

the potential content of antisemitism has been broadened to include opposition to Zionist doctrine, for example, or criticism of Israel . . . . complacency and confidence based on surveys, polls, and statistics are mistakes—potentially fatal mistakes.[22]

In any discussion of antisemitism, they conclude, reference to the Holocaust is the ultimate trump card, the unassailable justification for continued anxiety despite the apparent decline of antisemitism in America:

> Briefly stated the lesson goes like this: The German Jews thought (as we do today) that they were safe. They too believed they could assimilate. But look what happened. Don't make the mistake they made.[23]

But why, it must be asked, has Holocaust anxiety turned into a dominating presence only relatively recently, that is, roughly starting from the mid-1970s? Arthur Hertzberg, one of the sagest commentators on American Jewish life, suggests that the revival of American Jewish interest in the Holocaust coincides—not at all accidentally—with the dramatic decline in antisemitism.[24] Hertzberg observes:

> Middle-aged parents saw what freedom had wrought and became frightened at the evaporation of the Jewishness of their children. The parents evoked the one Jewish emotion that had tied their own generation together, the fear of antisemitism. The stark memory of Auschwitz needed to be evoked to make the point that Jews were different. Young Jews needed to be told that antisemitism had not disappeared, it was only quiescent and could return to destroy them. Holocaust courses, institutes, and museums suddenly became necessary, to evoke sharp, and instant, Jewish emotions among hundreds of thousands of younger Jews who had little connection with Jewish religion or Jewish learning.[25]

Much like parents seeking to preserve the Jewishness of their children, Jewish community leaders also felt the need to *use* the Holocaust to "bind Jews emotionally to the Jewish community, and to inspire identification and commitment to Jewish survival."[26] Because the Holocaust is, for many Jews, the "most vivid and ethnically alive" aspect of their Jewishness,[27] it is also the easiest and most accessible of Jewish themes to employ. But for all its efficiency as a community-rouser, preoccupation with the Holocaust has its limits and its potential pitfalls. The attempts to coax just one more tear, to instill fear once again will be eventually overwhelmed by the familiar

American realities of affluence and security. Moreover, for many sensitive young people, it will inevitably seem that

> the only place where there is real energy in the Jewish community is in commemorating the Holocaust and searching out real or imagined enemies who might, on further stretch of the imagination, threaten us once again.[28]

A variety of reasons account for the remarkable amounts of emotional energy invested by so many American Jews in Holocaust memorials. Perhaps the most important is the capacity of the Holocaust to mobilize all American Jews, each in his own way. "The vicarious memory of the Holocaust" is perhaps the single uniting experience that consolidates the "fractious" American community. Despite its unifying power, the fact that there is room for creative interpretation of the Holocaust, that all "may draw different conclusions" from it, only reinforces its position as a central focus of American Jewish identity.[29]

Yet whatever specific interpretation one chooses to place upon the Holocaust, the memory of "affliction" is never very distant. Jewish fund-raisers have learned long ago that nothing heightens the sense of Jewish vulnerability and energizes the Jewish philanthropic urge better than linking a specific project to the memory of the Holocaust. To illustrate: a full-page advertisement in the *New York Times* appeals for donations to support the exodus of Soviet Jews to Israel. Under a photo of Yad Va'shem's memorial hall the text reads: "It starts with hate mail, name calling and grave desecrations. . . . We all know how it ends. And now it looks like it's starting all over again in the Soviet Union."[30]

Nevertheless, it is clear that in the process of becoming a central American Jewish concern, the Holocaust took on some very distinctly American attributes—attributes that demonstrate the limits to which the Holocaust can be mobilized as part of a traditional, solidarity-enhancing Jewish survival strategy. What stands out most strikingly in American Jewish evocations of the Holocaust is the universal, generically human significance with which it has been invested. Although we shall return to this point in subsequent chapters, it seems nevertheless appropriate to adduce a number of illustrations. Discussing the Holocaust Museum in Washington, D.C., the most prominent authority on Holocaust memorials speaks of "the gradual integration of Holocaust memory into American civic culture" and the parallels between how America and Israel are projected into the Holocaust narrative as "lands of refuge and freedom."[31] A Holocaust curriculum volume, clearly produced for Jewish and non-Jewish use, comes to the following conclusion:

Perhaps the most important implication or lesson comes from the examples of the rescuers. In spite of pressures, non-Jews all over Europe refused to collaborate in the "Final Solution." These individuals chose to act according to a standard of behavior, a code of ethics, that put human life ahead of other considerations. As one scholar wrote, referring to the rescue of the Jews in Denmark, the history of the Holocaust shows us that "it could happen in most places but it did not happen everywhere."[32]

Nothing more famously illustrates the American inclination to invest the Holocaust with universalist meaning than Steven Spielberg's decision to tell the story of the genocide of Europe's Jews through the vehicle of a "righteous Gentile" in the movie *Schindler's List*.

Israel

Support for Israel and preoccupation with the Holocaust have a common root: Both focus upon the beleaguered nature of Jewish existence. American Jewish leaders regularly refer to Israel as "a spiritual homeland," "the focus for our sense of peoplehood," the exemplification of "the fundamental values of Judaism," and "a light unto the nations." But at the heart of these various images is a vision of Israel as "endangered." It is, these leaders quickly add, the responsibility of American Jews to assist it to survive. In a word: "When Israel is endangered . . . all Jews are endangered."[33]

Not only are Holocaust memorials and support for Israel similar in their emotional derivation; historically, they became major issues for American Jews at quite the same time. Both rose to the commanding position they now hold in the days and weeks preceding the 1967 Six-Day War. Prior to that time, neither Israel nor the Holocaust were major components in American Jewish identity. It has been regularly observed that analysts of American Jewish life—notably in the various *Commentary* symposia of American Jewish intellectuals on the state of Jewish belief and Jewish self-understanding—had little to say about either subject.[34] In the first edition of his popular book *American Judaism*, Nathan Glazer noted that "the two greatest events in modern Jewish history, the murder of six million Jews by Hitler and the creation of the Jewish state in Palestine, have had remarkably slight effects on the inner life of American Jewry."[35]

The weeks of tense anticipation and gnawing fear that preceded the outbreak of the Six-Day War brought home with incomparable force the ancient message of Jewish vulnerability. Those harrowing days catapulted

Israel into the center of American Jewish concerns and, simultaneously, placed a dramatic spotlight upon the event with which Israel's vulnerability had resonated: the Holocaust. The latter was destruction incarnate; the former destruction *in potentia*. At that moment, American Jews perceived themselves—in spite of their secure existence—as an inextricable part of this history of tribulation.[36]

In the late 1950s, Marshall Sklare and a number of his colleagues conducted a systematic analysis of American Jews in a midwestern suburb he spoke of as Lakeville.[37] It was a community of very prosperous third- and fourth-generation American Jews who encountered little anti-Jewish discrimination. They were largely assimilated; Jewishness in general and especially Israel seemed to play a minor role in their lives. Notably, Sklare tells us that he chose this community because it was a place where the kinds of Jews who would be increasingly encountered in tomorrow's Jewish communities were already very substantially represented.[38]

Following the Six-Day War, Sklare returned to Lakeville to assess the impact the war had had upon its members. He found a dramatically transformed reality.[39] The period preceding the war had electrified Lakeville's Jewish residents, bringing home the very real possibility that Israel might not survive. One anecdote he relates is worth a thousand words. One of Sklare's respondents had an Israeli house guest staying with him during the weeks prior to the war. The Israeli reassured him that everything would turn out all right. The American host reported becoming hostile toward the Israeli because "he was so lacking in feeling as not to experience the anxiety the respondent himself felt."[40]

During the war, there was an insatiable hunger for news. Radios were carried everywhere and the slightest shred of information passed like wildfire to anxious ears. There was an unprecedented outpouring of contributions to the United Jewish Appeal's Israel Emergency Fund. ("It is ingrained in the American Jewish soul," wrote Arthur Hertzberg, "that the correct response to a danger is to give money."[41]) In Lakeville, as in the rest of the United States, the response was staggering: from May 23 to June 10 over $100 million were raised—and it was in the form of cash and checks, not pledges.[42]

Sklare explains this unusual outpouring of cash and checks:

> By the time the first public (if not private) fund-raising meetings could be convened, victory was a foregone conclusion. But sober businessmen long experienced in problems of procurement, of manufacturing, and of transportation, acted as if the money they contributed one day could somehow miraculously be turned into the sinews of war the very next day. Because they wanted to believe in such a mira-

cle, the emphasis was not upon pledges—the usual form of Jewish fund-raising—but on a different approach: the giving of cash.[43]

One rabbi, reporting on a fund-raising meeting in his synagogue, explained that

> the entire meeting was cash oriented. A great many checks were handed in; people not only wanted to pledge money but they actually wanted to give cash at the meeting. Several people got up and said they had arranged for a bank loan so that they could give the cash. Another man got up to say that Baron Rothschild in Paris had sold his race horses to raise cash.[44]

The events in Israel touched Jews who had, heretofore, remained unmoved by anything Jewish. Sklare describes the most assimilated of the Lakeville respondents, a woman who had no contact with Jewish life. Her children had received no Jewish education; she worked on Yom Kippur; many of her close friends were Gentile. But, Sklare reports, she was as emotionally overpowered by the events as any other respondent. Since she was on no Jewish mailing list, she had to actively seek out where contributions to the Emergency Fund could be made. But it was her motivation, as she expressed it, that is interesting to consider. Israel's struggle against the vastly larger Arab armies was a symbolic portent: "No more does the Jew march to the ovens. Now he has something to fight for," Sklare records.[45] She declared: We have never fought back before. We always picked up our bundles and ran. Now we can fight back.[46] Her son in graduate school had the same reaction. She reported: "Bill wrote to me how proud he was to be a Jew at this time. He had told me before that he could not understand why the Jews walked to the gas chambers."[47]

Hertzberg analyzed the American Jewish response to the Six-Day War in similar terms. What was most important, he writes,

> was a revulsion against the passivity of the Jewish victims of the Holocaust. "Good" Jews have been largely arguing since 1945 that the passivity was a distinctively Jewish form of heroism, but it is now apparent that many who interpreted it in this way never really succeeded in convincing themselves.[48]

Sklare's position, although quite different in nuance, returns to these same Holocaust-related themes as well. Through no merit of their own, American Jews had avoided the agonies of the Holocaust. During the days leading up to the Six-Day War, the repetition of their fortuitous salvation appears to have been an entirely credible possibility. Sklare understands them as thinking:

> If we have the problem of justifying our escape from the first holocaust, the least we can do is make the gesture of helping to prevent a second one; at the very minimum such a gesture will indicate that some good purpose was served in our being spared. (And the possibility of a second holocaust presents us with an opportunity to cleanse the record of the 1930's and 40's—perhaps we are not entirely sure that we did all we could to avert that holocaust and to succor its victims.) Thus, our support of Israel is intimately connected with our desire to preserve a feeling of our worth as human beings.[49]

From 1967 until quite recently, massive support for Israel on the part of American Jews remained constant and constituted the most important single item on the Jewish communal agenda. (The rising level of indifference toward Israel, to which we allude in the next chapter, is of relatively recent origin.) Inevitably, the primacy of Israel was rooted in the traditional adversity-centered view of Jewish life. The foremost authority on American Jewish attitudes toward Israel notes that "American Jewish feelings about Israel are dominated by fear far more than by hope, by nightmares more than by dreams."[50] Rather than pride in Israel's achievements, American Jews are more deeply concerned with threats against Israel's security. Interestingly, there is a significant correlation between perceptions of Arab hostility and perceptions of American Gentile hostility. "For American Jews, caring about Israel is tied to worrying about the 'goyim.'"[51] It follows that those who view the world as generally antagonistic to Jews and to the Jewish state display a high levels of caring about Israel.

But American Jewish views of the world as antagonistic are on the decline—nowhere more so than among the youth. It should come as no surprise then that interest in Israel is declining as well. With the threat of antisemitism receding, the Holocaust universalized and fading into the past, the dislocation of Israel from the center of American Jewish identity, new strategies for Jewish survival in the United States become imperative. It is to these novel directions in Jewish self-understanding that we now turn.

american jews

New Images

> Like if the whooping crane ain't gonna make it; the
> whooping crane ain't gonna make it. No hatcheries
> are going to do it. That's what these Rabbis are trying
> to do, make hatcheries for whooping cranes.

Nothing manifests the residual power of the "ideology of affliction" more
starkly than American Jewry's preoccupation with the Holocaust and with
Israel's security. They form the axis of contemporary Jewish sensibilities for
many American Jews even though both of these concerns are far removed
from their existential immediacy. Not only are the Holocaust and Israel's
defenses unrelated to the daily activities and familiar challenges that confront America's Jews, in some important ways they run profoundly counter
to them.[1]

The self-understanding of Jewishness that emerges from the typical
Holocaust-generated perspective is clearly at odds with the firsthand reality that American Jews actually experience. And yet, despite the unprecedented confidence and power they enjoy, many American Jews choose to
center their identity and sensibilities on traumatic events that emphasize
powerlessness and victimhood. They understand as central to their own
existence events that took place at a great remove from them, that directly
affected only an aging handful of its members, and that are ineluctably
receding into the past. Despite the indisputable enormity of the Holocaust,
it is nevertheless intriguing that the rhetoric of precariousness and affliction should stubbornly persist in elegantly appointed community centers,
among acclaimed Hollywood moguls, and amidst Washington lobbyists
unequaled in their influence.

A community fully at home in one country—that reacts with fury when
charges of dual loyalty are raised—cannot discipline or mobilize itself
when its own needs are at stake with anything like the passion and solidarity that surge forward when Israel's security is threatened. Although American Jews have no intention of taking part in the Zionist enterprise and are
often woefully uninformed about Israel and its travails, when the Jewish
state's perils resonate with their collective memories of adversity, some
aboriginal Jewish loyalty is set into motion. What is more, these vicarious
concerns with tragedies and threats that are outside the American Jewish

experience tend to drive pressing issues like Jewish literacy to the margins of the public agenda.

Although remote from their immediate concerns, the "ideology of affliction" continues to retain a powerful grip on the American Jewish imagination. In the past, when adversity was painfully real, the "ideology of affliction" served to render it comprehensible and endurable. Gentile hostility was an essential part of the nature of things and, moreover, demonstrated the chosenness of the Jews. Paradoxically, although the idea of chosenness is often awkward and embarrassing to contemporary liberal American Jews, the uniqueness of Jewish suffering remains an unassailable given. In other words, for lack of a more substantive relation to the Jewish tradition, many American Jews remain wedded to the "ideology of affliction." With Jewish substance shallow and diluted, few other alternatives remain. They search for signs that sustain the credibility of Jewish precariousness, and, what is more, this search has become indispensable to their collective identity.

This does not augur well for the American Jewish future. Eventually, the familiar and immediate will overwhelm the unfamiliar and distant. What accords with real needs and experience will displace what does not. Cognitive dissonance, after all, has a lifespan of its own—especially when the beliefs in question are not part of a broader system of faith and practice that renders threats of persecution credible (as is the case with the Orthodox). The incongruity between experience and consciousness seems destined to lead to the kind of outbursts that Philip Roth puts into the mouth of an angry and graphic Alex Portnoy:

> "Jew Jew Jew Jew Jew Jew! It is coming out of my ears already, the saga of the suffering Jews. Do me a favor, my people, and stick your suffering heritage up your suffering ass— *I happen also to be a human being.*"[2]

It is, therefore, of the greatest significance for Jewish survival in America that alternate forms of Jewish identification—that are not products of the "ideology of affliction"—have, of late, been emerging. For a number of decades, and with greater intensity in recent years, there has been a proliferation of specifically American reinterpretations of Judaism and Jewishness that explicitly acknowledge the revolutionary impact of material prosperity and personal security. They underscore the novel circumstances created by almost limitless freedom of self-expression in America. Moreover, they recognize the wide-ranging implications of the disappearance of Jewish neighborhoods and the obsolescence of ghetto nostalgia. What, they ask, can it mean to be a Jew in these unprecedented conditions? Among the variety of responses, two are paramount: first, Jewish liberalism; second, the privatization/personalization of Jewishness. We shall explore each of them in turn.

American Jewish Liberalism

About half of American Jews identify themselves as political liberals.[3] This is a striking datum because it represents twice the number of non-Jews who do so.[4] And it must be added immediately that the affinity of Jewishness for liberal attitudes is more than happenstance. For many American Jews, the non-Orthodox in particular, political liberalism is constitutive of what it means to be a good and caring Jew. For them, the quest for social justice, civil and human rights, and the concern for the welfare of the disadvantaged are the moral and religious content of the Jewish tradition.

John Dos Passos has an imprisoned Jewish radical explain the source of his passion for social justice as follows:

> "There's something in it. You'd have to be a Jew like me to understand. You've heard of the Pale. Everyone of us has something fenced up way down in us. We've been in prison for two thousand years. I have the mind of a jailbird, that's why prison can't hurt me. That's why we throw ourselves into every movement of freedom. That's why I feel the slavery of the workers, I feel it as a worker and I feel it as a Jew."[5]

Many of these same sentiments are often given an overtly theological reading. Responding to black recriminations toward Jews in the early 1990s, a professor at the Jewish Theological Seminary of America recalls that for him and many of his associates, participating in the civil rights movement of the 1960s was the very heart of what they understood Judaism to be. He thought it no coincidence that he taught at a religious institute where Rabbi Abraham Joshua Heschel spent his career and that he sent his daughter to the Abraham Joshua Heschel religious day school "where the photo of Professor Heschel marching with Dr. King . . . served virtually as the emblem of the school." He writes:

> As a teenager in 1962, I remember the work that my synagogue youth group engaged in to do our small part for the great struggle that black Americans had mounted. For us at that time there was the sense that we were participating in the most important religious

challenge of our age . . . . I think that in certain significant ways, my *Jewish* identity was shaped by a connection to the civil rights movement—that "seeking Justice" was what my tradition demanded of me and that the fervor of those times allowed me the chance to go beyond myself.[6]

A nationwide survey of American Jews undertaken by the *Los Angeles Times* in 1988[7] fleshes out this affinity for liberal attitudes nicely. When asked: "As a Jew, which of the following qualities do you consider most important to your Jewish identity: a commitment to social equality, or religious observance, or support for Israel, or what?" Half answered "equality"; the rest were divided between religious observance, support for Israel, and a miscellany of other responses.

Answers were closely associated with denomination. The proportions answering "equality" were 18 percent of those defining themselves as Orthodox, 44 percent of those defining themselves Conservative, 65 percent of those defining themselves percent Reform, and 63 percent of those who were nondenominational. For many Jews of progressive and liberal persuasions, the part of their heritage with which they most closely identify and of which they are most especially proud is the dedication to social justice. They manifest a particular proclivity to identify the Jewish mission with a socially activist and reformist posture, with what they sometimes call "acting as humanity's conscience."

But if the Jewish tradition mandates pursuing social justice, we would naturally expect those with the greatest exposure to this tradition to evince the most ardent commitment to liberal causes. Those whose ties to the classical sources and to traditional Jewish observances are weaker would, by contrast, be expected to manifest declining commitments to progressive causes. The reality demonstrates quite the reverse. The Orthodox are dramatically underrepresented in the liberal camp—fewer than one in five—while the Reform and nondenominational (which usually means, in practice, entirely unaffiliated) are strikingly overrepresented—almost two out of three.

Interestingly, among Conservative and Reform Jews, many measures of liberalism were found to be inversely proportional to synagogue attendance. This leads us to the conclusion that contemporary American Jewish liberalism does not so much derive from a firsthand engagement with Jewish sources; rather, it should be understood as an alternate form of Jewish identity that issues from powerful socio-historical forces of relatively recent origin. For many progressive American Jews who are committed to this form of Jewish identity, pursuing the liberal mission is not something that Jews happen to do; it is, for them, the core of what it means to be Jewish.[8]

Having disposed of the contention that pursuing social justice is inherent in the Jewish tradition, many analysts turn to extrinsic factors to account for the remarkable affinity between Jews and liberal causes. The most popular alternate explanation relates Jewish liberalism to the status of Jews as a persecuted minority. When the Enlightenment and French Revolution presented the promise of equality and acceptance, Jews naturally flocked to progressive causes—as the Dos Passos quote above so cannily conveys. And yet we cannot help but feel that this is only a partial explanation. Without wishing to detract from the interpretive power of this very cogent account, we believe, nevertheless, that the Jewish tradition's endemic qualities should not be dismissed quite so hastily.

The Jewish tradition clearly does have a highly salient social justice motif. Caring for the poor, for orphans, widows, the stranger, the infirm, and the disadvantaged is too often enjoined and emphasized to be regarded as inconsequential. Philanthropy toward and compassion for the downtrodden are core Jewish values and they are justified in specifically Jewish terms, to wit, "for you too were strangers in the land of Egypt." The Orthodox fully internalize this message; among the ultra-Orthodox, for example, care for the disadvantaged is exemplary. Indeed, we doubt that there is another group in American society that is as densely saturated with philanthropic causes and benevolent organizations. Most Orthodox synagogues have a fund to provide interest-free loans for those who have fallen on hard times or who find themselves temporarily in an awkward financial position. Going to an ultra-Orthodox shul on a weekday means being personally confronted by a barrage of appeals from a small army of collectors. A host of itinerant charity solicitors with their distinctive traditional garb canvass the Orthodox neighborhoods and ring the bell of every door that has a mezuzah (a housed piece of parchment on which certain biblical passages are inscribed) on the doorpost. (Growing up in these neighborhoods means knowing that a ring at the door is as likely as not someone seeking a donation.) Solicitors occasionally venture outside their own well-worked territory into the more cosmopolitan suburbs, to the acute distress of genteel Jewish residents. Sifting through the mail received in Orthodox homes would reveal that it contains its equivalent of suburban/commercial junk mail in appeals for charitable causes representing everything from endowments to support Jewish learning, to funds that support homes for the aged, to campaigns that aim at furnishing dowries for impecunious brides.

A study by the sociologist Chaim Waxman of Jewish baby boomers finds that over 80 percent of the Orthodox reported contributing to Jewish charities of one kind or another—compared with 56 percent of the Conservative, 43 percent of the Reform, and 25 percent of the unaffiliated. Waxman notes that Orthodox baby boomers reported larger families and lower annual family incomes than Conservative and Reform (an average of about $10,000 a year less than the Conservative and $20,000 less than the Reform). Yet 71 percent reported contributing $500 or more to Jewish charities. Comparable figures for the Conservative were 18 percent and for the Reform 12 percent.[9]

Nevertheless, all this charity and compassion does not translate into liberal attitudes. Because it is turned inward, directed virtually exclusively toward other Jews—if not actually limited to other Orthodox Jews—the social justice motif tends to strengthen communitarian concerns rather than universal ones. Orthodox philanthropy begins and ends at home. Waxman reports that over two-thirds of the non-Orthodox and fully 75 percent of the unaffiliated reported making contributions to non-Jewish charities during the past year; only 57 percent of the Orthodox reported doing so.

One might say that the internal organization of the Orthodox world manifests many of the same benevolent, welfarist, social justice commitments that dominate the thinking of their more liberal co-religionists. But with Orthodox suspicion and hostility toward non-Jews and their rejection of the non-Orthodox, the drive toward social justice remains largely an "in-house" affair.

When the boundaries sealing off Jewish community life from society at large were breached by the Enlightenment and Emancipation, the drive for social justice, so long an internal concern, was propelled outward. Since then it has served as an all-purpose catalyst for progressive causes. Justifications for this kind of universalized social activism were not difficult to come by; Jewish particularism, it was reasonably argued, represented the natural Jewish reaction to special times and circumstances. Given a borderless world, however, the commendable Jewish instinct for mutual support needed to be given more global import. This new reading of the old sources, it was contended, liberated them from the obscurity of tribalist particularism and catapulted them into the light of universal human significance.[10]

In much the same way that Jewish intellectualism turned from Talmud and halachic law to philosophy and literature, so the Jewish emphasis on the mutual responsibility of community members for one another became, in the "emancipated" version, a universalist pursuit of fraternity and mutuality—often with the older religious-messianic dreams recycled and secularized. The notion of *tikkun olam* (repairing or reforming the world) that heretofore was understood in mystical or community-centered terms takes on programmatic, activist, and universalist significance. This world-affirming Jewish stance—so at odds with Christian other-worldliness—transcends its specifically religious sources and serves to invigorate generations of Jewish radicals, progressives and liberals.

To the degree that Jewish particularism recedes, this socially activist elan takes on more ecumenical and broadly humanitarian characteristics. As we have seen, among the Orthodox the social justice theme works itself out mainly within the Orthodox community itself. At the other end of the Jewish spectrum, the Reform and unaffiliated identify social activism with what might be described as "benevolent cosmopolitanism," that is, with caring for the sufferings of humankind in general.

As unique Jewish content is lost and ignorance of the tradition becomes the norm, however, the specifically Jewish sources that feed this liberal current are drying up. Without knowledge of the Jewish ideas that ostensibly inspire liberalism, it would be very odd to claim that just these ideas are its source. If we add to growing illiteracy the secure position of American Jews that gives the lie to the sense of vulnerability, the historical verdict would have to be that Jewish liberalism will lose its hold. In the interim, a mixture of partially retained religious messages, a residual sense of vulnerability, and, not least, simple historical inertia sustain the Jewish-liberal symbiosis. But inertia, in the form of habitual transmission from generation to generation, can last only so long—especially when its sources have disappeared from view and the reality in which it operates is inimical to the transmitted message. The future of Jewish liberalism appears precarious not because Jews will begin to "vote their pocketbook" (as neo-conservatives like Irving Kristol and Norman Podhoretz have predicted) but because both the substantive and the circumstantial sources of Jewish liberalism are showing symptoms of exhaustion. Indeed, there are distinct signs that this is already happening.

A recent study that compares the political attitudes of Jews with non-Jews over the course of the past few decades finds that, broadly speaking, Jews are only marginally more liberal than non-Jews of similar educational and socio-economic status, and when years of education are held constant, most of the differences disappear.[11] What distinguishes Jews from non-Jews appears to be not so much some primal liberal instinct but the fact that they are the most highly educated ethnic group in the United States. If the non-Jews in question are members of liberal churches or not church members at all, that is, if their religious exposures are roughly parallel to Conservative/Reform or nonaffiliated Jews, differences on virtually all measures of liberalism disappear.

Jewish uniqueness does, nevertheless, remain but it is not related to classical liberal concerns such as egalitarianism and compassion for the underprivileged. Jews and non-Jews tend to part company in regard to two issues: the separation of church and state—with Jews considerably more insistent upon a rigorous separation—and sexual codes of behavior. Jews are far more inclined to register understanding for homosexuality, abortion, and extra-marital sexual activity.

Furthermore, this kind of educationally and socio-economically based Jewish liberalism has a fatal weakness: It can no longer distinguish between Jews and non-Jews. There is nothing in the liberalizing educational process that relates liberal sentiments to one's Jewish identity; on the contrary, the overwhelming thrust of contemporary higher education (particularly in the more prestigious institutions of learning that Jews are more likely to attend) is to deracinate, that is, to attribute liberal ideas to generically human sources. Paradoxically, therefore, even when their Jewish cultural sensibilities lead Jews to join liberal causes, the source of their own behavior often remains obscured. Liberalism seems to them no more an essentially *Jewish* phenomenon than the greater proclivity of Jews to go to therapists or their alleged weakness for Chinese food. How ironic that Jews, finding themselves dramatically overrepresented in a liberal organization, will often willfully ignore this question-begging disproportion (which threatens to convict them of insularity) or at least relate to it with no more than casual curiosity. Jewishness, they protest, despite its palpable presence, has nothing to do with our being here.

Liberalism as the content of Jewishness fails, therefore, because it is self-undermining. As a survival strategy it may, temporarily, provide much needed sustenance for modern Jews who are skeptical, morally earnest, and disoriented, but it cannot sustain Jewishness because, by its very nature, it finds it awkward, if not actually mortifying, to justify communitarian boundaries. If ecumenical humanitarianism, benevolent cosmopolitanism, and enlightened nonsectarianism are what Jewishness purveys, it would be incongruous, even hypocritical for the purveyors to insist on their own uniqueness and to encourage their separation from others. A strategy for Jewish survival that does not provide the resources to vindicate difference, borders, and internal community cohesion (a fortiori, one that celebrates universalism) may possess the noblest of motives and the most commendable of intentions, but it paves the way to Jewish dissolution. A Jewish community claiming liberal humanitarianism as its content will quickly learn that its members are adept at finding the sources of their liberalism elsewhere.

The Privatization of Jewishness

Jewishness survived the decline of religious belief (as we argued in Chapter 3) because ethnic solidarity filled the vacuum caused by secularization. Even though Judaism as a religious system suffered renunciations and defections, the persistence of antisemitism and the community-enhancing effects of densely populated Jewish neighborhoods provided adequate support for a robust Jewish identity. In this insular context, even Jewish universalism (!), radicalism, and liberalism could be interpreted in specifically Jewish terms by those who chose to remain Jewish and looked for excuses to do so.

Jewish illiteracy, the decline of Jewish neighborhoods, and the growing security of American Jews have rendered the liberal-Jewish symbiosis increasingly problematic. Despite our claim that liberalism does, indeed, draw upon an authentic Jewish proclivity for social justice, it fails as a strategy for Jewish survival because it lacks the resources to justify Jewish cohesion and particularism. Moreover, because of its cosmopolitan thrust, its logic undercuts the very Jewish sensibilities that ostensibly lie at its source.

Liberalism as the vehicle for Jewish identity has run into other difficulties as well. It suffers because the public, ethnic, political, and organizational understanding of Jewishness does not sit well with the personalist and experientialist vogue that has recently overtaken much of the American Jewish world.[12] The ethnic-organizational form of Jewish identity speaks in civic, rational, systematic, and strategic terms; the private-experiential variety, by contrast, is cast in considerably more intimate, stirring, and spiritualist language.

The rhetoric of ethnicity concentrates on themes such as peoplehood, community, and solidarity. Its message centers on slogans such as "We are one" and "Keep the promise." Its surpassing moments are Super Sundays, collective mobilizations for Israel, and well-orchestrated political campaigns for or against some specific public policy. It is necessarily combative, impersonal, and ideologically articulate. The language of privatized Jewishness, on the other hand, speaks in the hushed, softer terms of individual meaning, journeys of discovery, and the search for fulfillment. It is concretely interpersonal rather than abstractly collective in its emphases. Its favored qualities are authenticity and sincerity rather than achievement or efficiency. Typically it is consoling, nonjudgmental, intuitive, and nonobligating.

How deep are the inroads that privatized Jewishness has made? Although a definitive answer would require a great deal of information that is not yet available, there are distinct signs that it is having a substantial effect, especially on Jews in the younger age brackets. Contributions to the Federations of Jewish Philanthropy—a major form of public Jewish expression—are stagnating if not actually declining. Mobilization for political causes of all kinds is reported to be more and more difficult to justify and sustain. Jewish organizations are increasingly made up of and supported by an aging membership. Organizational work, once a commonplace Jewish avocation, appears to be eschewed by many; it is for them excessively impersonal, power-centered, and perfunctory.[13]

In place of the declining public face of Jewishness, a burgeoning private sphere offering a new understanding of the Jewish tradition has begun to make itself felt. Notably, it is very much a post- "ideology of affliction" phenomenon. It centers itself neither on perceptions of Gentile hostility nor on the precariousness of Jewish existence. Affluence and security are implicit in all of its pronouncements. It is the voice of a distinctively American cohort whose initial inspiration can be traced back to the counterculture of the sixties. Since then this "greening of Judaism" has lost many of its rebellious and antinomian qualities but still presents a picture of creative diversity and moral enthusiasm.

For all of its disarray, however, this new privatized form of Jewishness does have a number of recognized spokesmen. Arthur Green, currently Professor of Philosophy at Brandeis University, is generally acknowledged to have been the major voice in the movement's earlier years. Centering on the various university communities in the Boston area, a *havura* (literally, association or fellowship) of Jewish students and young faculty began experimenting with communal Jewish living, with novel approaches to the liturgy and holidays, and with a mildly mystical and highly personalistic version of the Jewish experience. They rejected the formalities of the large established synagogues as impediments to religious feeling, preferring small face-to-face groups and the intensely immediate spiritual experience.[14] Another highly colorful and inspirational personality associated with the personalist, havura movement is Zalman Shachter, an ordained Orthodox Rabbi who long ago abandoned the rigors of traditional observance while preserving a neo-Hasidic atmosphere and an extravagantly exuberant guru style. Especially interesting is Michael Lerner, founder and editor of *Tikkun*, a monthly that espouses liberal causes of both a Jewish and a general character. Lerner has recently projected his own conception of Judaism under the revealing title *Jewish Renewal: A Path to Healing and Transformation*.[15]

Like so much else that derived from the cultural creativity of the sixties, the *havura* and what it stood for has been imitated, bowdlerized, and coopted. From the seditious margins of Jewishness it has moved into its respectable center. Today, the privatized version of Jewishness has become a major, if not actually cliched, presence in virtually all of non-Orthodox American Judaism. Ironically, many established mainstream synagogues— of precisely the type the personalists rejected—have sponsored their own *havurot* (pl. of *havura*), even organized the entire synagogue along *havura* lines, in order to overcome the sense of remoteness and decorous indifference felt by so many of their members. Nevertheless, many *havurot* remain independent of or only marginally connected to a larger synagogue.

Variety dominates. Being experimental and given to personalized, experiential criteria for accepting or rejecting practices, it is only to be expected that the fundamental religious impulse that lies at its source will work itself out in strikingly different ways. Some of the *havurot* are centrally organized, others are entirely independent and probably unaware of one another's existence. Normally, they consist of a relatively small number of participants (five to fifty) who attempt to create in miniature the firsthand communitarian immediacy that urban anonymity discourages. They may gather as often as once a week for Sabbath services or as infrequently as once a year for the High Holidays. Often they celebrate life-cycle events—births, deaths, marriages, bar and bat mitzvahs—as if they constituted an extended family. The most ambitious may endeavor to create a full-scale Jewish life in common; others are content with establishing voluntary Jewish social clubs. (The latter can be sports-oriented—such as cycling or attending ball games together—or perhaps center on playing bridge.)

Weekend retreats, in which Jewishness is celebrated communally through prayer, learning, and ceremony, are a staple. It might be said that they try to synthesize the religious fervor and intimacy of a hasidic *shtiebl* (a small, informal synogogue of the traditional kind), with the intellectual openness and experimental freshness of the most progressive elements in the Jewish world. Some are formed by unassociated individuals with a specific religious agenda, others are created almost bureaucratically by synagogues seeking to introduce a degree of informality into the facelessness of a large congregation. Nor has the profit motive been excluded: Summer camps and retreats promising all manner of religious experiences have proliferated. Indeed, the new mood has not entirely passed over American Orthodoxy. Here, too, albeit in very restrained and moderate forms, the quest for religious immediacy is pursued in an assortment of ways. At the other end of the spectrum, Jewish content dwindles to a negligible residue and the age of Aquarius takes over—at times featuring overtly pagan rites and orgiastic sexuality.

Yet despite the lack of intellectual coherence, a number of very general characteristics are discernible. Four intertwining features, that together constitute a familiar syndrome, should be mentioned: universalism, moralism, personalism, and voluntarism. Most of these qualities are present in the more conventional, progressive religious denominations; still, they are especially conspicuous and dominant in the chaotic amalgam of Jews (sometimes joined by non-Jews) that has sprung up throughout North America and that goes under the portentous rubric of the "Jewish Renaissance."

We shall exclude both the Orthodox and the peripherally Jewish from our considerations; our concern here is with those groups whose experimentation is, on the one hand, recognizably Jewish in character and yet, on the other, not decisively constrained by the authority of halacha.[16] We include both the more conventional progressive forms of Judaism where these tendencies are mixed with more traditional elements, as well as "renaissance" phenomena where exploration and experimentation predominate.

Within this compass, the universalist ideal is clearly preeminent. By universalism we mean allegiance to the proposition that Jewish tradition is directed to all peoples and not to Jews alone. Although not overtly missionary in its practice, Judaism is understood to be anything but a tribal or narrowly communitarian religion; its universalist monotheistic character, its pursuit of social justice, its world-affirming character, its messianic yearnings all point to a boundless message of peace, hope, and human dignity.

Universalism also entails openness to other religious traditions. Judaism, so it is maintained, may be consummate and precious, but it is not exclusively in possession of the truth. Although interfaith activities require that one first be solidly rooted in a single faith, the exquisite spiritual beauty of other religious traditions cannot be dismissed in the name of insular loyalties. Indeed, universalists insist that Judaism will be positively enhanced by seeking to learn from other traditions, cultures, and religions. We must, as one advocate put it, "emphasize the things that . . . religions have in common, rather than dwelling only on the differences."[17] Ideas and practices deriving from Eastern religions, Islam, and even Christianity are, therefore, commonly present in services and ceremonies.

Furthermore, Judaism's universal significance obligates Jews to care for all peoples of the world, that is, to be acutely sensitive to the misery and indignities suffered by human beings as such. Being a caring Jew means deriving from one's specifically Jewish roots a sense of responsibility for the fate of humankind as a whole. For example, to the list of sins that Jews ask to be forgiven for in the High Holy Days liturgy, one experimental congregation added the following items:

> For the sins we have committed before you and before us by being so preoccupied with ourselves that we ignored the social world in which we live . . . .
> And for sins we have committed by participating in a racist society and not dedicating more energy to fight it.
> And for sins we have committed by not putting more energy into the struggle against proliferation of nuclear energy throughout society.[18]

Although more conspicuously present among those dedicated to the Jewish Renaissance, this universalist impulse is ubiquitous among most non-Orthodox American Jews. It saturates their political rhetoric as well as their

theology. A West Coast regional meeting of Conservative synagogues prepared its own booklet of supplementary readings and prayers, which included
the chant: "From one group to one humanity has been our goal . . . . "[19] The
universalist idea, moreover, finds its way into virtually every corner of Jewish ceremony and practice. Jewish holidays are regularly transformed, their
traditional messages reformulated, so as to diminish their particularistic
Jewish content and infuse them with universal significance. Clearly, some
holidays lend themselves to such modifications more readily than others.
Passover, the holiday commemorating the Jewish Exodus from Egypt, and
Hanukkah, which recalls the Jewish revolt against the Syrian-Greeks can,
for example, easily be construed as holidays of freedom. They both tell tales
of liberation from the yoke of foreign domination and, significantly, recall
similar struggles for emancipation and independence in our own day. The
less palatable, that is, the more particularistic aspects of the historical narrative tend to be given short shrift.

Passover is probably the best example. The narrative of liberation from
slavery becomes the preeminent, if not actually the sole, message of the holiday. The more particularistic nation-creating significance of the Exodus, its
being a necessary prelude to the revelation at Sinai in which the Jews are
uniquely chosen as guardians of God's Law, the painfully devastating
plagues visited upon the Egyptians, the mass drowning of the Egyptian army
in the sea, the destruction of the peoples of Canaan, and so on, all become
shadowy presences, overwhelmed by the universal message of liberation
and independence. Nowhere, perhaps, was this universalist impulse more
manifest than in the "freedom seder" developed by Jewish civil rights
activists during the 1960s. Non-Jews, blacks in particular, were invited to
jointly celebrate the seder. The text of the Passover Haggadah was substantially edited to emphasize the liberationist core of the holiday and new symbols and themes were added to reflect the commonality of Jewish and black
slavery as well their shared yearnings toward freedom and dignity.

A more contemporary transformation, one that includes the values of
personalism (to be described below) as well as universalism, is described in a
Wall Street Journal article. The newspaper's Boston bureau reported on a
Cambridge seder in which the majority of those attending were non-Jews:

> We used modern Haggadot, which describe the exodus from Egypt,
> but they were not modern enough. Someone complained that refer-
> ences to "light and darkness" carried negative connotation for peo-
> ple of color. Susan, an Episcopalian, was complimented on her
> skillful reading of Hebrew. "I went to divinity school," she
> explained. . . . We improvised on other matters. A Passover song,

"The Ballad of the Four Children," was sung to the tunes of "My Darling Clementine" and "La Cucaracha." A new-age prayer was read decrying alienation, anomie, and the "pharaohs of technology." Individuals read special poems or literary passages. We heard a selection from e. e. cummings and a few words from "Candide." A friend suggested I read "The Midnight Ride of Paul Revere," as it combines the theme of exodus with a New England twist . . . . [20]

Hanukkah has also undergone its own form of metamorphosis. From a holiday celebrating the victory of the zealously anti-assimilationist Hasmoneans over the more worldly and cosmopolitan Hellenizers, it has become a tale of political liberation, with nonsectarian human significance. In this case (given the need to provide an adequate Jewish rejoinder to "peace on earth, good will to men") the historical realities have not merely been recycled; they have been quite reversed. The vindication of Jewish particularism that the holiday commemorates is replaced by the universal significance of freedom. The irreducible distinctiveness of the Jews becomes an integral part of the "holiday season." Lighting the Hanukkah menorah, which symbolizes the re-consecration of the temple and the return to Jewish ritual sacrifice, is transformed into a celebration centering on the "light of freedom." For those Jews who fear that the omnipresent Christmas spirit will weaken their children's sense of Jewish distinctiveness, Hanukkah is a godsend. It becomes a time for gift giving that rivals and sometimes exceeds that of Christmas. Indeed, invidious comparisons are sometimes drawn between Christian children who receive gifts only once and the fortunate Jewish children who receive them on each of the eight nights of Hanukkah. (Nevertheless, Hanukkah's indispensability as a counter-holiday may well be on the wane as more Jewish homes, particularly among the intermarried, accept Christmas celebrations as natural and legitimate.)

We recall our children's disappointment at their first Hanukkah in Israel. We happily adopted the Israeli custom of presenting the children with the equivalent of a few pennies (Hanukkah gelt) on the first night of Hanukkah, and nothing more. Actually, the custom in Israel is to give smaller children chocolate candies wrapped in gold paper that simulate Israeli coins. Our children assumed that the American Jewish custom of engaging in an eight-day orgy of gift-giving was the Jewish norm. They were not only disappointed but a bit shocked by our cavalier violation of hoary traditions.

If some holidays are easily translated into the universalist idiom, others are far more resistant to such alterations. The fast day of Tish'a B'av seems singularly inhospitable to such mutations. This midsummer fast day is the most somber day in the Jewish calendar; it memorializes the destruction of the two temples, the calamity of Exile, and the recurrent tragedies that have disfigured Jewish history. (It says a great deal about American Jewry that not only do most not observe the day, they have probably never heard of it.) Despite the obviously and narrowly Jewish character of these events, some Conservative and Reform synagogues have sought to revive the fast day and infuse it with contemporary, universal significance. In New Haven, Connecticut, for example, all of the Conservative and Reform synagogues cooperate in sponsoring a Tish'a B'av ceremony. In 1986, the chairperson made it clear that although "originally, the observance of Tish'a Be'a recalled only the destruction of the Holy Temple," it is no longer sectarian in significance. Jewish as well as non-Jewish calamities are now included. Stretching the point further still he went on to conclude:

> This year, in honor of the 100th anniversary of Miss Liberty, special recognition will be included of our great debt to the United States of America for the opportunity that this country has given our people.[21]

Another Conservative rabbi, writing about the day in the local Jewish weekly, explains the meaning of the term *golus*, Hebrew for "exile," in the following way:

> While *golus* is a Jewish word it is not only a Jewish issue. It is a human issue as well. *Golus* in 1986 is children going to sleep hungry night after night. It is approximately 30 armed conflicts raging around the globe. It is the continuing deterioration of our habitat and ecosystem. . . . And most alarmingly, it is thousands of nuclear warheads ready at this moment to annihilate us all.[22]

The proclivity to universalize the Jewish message and present it in an ecumenical American idiom is especially present in many progressive synagogues that feel the need to appeal to the young, the educated, and the affluent. The rabbi of one such suburban "traditional progressive" synagogue in New Jersey reminisced[23] that the congregation's membership had been both falling and aging. Recognizing that "God doesn't play a role" in the life of the congregants, that if they affirm a belief in God it is only "because that's the American way," he undertook some dramatic renovations of the liturgy and of general character of the synagogue. He reports rewriting the High Holy Day services. The Hebrew liturgy was eliminated—except for some selections chanted by the cantor "which had nostalgic value." In its place he introduced "some poems, a piece by Einstein that was very religious in spirit, a few of my own writings." But since there "isn't enough in the prayer book to carry you through to sunset," he put together "a collection of meditations and readings—Hasidic stories, Rabindranath Tagore, Stephen Vincent Benet, and Martin Buber—very beautiful things." Moreover, "we hired a string quartet to play relaxing classical and liturgical music and put benches outside in the gardens, so if you want to go out, go out."

The Passover liturgy, he continues, did not mean very much to his congregation:

> So we took that service, with its powerful theme of freedom, brought in the American Revolution and the idea of the heroic with the Warsaw Ghetto Uprising, and wrote a service around these themes. We took music—from Beethoven to Yiddish melodies—and brought in part of the brass section of the New York Philharmonic.

Reflecting on the success of such practices in filling the pews, he notes that what is important is that "it has to be a class act or it's embarrassing and they won't come again."

The rabbi articulated his position as follows: "I say that a synagogue should be all things to all people." The synagogue was successful in attracting a large membership, he believes, because "we had the courage to make a statement—that Judaism does not stagnate, that it can incorporate anything of value." Putting this pluralist conception into practice, he tells of the many speakers who have addressed the congregation. Among them were Jane Fonda, Roy Cohen, Al Goldstein (the editor of *Screw* magazine), and Mrs. Anwar Sadat. He concludes: "If you want to be in the tradition of Isaiah, you've got to go out on a limb. The Jewish tradition says, go out on a limb, baby, and you pay the price; but 'justice, justice, shall you pursue'!"

Our second category, moralism, is rather closely related to universalism. Marshall Sklare, the distinguished sociologist of American Jewry, defined moralism as follows:

> Religious man is distinguished not by his observance of rituals but rather by the scrupulousness of his ethical behavior. While the follower of sacramentalism sees ethical conduct as an integral part of observance, the follower of moralism feels that such conduct may be impeded rather than stimulated by the stress on sacramentalism. At the very least, sacramentalism is seen as irrelevant to motivating ethical conduct.[24]

The likeness of moralism to universalism resides in their common inclination to reject particularistic ritual, that is, to transcend specific, prescribed, and mandatory observances deriving from a natal culture in favor of universally available humanistic and ethical qualities. The tendency, noted above, to recast the Jewish holidays, liturgy, synagogue life, and soon, in inclusive, cosmopolitan moral terms is a conspicuous case in point.

This moralistic streak is vividly manifest in a recent random sample survey of Conservative congregations. Asked for their reaction to the statement: "A Jew can be religious even if he or she isn't particularly observant," a striking 76 percent expressed their agreement. Two details are notable in this response. First, the question did not ask about what it means to be a *good* Jew but rather what it means to be a *religious* Jew. Second, the survey was conducted among Conservative Jews who, as opposed to Reform and nondenominational Jews, pride themselves on their conservation of tradition.[25]

For those of a moralist persuasion, therefore, fulfilling one's duties as a Jew entails, above all, being a *good person*. "Good" in this sense does not signify observing specific mitzvoth, nor even conforming to some specifically Jewish form of the ethical life; it means little more or less than living in accordance with the moral sensibilities prescribed by the modern liberal worldview. In deliberating the moral dilemmas that confront them, moralists do not make systematic efforts to draw upon the reservoir of Jewish ethical discourse in order to light the way to a resolution. Jewish thinking, it is assumed, conforms to what a liberal, right-thinking, decent, rational, humanistic individual would in any case believe. Sylvia Fishman refers to this process as "coalescence." She writes:

> It is not just that for most contemporary American Jews the authority of historical Judaism has been diminished, not just that the past has a vote but not a veto. For most American Jews today, the distinction between what is Jewish and what is American is not recognized. . . . Rather, in many ways the boundaries have disappeared and the two belief systems have merged into one coalesced whole widely known as "Judaism."[26]

Notably, even when ritual practices are, in fact, preserved, the moralist has little concern with the specific, formal requisites set down by religious law. The "proper" or "valid" manner of executing the ritual is entirely secondary to the moral and broadly human significance that is attached to it. Rituals lose their status as God-prescribed observances and become symbols exemplifying human ethical imperatives. Fasting on Yom Kippur—be it only for an hour or two—becomes a way of vindicating the capacity for human control over pressing creaturely urges; Sabbath rest—in whatever form it takes—becomes a metaphor for periodic human renewal; even prayer becomes less a medium for communion between humankind and God and more a means of human self-expression, meditation, and reflection. Understandably, those practices easily amenable to moral construal are more likely to be adopted than those that are morally opaque, that demand recurrent observance, or that attempt to rigorously structure individual lives. Systematic study or the exacting discipline of kashrut do not sit well with this regimen.

De-theologizing religious observances, that is, replacing human for Divine content or making rituals over into ceremonies signifies that what is actually experienced by concrete individuals in religious life takes precedence over self-standing, objective religious obligations. This is the heart of our third category, what we have called "personalism." With individual experience situated at the very center of religious life, it comes as no surprise that Jewish rites are subject to radical innovation, indeed to outright invention. From a personalist perspective, departures from the established and traditional should be undertaken if they heighten religious immediacy or foster the sense of relevance. There can be no logically justifiable limits to such experimentation; the legitimacy of practices is subject only to whether it "works for you."

To illustrate: Kaddish is a prayer traditionally recited for close family members who have died. One early *havura* member recalls a debate over whether to say kaddish for the slain (non-Jewish) John Lennon. It was resolved in the following way: "We just said, 'Oh yes, that feels right, let's do it.' "[27] Another "Jewish revival movement" synagogue in Manhattan advertises itself as a "four ring circus" that "simultaneously offers a service for every sensibility—intellectual, spiritual, formal, informal."[28]

At times the source of the observances can be located within the Jewish tradition, at others it involves such a profound jumble of so great a variety of sources that we might well characterize them as new creations. For example, an elaborate folder advertises a weekend retreat under the rubric, "The Living Waters Weekend." The weekend is directed by Rabbis Philip and Shoni Labowitz, co-Rabbis of Temple Adath Or in Fort Lauderdale, Florida, who are the "creators of healing rituals in Jewish Renewal." The following is the Saturday program:

> Optional Sunrise walk and meditation. Musical Worship Service at the Ocean. Guided Conscious Eating at Breakfast. Water Exercises for Body Toning. Yoga with Kabbalah. Relaxation Time. Luncheon Recalling Our Heroes. Outdoor Games, Informal Talk, Time for Massage. Sacred Gathering for Men and Women. Poetry Reading and Pre-dinner Music. Sunset Barbecue with Folk Dancing. Havdalah Ritual on the Beach. Kabbalistic Meditation.

Although this program is extreme, it is hardly unique.

Another highly eccentric but suggestive form of personalized Jewishness comes across in the following account of a Los Angeles man who, finding that the sources of his religious inspiration had dried up, adopted some radical innovations. He reports that he could no longer pray with fervor, so he began to listen to music with his tefillin on.

> There are a couple of songs I've been able to pray to: a song called "Long Promised Road," by the Beach Boys and some James Taylor songs . . . . I don't use the songs for background music; I give my attention to them and to what they are leading me to think about . . . . I also sometimes do this praying to Dvořák, to a bluegrass version of one of the *Slavonic Dances*. I listen and either conduct or dance around. I mean, I really jump all over the place.[29]

Personalism, as the word suggests, focuses religious life on the actual experiences of the individual person. Even when, as with the Florida weekend retreat, the experience is undergone in the company of others—indeed, requires others for its consummation—it remains the individual's experience of the group encounter that is central. "Immediacy," "authenticity," the "here and now," the "face-to-face" encounter, the "actually lived moment," the "meaningful experience"—all the verbal insignia of personalism—run against the grain of responsibilities to either an abstract collectivity or an impersonal codex of do's and don'ts. If it is not meaningful, there is little sense in doing it, customary duties notwithstanding.

Hence, the personalist life-style is indeed a "style," that is, a form of life given to sharp fluctuations and not a structure that is stable and continuous. It tends to be constituted out of episodic and exceptional experiences that light up the workaday and lackluster rather than out of a fixed position that encourages disciplined regularity or patterned coherence. Simply put: Personalism detaches individuals from the larger social collectives of which they are a part, releases them from the binding duties these collectives impose, and leads them toward self-directed lives that pursue rare moments of meaning and growth.

This emphasis on the self and its realization rather than on obligations transcending the individual person entails a turning away from the kinds of commonplace commitments that lack the special cachet of personal authenticity or inner growth. What are called "traditional family values," for example, suffer accordingly. Once thought to be natural and sacred, these bonds are weakening apace. What seemed mandatory only a generation or two ago—that parents forgo their own needs for the sake of their children's, that grown children bear the responsibility for the welfare of their aging parents, that husband and wife renounce and compromise for each other's sake—have become questionable propositions for many. Accordingly, rates of divorce among Jews, once just about the lowest among all ethnic groups in the United States, are now rapidly approaching the national norm. Considering that Jews are far more understanding of abortion, homosexuality, and extramarital sexuality than other Americans, this tendency seems likely to become even more pronounced in the future.

Much the same can be said in regard to responsibilities toward abstract collectivities such as the Jewish people. From the personalist perspectives, true love, the ultimate personal experience, far outweighs it. Indeed, to the degree that love needs to overcome obstacles (ethnic or religious) in order to be realized, it is considered the more authentic and marvelous. Understood in terms of personal meaning, Jewishness becomes—even for Jews—an acquired taste, a take it or leave it affair. Moreover, experience-based religiosity has no intrinsic justification for exclusion or boundaries; it necessarily includes all who are partner to the inspirational moment.[30]

Voluntarism, our fourth attribute, relates closely to moralism and personalism in that Jewish identity is understood to be chosen rather than given, accepted rather than received. The very idea that an identity is imposed by the accident of birth rather than adopted voluntarily by each individual seeking to realize his or her own potential is understood as a burdensome anachronism. A fortiori, actual practices and responsibilities need to be consciously adopted and made one's own; obligations, the voluntarist might say, are not bequeathed from generation to generation.

Even when an inherited identity is, in fact, accepted, the degree of intensity with which one chooses to exercise it can vary quite substantially. It can be central or marginal, residual or energetic—generally with little social sanction attached to the choice. It can vary greatly across time, whether measured in weeks and months, or in years and decades. There is also a choice to be made within the tradition itself; it too must be evaluated in terms of its utility and meaningfulness to the individual. "The modern Jew selects from the vast storehouse of the past what is not only objectively possible for him to practice but subjectively possible for him to 'identify' with."[31]

Voluntarism of this kind is statistically corroborated in the 1990 National Jewish Population Survey conducted by the Council of Jewish Federations and Welfare Funds.[32] (Notably, a significant number of respondents who identified themselves as Jewish in the 1990 survey denied such an identity when re-surveyed in 1993.[33]) In this, the Jews are not exceptional. Research on other ethnic groups, especially among those with complex, multiple ancestries, demonstrates that group identity in the United States is fluid and situational.[34] Ethnic identity may peak and plummet depending on the needs of the moment, the specific social context in which one finds oneself, or even according to rhythms of the calendar and the holiday seasons.

The voluntarist (and personalist) perspective signifies that practices are never mandated and, obversely, that nonobservance is never sinful. Indeed, the euphemistic lengths to which Jewish leaders will go to in order to avoid labeling anything as wrong or sinful is highly creative. *Tashlikh* is the custom in which, on Rosh Hashana, bread crumbs, which symbolize sins, are tossed into a flowing body of water. It is meant to represent a departure and purification from the sins of the past that are said to be dissolved and washed away. The central motif in *Tashlikh* is repentance and its overwhelming focus is on sin. In a circular distributed by one of the largest Hillels (Jewish organizations on college campuses) in the United States, the director, trying to convey the meaning of the *Tashlikh* ceremony, apparently could not bring himself to use the word "sin." Instead, he personalized the observance by referring to the bread crumbs as symbolizing "acts which we performed in the past year and which we now regret."

The voluntarist form of discourse pervades the rhetoric of rabbis, educators, and parents who, spurning the imperative mood, prefer to cajole, encourage, urge, and inspire. Ceremonial acts are presented as meaningful and contributing to personal growth, but not as obligatory. Congregations, classrooms, and children are assured that whatever they do is legitimate only if they have truly chosen it. Authentic personal choice, regardless of its specific substance, is endowed with a privileged spiritual status—indeed, it is held to be superior to actions deriving from a subordination of the self to a religious code or obedience to God.

One marvelously candid observer, wrestling with his own complex Jewish faith, suggests that rather than centering our concern on whether the Revelation at Mount Sinai actually took place—which is a "faith I do not have, cannot invent, and regard (perhaps for that reason) as irrelevant"—we should focus on the far more amenable human question: "Do you *choose* [emphasis added] to associate yourself with the event/story/idea?" In choosing to accept the Revelation, I remain "faithful" to the event, even though I lack "faith" in its empirical veracity:

> I am offering my consent. I am freely choosing to associate myself with a myth I find uplifting, informative. I am choosing to accept the implications of a legend as if it were no legend at all. . . . I am never entirely unaware of the as-ifness of my choice, but neither am I much impeded by it.[35]

Prayer, as we noted above, ceases to be an act of supplication directed by mortal man to an infinite and omnipotent God; instead, it becomes a Jewish language that need not be believed to be spoken, any more than we need to "believe" in the specific language we happen to speak. When we chose to pray it is "not faith, but fluency in the language of Jewish moral imagination [that] is the measure."[36] We are not so much asked to believe in the God to whom we pray as we are enjoined to become "godly." We are urged not so much to believe in the metaphysical implications of prayer, as to choose the "elaborate system of metaphors" offered by the venerable Jewish texts and, by internalizing them, gain entry into a wondrous world of meaning and profundity.

Prayer can be transposed into even more crassly human terms. One writer asks, for example, "How, practically, can Jewish prayer function to help one confront anger and utilize it for personal transformation and social change?"[37] Prayer, here, has been fully personalized, made into an avenue for therapeutic self-help.

Another piquant example of this individualized version of Judaism comes from the Conservative Temple Beth Ami in Reseda, California. Advised by a faculty member of the University of Judaism, the West Coast Rabbinical Seminary of the Conservative movement, the temple prepared a booklet on the subject of "ritual observance" that it distributed widely to other Conservative congregations. The program advocated in the booklet was built around voluntary groups patterned on Weight Watchers. Each member of the group would undertake to perform certain rituals and make a progress report to the group at monthly meetings. Members were to fill out a "12 Month Goal Sheet" in which

> they should determine which rituals they would like to involve themselves in during the coming year. The members should understand that the goal of this program is not to make them become more Jewish than what they will be comfortable with.

Among those rituals the program prescribes, some are entirely marginal to Jewish law, others are customs rather than obligatory rituals, and yet others are, on their face, contrary to Jewish law. It is, of course, not the lack of strict Orthodoxy that is of interest here; what stands out is the customized, tailored Jewishness that seeks out those practices that are likely to resonate with late twentieth-century American sensibilities—regardless of their sources or their importance. They were *chosen* out of the reservoir of tradition for their contributions to the much desired sense of family harmony and personal fulfillment. Among the eighteen Sabbath rituals, we find, for example: "playing Shabbat music to set the mood," "blessing children," "blessing wife," "blessing husband," "having a special Shabbosdik meal," "using a white tablecloth and good dishes," and "singing Shabbat songs around the table."[38]

Consistent with our understanding of personalism and voluntarism, there is great elasticity and variability in the definition of "who is a Jew" among the non-Orthodox. After all, personalism and voluntarism do not sit well with objective, legal-formal boundaries. Legally prescribed or traditionally imposed definitions are, in their eyes, stilted and unauthentic. It is only to be expected that those who are sympathetic to our fourfold personalist syndrome would tend to accept characterizations of Jewishness that rely heavily on self-definition, on *feeling* rather than on *being* Jewish. Jews, they would say, are those who choose to call themselves Jews.

This pliant characterization of Jewishness received a substantial boost when Goldscheider and Zuckerman[39] dismissed as demographic nonsense the fear that assimilation and intermarriage were seriously attenuating the American Jewish community. Jewishness, they claimed, is not necessarily a matter of birth or belief or practice. Hence, assimilation and intermarriage by themselves do not, as the alarmists threaten, foreshadow the growing debilitation of the American Jewish community. Jews remain a flourishing and cohesive community because they are socio-economically distinctive; they adopt similar life-styles, career and residence patterns, liberal values, and educational goals. It is not the substance of Jewishness (however defined) that binds Jews together so much as their similar placement in the American social structure. Jews constitute a vital community because they tend to act in similar ways. In short, Jews are as Jews behave. (Presumably then, Jewish cohesion would be similarly maintained were Jews distinctively poor, ignorant, and reactionary—or, for that matter, if they had a collective weakness for mah-jongg or Sunday morning golf.)

Although Goldscheider and Zuckerman's approach blurs the boundaries of Jewish identity to encompass many who might otherwise be excluded, they do not adopt a truly voluntarist understanding of Jewishness. If Jewishness is concomitant of certain objective social structures, feeling Jewish is not entirely a personal choice. A giant step in the direction of expanding the category "Jew" in the voluntarist direction was recently taken by the Reform movement. As opposed to the halachic definition of Jewishness as one born of a Jewish mother or converted, the Reform included those born of a Jewish father as well. Their decision broadened but also simultaneously narrowed the category "Jew." "Broadened" because the spirit of contemporary liberal egalitarianism does not sit well with gender-specific categories. "Narrowed" because congruent with personalist sensibilities, the Reform declared that Jewishness, even for those born of a Jewish mother, ought not be a congenital datum; it must be actively and consciously chosen. Hence, in Reform practice, even those born of a Jewish mother must personally and voluntarily accept their Jewishness in order for it to be recognized. Jewishness ceases to be a given; it must always be deliberately taken.

For all of its ostensible magnitude, the Reform decision to accept patrilineal definitions of Jewishness was not a truly revolutionary step. In fact, many if not most Reform temples had adopted the principle long before—the formal decision only legitimated a prevalent practice. (Notably, 58 percent of American Jews approved this step in 1987. We may confidently assume that the number would be substantially higher in the late 1990s.[40]) Accepting patrilineal Jewishness represented a formal recognition of the reality that mixed marriages—the marriage of a Jew and a non-Jew in which neither partner converts to the other's religion—had become so common they could no longer be ignored. Indeed, it became increasingly difficult for the Reform clergy to express public reservations about mixed marriage because so many of their own congregants were themselves married to non-Jews.

Mixed marriage created an unprecedented set of challenges for the Reform leadership. Many mixed couples expressed their desire to affiliate with the temple and to raise their children in a Jewish ambience. Others sought to incorporate their non-Jewish (at times believing, practicing Christian) spouse into the temple's religious life. The Reform decision to accept a patrilineal definition of Jewishness is in large measure a response to the pressure exerted by Jews in mixed marriages to normalize, even legitimize the status of their family within the Jewish community.

In this vein, the authors of a study on conversion report that over half of the "non-converts" in mixed marriages "felt that one could be a part of the Jewish people and community without undergoing a formal conversion process."[41] This personalist-voluntarist spirit is brought home sharply in the writings of converts to Judaism who remain married to non-Jews—a condition facilitated by an increasingly tolerant and ecumenical Jewish community. Thus, a convert to Judaism writes:

> Chanuka and Christmas will probably both be observed, simply because the family ties my husband associates with the mid-winter holiday are too significant to abandon.[42]

Another convert has this to say:

> I am very fortunate because my husband supports my decision to convert to Judaism. . . . His main concern was that I might expect him to convert also, or that the rabbi might expect it . . . . Tom is a

very spiritual person and I had no expectation that he would have to take the same journey. I knew that we could still share much of Judaism as a couple and as a family.[43]

And later, describing her synagogue:

At Beth Shalom there are many non-Jewish spouses and so there is a great deal of concern that these non-Jewish family members feel accepted and a part of the community. Our religious school also is very supportive of the children who have a non-Jewish parent or relative and every effort is made to make those children feel they belong.[44]

She presents the heart of her credo strikingly:

I refuse to let my religious choice cause strife in my family. I made a personal religious choice and if I expect people to honor my choice then I must honor theirs.[45]

Finally, another writer says in a similar vein:

As for synagogue and community involvement, I do not see a need for the gentile spouse to feel excluded. While there are definite honors from which one would be excluded, there are plenty of meaningful opportunities to involve the non-Jew in synagogue life and congregations should do that. Though these people may not be Jewish, that does not mean they do not want our synagogue and organizational activities to be successful. Because their families are involved, they do want to see us reach our goals.[46]

Much the same message comes across in a recent book entitled *Raising Your Jewish Christian Child: Wise Choices for Interfaith Parents*. It was advertised in *Commentary*—a magazine noted in recent years for its militantly Jewish stance—as offering the reader ways in which "to give your children the best of both heritages." It urges readers to "act now to enrich your children's spiritual lives. This year's holidays can be the richest, most harmonious ones your family has ever celebrated."[47] What stands out in all of this personal testimony is its very ordinary, even commonplace, tone. From a revolutionary reading of Jewishness just a generation ago, privatized Judaism has become mainstream and legitimate—accepted, no doubt, by a solid majority of American Jews.[48]

Our concern is not that American Jews are failing to act in accordance with Jewish law. If an innovative, alternate form of Jewishness could sustain Jewish survival, we might welcome it. Nor do we have any principled antagonism to the regnant spirit of privatism. In many ways, the experientialist, personalist temper is quite attractive and does, in fact, pose an important challenge to Jewishness in its official, traditional mode. Our question is another: Are privatized readings of Jewish identity compatible with Jewish survival?

We doubt it. In our view, privatizing Judaism places the survival of the American Jewish community in serious jeopardy. Even if we set aside some of the more exotic, radical positions described above, it is difficult to see Jewish cohesion maintaining itself over time in the face of the atomizing and open-textured qualities of the privatizing syndrome. A number of complementary arguments lead us to this conclusion.

First, the privatized style is unable to block the advance of intermarriage. Its universalist sympathies actually encourage it. The primary concern becomes, in fact, not offending the intermarried couple or the non-Jewish spouse. For example, a brochure entitled *Gateways*, printed by the Jewish Theological Seminary, announces grants for synagogue programs that encourage intermarried families "even when conversion is not being contemplated" and asks whether "we can help the non-Jewish partners in such a marriage overcome feelings of being unwanted, alienated or frightened by what might be expected of them by a Conservative rabbi and his/her congregations." A B'nai Brith publication, *Mingled Roots: A Guide to Jewish Grandparents of Interfaith Grandchildren*, urges grandparents to assure their intermarried children "that you [the grandparent] will not try to 'convert' the child to your religious beliefs . . . that you accept and respect their way of doing things in their home."[49]

There is no cogent rationale, from the perspective of privatism, with which to challenge the decision of an individual Jew, deeply in love with a Gentile, from intermarrying. In fact, privatism renders conversion for the sake of a prospective spouse dubious, even disreputable. If there is no genuine personal drive motivating an individual to enter the communal-religious identity of one's partner, doing so for the sake of convenience, or because of demanding in-laws, or in order to reduce areas of conjugal friction, appears—from the privatized perspective—rather spineless and deceitful.

Only a few years ago, those Reform rabbis who reluctantly consented to or even openly approved of officiating at mixed marriages did so in the hope that the non-Jewish partner would eventually convert. Since it was understood that conversion constituted the critical divide that distinguished those parents who would raise their children as Jews and those who would not,[50] Reform rabbis were hopeful that in presiding over mixed marriages they were encouraging the prospect of conversion. There was even the anticipation that through mixed marriages eventuating in conversions the Jewish people would add substantial numbers to its ranks. These hopes have been cruelly dashed. Today, even the Conservative movement, ostensibly much more traditional than Reform, is in the process of blurring its insistence on conversion among the spouses of its own synagogue members.

Second, the logic of universalism, moralism, personalism, and voluntarism undermines Jewish particularism and accelerates the tendency to assimilation. One can at least say of those liberals (dealt with at this chapter's outset) who attempt to constitute Judaism out of liberal substance that they understand Jewish identity in a normatively unique way. There is a specific Jewish mission and liberalism is its content. But what can be said about the privatized syndrome that cannot be equally said of dozens of other garden-variety forms of modern consciousness? What are its differentia? That Judaism and Jewishness are more flexible, more given to protean reinterpretations, less wedded to any particular symbol or theological system, less obligating or judgmental, more modern and au courant, more relevant, more sensitive to trends as they develop, that is, more chameleon-like than any other religious community? That it simulates a kind of Unitarianism ornamented with Jewish peculiarities? It hardly needs saying that all of this does not add up to a recipe for success.

To be sure, we are not intimating that these are the beliefs to which American Jewish leaders actually subscribe. In this specific regard, the above description, we would concede, contains elements of polemic and caricature. We believe, nevertheless, that these views do not represent a caricature if they are understood as the logical denouement of current belief and practice. The privatized style of Jewishness, we contend, contains an inner dynamic that leads it ultimately toward these kinds of self-undermining conclusions.

What lies beneath the surface of this critical assessment is our conviction that Judaism and America represent two cultures, not one. This would be so axiomatically manifest as to be undeserving of mention were it not for the equally obvious fact that what appears to be a blatant truism is very often ignored or violated in practice. Judaism and America are regularly dealt with as if it were inconceivable that they might have divergent worldviews or sanction different forms of life—to say nothing about being inimical to one another in important regards. In the prevalent American Jewish "civil religion," Judaism is represented as a facsimile of Americana, America read from right to left. It is only the boldest of progressive religious leaders who are rash enough to suggest otherwise. Let us take the privatized version of Judaism as our case in point: Is there a single assumption, implication, or conclusion adopted by the privatizers that runs against the grain of an urban, upper-middle-class American consensus?

When Judaism is made over in the American image, both the American and the Jewish components suffer. The American because it is deprived of the yea and nay-saying power, the independent critical voice of a venerable cultural and religious civilization. The Jewish because, denuded of all independent content and rendered compatible with all current vogues, it becomes a pure figment of the American imagination. And lacking any differentia, being all sail and no anchor, it is sooner or later swallowed up and overwhelmed. To paraphrase what was said earlier in regard to liberalism: A Jewish community claiming personalism, universalism, and so on, as its content will quickly learn that its members are adept at finding their personalism, universalism, and so on, elsewhere.

Judaism, to be sure, learned from and was enriched by the many cultural legacies it inherited from the dozens of countries through which Jews passed. It is precisely this multinational legacy, the confrontation with so many of the world's great cultures, that may well lie at the source of Jewish cultural creativity. It would surely be an act of perverse ingratitude were Judaism to shun just the American influences, that is, reject the humane message purveyed by the most benevolent and hospitable country in the history of Jewish wanderings.

To incorporate American values, however, it is obviously necessary for there to be a Jewish corpus into which they can be synthesized. Confrontation of cultures requires two cultures. Dialogue involves relating and withstanding simultaneously. For those lacking Jewish cultural content, the ability to confront and withstand is forfeited.

What remains for them is only an American monologue. Widespread Jewish illiteracy means that the vast majority of American Jews are adept at only one cultural language: American. Insofar as their Jewishness intrudes onto their Americanism, it is often in only incidental ways, ways that Goldscheider and Zuckerman sought to inflate into a full-blown Jewish identity. Being monocultural, the mandatory framework of reference for their Jewish identity is afforded by American categories. Without access to Jewish sources or to a naturally lived Jewish life, whatever is Jewish is received third- and fourthhand, mediated through the many layers of the American experience. (As Voltaire said of triangles: If they had to conceive of God, He would have three sides.) Can we wonder then that so much of American Judaism proves to be remarkably faithful to the original model?

Privatism fails, therefore, not because it lacks a worthy message. Indeed, the introduction of personalist authenticity into a well-grounded Jewish personality might well create fascinating intellectual sparks. It fails because it does not so much engage Jewishness as overwhelm it. Privatism cannot catalyze Jewish culture because it makes no serious effort to confront it. It cannot be a vehicle for Jewish survival in America because it already represents the unconditional victory of the American.

There are many progressive religious and lay Jewish leaders in America who are coming to understand that critiques of this kind are not the ventilations of cranky conservatives. Trying to please by appealing to the most fashionable and current cultural tastes, they find that they are competing in a market in which they cannot win, in which success involves becoming more and more indistinguishable from the middle-class America that surrounds them. Trying to fill the pews, they learn that they need to camouflage, even subvert Jewish content. Success, in the form of full synagogues, comes to those who are willing to take the most radical steps in this direction. (Affiliations bought at the cost of content are very much like the good intentions with which hell is said to be paved.) And yet, in the end, they recognize that since synagogues can never be more American than America, the appeal of the original will always be more potent than that of the clone.

To repeat: None of this means to imply that liberalism or personalism are unworthy. Clearly, they can be noble sentiments and we often find ourselves in deep sympathy with them and with many of the admirable people who espouse them. Our interest in them here relates to their viability as strategies for Jewish survival. And as such we believe they fail. Neither is able to meet the minimal requisites of a workable Jewish survival strategy: the justification of boundaries, the sanctioning of communal difference, and the vindication of specifically Jewish cultural content.

This may well be a case in which the truth proves to be not particularly happy, in which the very alternatives we are forced to decide between are vexing and disagreeable. It is therefore especially crucial to face them squarely. We may not possess the latitude to fully and simultaneously maintain both our cosmopolitan pluralist and our Jewish identities intact. Our choices may well be starker and more radical than most of us would like to admit.

israeli jews

Preserving the Old

O n its face, the problem of Jewish survival in Israel seems a perverse one. In what sense can Jewish survival be threatened in the Jewish state, a Hebrew-speaking nation that celebrates Jewish holidays, ingathers Jewish "exiles," names its streets after Jewish notables, teaches Bible in its secular school system, serves as a touchstone for Diaspora Jewish identity, and understands itself as the logical closure to two millennia of Jewish wanderings? With the Menorah emblazoned on all official documents, the flag recalling King David, and its anthem telling of awaiting the return to Zion for a "hundred generations," Israel's Jewishness seems both manifest and assured. Besides, with Jews comprising more than 80 percent of the population and with little cultural commerce between the Israeli Jewish majority and the Israeli Arab minority, into which groups are Israeli Jews about to intermarry and assimilate?[1]

Nevertheless, the question of Jewish survival has rarely been far from the center of Israeli public debate—perhaps never more than at present. A recent experience, although quite minor and mundane in character, catches the sense of the issues involved in this debate with especial force and clarity. Neighbors, veteran *olim* (immigrants) from Stockholm, Sweden, recounted a discussion they had with their two older daughters, one just about to finish army service, the second with a year or so left until discharge. The family was talking about what the young women would do after their military service. After some private exchanges between the two daughters, they informed their parents that they were seriously considering going back to Stockholm for a few years in order to work for the local Jewish community. When questioned by their perplexed parents as to their motive, they answered: "We want to feel Jewish again."

Two of the central foundations upon which Jewish survival rested throughout the ages were, first, the sense of Gentile hostility and, second, the physical and cultural propinquity of Jews with one another. Antisemitism, as we suggested in Chapter 3, suffused Jewish history with meaning, rendering Jewish survival both logical and imperative. It lent credibility to Jewish religious beliefs and condemned those who would abandon them to bewilderment and marginality. In addition, the pressing immediacy and densely communitarian quality of Jewish life provided a common space in which basic beliefs were consensually validated and traditional practices collectively sanctioned. The serious threats to Jewish survival in the United

States (discussed in the two foregoing chapters) can be traced, inter alia, to the decline of both these circumstances: Antisemitism is in steep decline and Jewish neighborhoods are largely a nostalgic memory.

By contrast, the relative success of Israeli Jewishness in perpetuating itself is attributable to the continued presence of both these conditions. As to Jewish propinquity in Israel, little needs to be said. Whereas, according to every survey we have on American Jews, they report a sharp decrease in their social ties with other Jews and a concomitant rise of associations with non-Jews, Israeli Jews live in a largely self-enclosed Jewish world. Deep personal ties with Israeli Arabs are very rare and friendships with non-Jews abroad are atypical and limited in scope and intensity by the constraints of distance. It would not be entirely facetious to describe Israel as the largest Jewish neighborhood in the world or, less generously, as a "sovereign ghetto."

Antisemitism in America is clearly on the wane. Although it surely would be unwise to dismiss it as a defeated anachronism, it requires something of an imaginative leap for Gentile hostility to be perceived as posing an imminent threat to Jewish life and limb. Israeli Jews, in sharp contrast, are manifestly a beleaguered people. Here—whatever one's political persuasion—the burden of proof lies heavily upon those who would dismiss Israel's security problems as imaginary. Whether, in fact, Arab hostility is legitimately subsumed under the antisemitic rubric or not is hardly the point. What counts rather is how easily threats and hostility from the surrounding Arab and Moslem states can be reworked into traditional antisemitic categories. Jewish history, so the familiar argument goes, has always involved a struggle to survive; it regularly pitted the numerous against the few, the just against the unjust, the weak against the strong.[2] The Jews were surrounded, reviled, and beset—and, as if to prove that the Jewish fate has not changed, all of this is reenacted in our time (with the Holocaust still a vivid memory) by the new Middle Eastern incarnations of oppression and affliction.

Even secular, cosmopolitan Israeli Jews who reject traditional rhetoric of this kind as self-righteous and unreflective cannot avoid the striking parallels with the past. The existence of a sovereign Israel, to be sure, has transposed Jewish history into a new key, but the old melodies stubbornly linger on. "The whole world is against us; not to worry, we'll be O.K." went a popular army song of the early seventies. As in days gone by, Israeli Jews find themselves once again in the eye of the storm, buffeted by intractable enmities and impending dangers. Even Zionism itself—which was to be the vehicle of liberation from the lamentable tragedies of Jewish history—has often become a convenient modern foil for ancient hostilities, a sanitized, politically correct form of antisemitism. In short, the Jewish state has not, as Herzl hoped, put an end to the long-suffering and perilous nature of Jewish existence; it has only reconstructed it in a new form. It is no surprise then that worldviews grounded in antisemitism continue to resonate richly with the realities of Israeli public life.

Whatever the momentous differences between contemporary Israeli Jewishness and that of the old Diaspora ghetto, both realities include two critical pillars of Jewish identity: the preoccupation with precariousness and the propinquity with other Jews. Together they create a favorable climate for the perpetuation of Jewish loyalties and of Jewish perceptions. The "old" is preserved because, mutatis mutandis, Israeli realities recall traditional forms of Jewish existence. Hence, Israeli Jews are more likely to retain "traditional" perspectives and to engage in expressly Jewish behavior than their American cousins. Jewishness is usually more central to their lives and more palpably present in their calculations and worldviews.

Moreover, because daily life in Israel is saturated with a rich variety of Jewish themes, a certain rudimentary Jewish literacy is widespread. Although many Israeli Jews are notoriously ill-informed in regard to Jewish religious belief and practice, even militantly secular Israeli Jews are unlikely to be ignorant of the broad contours of Jewish history, the Hebrew Bible, or the Jewish calendar with its specific rhythm of holidays and observances. Whether it is absorbed via formal education in the school system (where Bible, Jewish history and literature, etc., are staples of the curriculum), or through the public domain which is suffused with a myriad of Jewish references, Jewishness is so tangibly present as to be unavoidable.

Israeli public discourse is regularly conducted in terminology, categories, and concepts that echo with Jewish history and experience. To adduce a number of random illustrations from the days in which this text is being written: In the context of violent confrontations over closing certain streets to motorized traffic on the Sabbath, haredim (ultra-Orthodox) regularly refer to police actions as "pogroms."[3] One leader of the extreme right asserted that when he walks the streets of the Gaza Strip, he sees it through the prism of Auschwitz.[4] On the other side of the political divide, one of the academic drafters of the Oslo agreements, discussing what he sees as the Netanyahu government's intransigence, warned that this behavior was alarmingly similar to the collective suicides at Masada and the tragic Bar Kochba revolt.[5]

Indeed, territorial issues are regularly debated in dense and contentious Jewish terms. The one side cites Biblical promises to the Land of Israel and adduces the halachic expertise of authorities past and present. Although important changes have been taking place of late (more on this in the next chapter), until recently the other side would have been expected to respond with the Biblical injunctions to actively pursue justice and peace, and with historical instances in which the rabbis chose realism and prudence over perilous stands of principle.[6] If we add this basic literacy to precariousness and propinquity, our portrait of Israeli Jews reveals further lines of continuity with traditional Jewry. (Indeed, it would be ironically amusing and not at all surprising were we to find that many Israeli Arabs, having absorbed a great deal of Jewish culture through personal contacts, the media, and the marketplace, are more Jewishly literate than the bulk of American Jews.)

Even the controversy between the religious and the secular communities in Israel does not take place between those inside and those outside the Jewish context; it is regularly fought out with Jewish weaponry, Jewish attacks, and Jewish defenses. And it is fought out against the background of general agreement on the value and importance of the Jewish tradition to Israel's cultural identity.[7] Herein lies the irony of a Jewish state: Its fiercest controversies and enmities are Jewish as well. To paraphrase Oscar Wilde's famous quip about the English and the Americans, Israeli Jews are two peoples divided by a single (Jewish) language.

"Operation Solomon," the stirring airlift of thousands of Ethiopian Jews to Israel in 1991 as well as the much larger emigration from the ex-Soviet Union are especially telling illustrations of how Jewish themes resonate in Israeli public life. The arrival of these immigrants did not signify, for the popular imagination of Israeli Jews, merely another movement of peoples from here to there; their arrival was greeted with nothing less than heroic Biblical exultation. The story of David and Bat Sheba was repeatedly recounted. Hushed talk about the "ingathering of the exiles" from the "four corners of the earth" caught the sense of awe at a Biblical prophesy come true. For some it was a breathtaking messianic portent. In fact, Israeli Jews were certain that the meaning of what they were watching on their TV screens—exotic, robed black Africans kissing the soil of the Holy Land as they alighted from the aircraft, and blond, Slavic-looking Russian Jews and oriental-looking Central Asian Jews being taken to their first homes in Israel—could be accounted for only in terms that engaged all the grandeur and poignancy of Jewish history. The fact that many of these immigrants arrived in the bomb-shelter, gas-mask days of the Gulf War and were immediately initiated into the stark realities of those trying days only heightened the sense of Jewish solidarity, of the magical Jewish drama that was unfolding before their eyes.[8]

The sense of living in densely Jewish surroundings also affects the nature of public discourse in subtle but profound ways. Not only is the substantive historical and cultural material of communal dialogue often high in Jewish content, the fact that it is directed to a virtually all-Jewish audience affects the tenor and style of the discourse as well. To be sure, with contemporary communication networks there is no longer any truly "in house" debate. Nevertheless, the immediate presence of only Jewish auditors inevitably creates a more self-directed and spontaneous dynamic of discourse. There are no intrusive strangers looking over the Jewish communal shoulder; one need not censor one's thoughts and feelings to accord with the fashions and standards that prevail in the world at large.

In the premodern era, Jews spoke to themselves in their own languages and in terms afforded by their own insular communal self-understanding. When they spoke to the enveloping Gentile world, it was already mediated speech—ideas born in exclusively Jewish contexts that were translated, at times even tactically redesigned or obscured, to have the proper effect on the non-Jewish powers-that-be. The disparity between inner-communal and Gentile-directed discourse was necessarily very great.

Since the Enlightenment, Jews have gradually lost the ability to conduct their affairs in their own sequestered and private communal space. In the United States, for example, there is no Jewish tongue in which to express communal concerns in an intimate setting. Neither is there a common cultural idiom known to all discussants that might provide some degree of opaqueness to Jewish discourse. Nothing shields Jewish communal debate from peering Gentile eyes. It is inevitably directed to mixed Jewish-Gentile audiences. Indeed, for good and for ill, Jews themselves have so entirely assimilated the standards of propriety that prevail in American society that they no longer have any need to dissimulate the inappropriately "Jewish" opinions they express behind closed doors.

Here again, Israel is closer to the Jewish status quo ante: Discourse takes place within a relatively closed Jewish perimeter. Sleeves are rolled up, communal camaraderie is assumed, and the tone of debate tends to be unrestrained and unself-consciously direct. There is no felt need to universalize the message for non-Jewish consumption. Neither is there any sense in prudently withholding the hidden Jewish agenda lurking in the message lest it give umbrage to those Gentiles within earshot. Lacking the ecumenical qualities that mark the discourse of Diaspora Jews, Israeli public discussion is uncompromised by (or, perhaps, lacking the enrichment afforded by) the presence of detached, extracommunal observers. In practical terms, the effect of this narrowing of horizons is to greatly fortify the Jewish-centered perspective and to encourage Jewish behavior to match.

A single illustration will have to do. Both Israel and American Jewry are passionate about the Holocaust and its significance. And yet there are clear differences of emphasis that separate their views. The Washington, D.C., Holocaust Museum as well as Steven Spielberg's film *Schindler's List*—certainly the most salient Holocaust-related cultural monuments of the past decade—contain a substantial component that speaks to the generically human significance of Nazi barbarity and Jewish slaughter.

The Holocaust Museum, which continues to be visited by a majority of non-Jews, emphasizes the potential for cruelty and evil that may overcome humankind. Although it is surely in need of important reservations, there is a certain subtle sense in which the Holocaust becomes a symbol for cruelty, a metaphor for human depravity and in which the Nazis and Jews could be replaced by other villain and victim peoples. Hence, its purport lies less in the Holocaust's being a Jewish tragedy and more in a message of universal tolerance, and of unending alertness lest humankind be overcome once again. Other genocidal experiences are never far from the museum's doors. In fact, Elie Wiesel, a Holocaust survivor himself, used the dedication ceremony of the museum to implore President Clinton to do whatever possible to stop the carnage in the states of the former Yugoslavia.

Spielberg, for his part, chose the tale of a "righteous Gentile" who heroically saved Jewish lives as the vehicle through which to convey the horrors of those years. It is as much his story as it is theirs. It is not the story of a Jewish tragedy told from a Jewish point of view. The film's message is surely not that the Holocaust ought to strengthen Jewish resolve not to give Hitler a posthumous victory or that the Gentile world generally is somehow responsible for the Holocaust. Its intended audience as well as its intended theme is universal and ecumenical.

Israeli observers have expressed reservations about both these attempts to perpetuate the memory of the Holocaust. The Holocaust, one might encapsulate their views, is a Jewish tragedy before it is a universal one. It will not do to "dejudaize" it or to expropriate it from Jewish history where it rightly belongs. Righteous gentiles, whatever commendation they deserve, belong to the historical marginalia of the Holocaust, not to its center. Universalizing the Holocaust's message must be preceded by a recognition of the universal guilt of European-Christian culture for its horrors. If the Gentiles want to use the Holocaust as a cautionary tale, let them first acknowledge that the European tradition of antisemitism is what made it possible; indeed, let them recognize that guilt for the Holocaust goes far beyond the Nazis.

The Israeli memorial for the six million, Yad Va'shem, has a more narrowly Jewish focus. Although it is visited annually by hundreds of thousands of non-Jewish tourists, there is no attempt to present the Holocaust in universal human terms. Little speaks of the need for universal toleration or of the importance of human rights or of the generically human significance of the Holocaust. Its exhibits and observances are Jewish-specific: A Jewish funeral prayer is recited in a large memorial sanctuary; the names of the hundreds of Jewish communities that perished are engraved in a tomb-like city; the names of the million and a half children who were killed are read one at a time in a hall of mirrors and candles; the names of the millions who perished are perpetuated in vast card and computer catalogues.

Even those Israeli Jews with little interest in Jewish tradition cannot help but be carried along by these dominant, omnipresent cultural patterns. Even if they manage to elude their grasp, it is quite likely that the prevailing Jewish-centered educational and cultural forces will succeed in drawing their children into the fold. If being drawn into Jewish patterns of thinking and acting is the social norm, parting from the Jewish context in Israel requires mutiny aforethought, an active and resolute decision to eschew things Jewish and to systematically create an island on to which they do not intrude. (They form an almost exact mirror image to what ultra-Orthodox Jews need to do in the United States.) It is no easy task even for those who are ideologically dedicated to its achievement. This is the very essence of a dominant culture that is able to define and constitute the public sphere: It creates powerful force fields that are extraordinarily difficult to avoid or resist.

By contrast, there is little in the way of an explicit ideology of assimilation in the United States, nor is there any need for one. One ceases actively pursuing Jewish identification, and the great homogenizing machine of urban middle-class American culture will do its work. When Jewish solidarity loses its grip, other interests and identities rush in to take its place. In a word, retaining a rich Jewish identity in America requires a conscious choice and a special effort. Being neutral means leaving the Jewish fold. Assimilation simply happens; it need not be planned. The powerful pressures of the dominant American culture—like the dominant Jewish culture in Israel—act to draw the marginal and uncommitted into its orbit.

Moreover, Jewish self-identification in America means, for the most part, affiliation with a synagogue. Very little is available in the way of real ethnic or cultural loyalties that do not substantially impinge upon religious institutions. (Even those concerned with the welfare of Israel or with Holocaust-related issues are overwhelmingly affiliated with and often work through synagogues.) Among those who fill synagogues on the High Holy Days, a very significant percentage are there not to pray to a God about whose existence they harbor significant doubts but rather in order to identify ethnically, historically, and culturally in the only way they know. Indeed, we would not at all be surprised if, in affiliating with a synagogue, the greater part of American Conservative and Reform Jews understand themselves as making an ethno-cultural statement rather than a religious one.

With the steep decline in religious belief among American Jews, trouble is inevitable. First, because religion cum ethnicity is, inherently, a dubious match. Lacking any autonomous ethno-cultural alternatives to the Jewish religion in America, great pressure falls on synagogues to act as "ethnic clubs" even though they are ostensibly religious institutions. They need to regularly dilute and adjust the religious message so as not to alienate the many for whom Judaism is the necessary vehicle through which they identify Jewishly.

More important, those who can no longer accept the religious medium through which they express their ethno-cultural identity are, over time, doomed to Jewish oblivion. Institutionally and religiously, lapsed Jews in America are homeless and without recourse; they have no secular Jewish culture to fall back upon. When they repudiate their religious affiliations, the American mainstream will, sooner or later, claim them as its own. By contrast, the obvious strength of Israeli Jewish culture lies in its ability to provide a secular Jewish alternative for the nationally committed, the skeptic, and the nonbeliever. It offers an often highly animated and intense Jewish culture that functions with an entirely optional religious component. Non-, or even anti-religious Israelis, have little trouble in understanding their lives and activities in Jewish terms, although as we shall see in the following chapter, this is now less clear-cut than it was in the past. They are able to transform religious observances into national ones, to continue to see themselves as an integral part of the Jewish historical saga. Becoming a lapsed Jew in Israel has little meaning; if it has any referent at all it is to those individuals who, with determination and system, repulse everything that smacks of Jewish culture—an infinitesimal group in Israeli society.

One of the more interesting consequences of these two very different Jewish realities is the degree to which the respective religious hierarchies in the two countries are vulnerable to popular pressure for reform and modernization. In the American context, because religious affiliation is overwhelmingly the most accessible avenue of Jewish identification, there is great pressure on the rabbinical establishment to adjust religious practice to popular demands. If there are no real alternatives to the synagogue for Jewish self-identification, synagogues willy-nilly bear the brunt of the pressure for change exerted by a heterogeneous Jewish public—including the many Jews for whom religiosity is a conduit to ethnic identification. The result is a religious establishment that is highly sensitive to the relevance of its activities and very accommodating to popular pressures for reform.[9]

The Jewish religious scene in Israel could not be more different. Israeli Jews do not feel that they must join or participate in a synagogue in order to express their Jewishness. As a result, synagogues and other religious institutions are peopled almost exclusively by those who accept the observant (Orthodox) version of Judaism. Those outside the pale of Orthodoxy place little pressure on the rabbis to accommodate themselves to their needs; they take the beckoning national-secular route to Jewishness and/or pick and choose from the rituals, customs, and services that the religious establishment makes available.

Most Israeli Jews are uncomfortable with what they term "religious coercion," that is, the restrictions that law and municipal regulations impose in areas such as Sabbath closings or in the monopoly that the rabbis have in matters of marriage and divorce. But in matters that fall within the ken of personal practice or synagogue ritual there is almost no pressure on the religious establishment to make accommodations and, hence, relatively little urgency to initiate reforms that would bring Judaism in line with contemporary popular tastes. With regard to matters of ritual and religious practice, the rabbis remain fundamentally insulated from public pressures and hence without motivation to revise its religious agenda.[10]

A last and weighty historical reason for the successful preservation of Jewish identity and tradition in Israel and its more conservative character has to do with the distinctive characteristics of those who made up the preponderance of the country's immigrants. The first and most influential wave of immigration came from the East European Pale in the early decades of this century. The second major wave arrived in the early state years from North Africa and the Middle East. Neither of them had undergone the liberal/pluralist and individualist revolutions that later transformed the Western world.[11] They had little or no contact with those pluralist and universalist forces that created the assimilation-prone character of Western Jews. Of course, many of the East European Jews had experience with Enlightenment themes and with radical emancipatory rhetoric, and many of them were even antireligious, but they arrived in Palestine from locales where national identity had not been diluted by the ecumenical liberalism that would develop in the West. When they arrived in Palestine/Israel, therefore, it was with an uncompromised and unchallenged sense of national belonging. Although many of them were involved in some of the most extravagant forms of social experiment in our time, they made no significant attempt to weaken the Jewish national bond. It comes as no surprise then that their affinity for Jewish self-identification is deep and abiding.

How then does this blend of precariousness, propinquity, literacy, and cultural insulation express itself in contemporary Israeli Jewish thinking and practice? How do modern Israeli Jews see themselves, both as Israelis and as Jews? We are in the fortunate position of being able to answer these questions with some degree of authority because of an unprecedentedly comprehensive study of religious and national attitudes of Israeli Jews that was recently undertaken by the Louis Guttman Israel Institute of Applied Social Research.[12]

The study's objective was to explore the degree and character of religious traditionalism among Israeli Jews. The respondents fell into four distinct categories: those who identified themselves as "strictly observant" (14%), those who said they were "observant to a great extent" (24%), those who characterized themselves as "somewhat observant" (41%), and those who reported that they were "totally non-observant" (21%). What emerges from this data is a striking picture of widespread if uneven traditionalism: Although only about a sixth of Israeli Jews characterize themselves as "strictly observant," about four-fifths report being traditional in some way or another. Even among the remaining fifth who identify themselves as "totally non-observant," a majority report observing at least some aspects of tradition. For example, only 6 percent of the total sample relate that they seldom or never take part in a Passover seder. Only 12 percent indicate that they seldom or never light Hanukkah candles. It is important to add that the study did not include most of the recent immigrants from the former Soviet Union who, at the time of their arrival, were overwhelmingly nontraditional. Overall, however, Israeli Jews, as they are depicted in the Guttman Report, turn out to be a rather traditional and observant people.

This image of tradition-preserving Israeli Jews is quite remarkable when seen against the background of Zionist history. Israel's founders and ideologues were a combatively antireligious, antitraditional lot, in open revolt against the Jewish past. Classical Zionism in its dominant forms attempted to sever the secular Jewish future from its religious past, to create a new "Hebrew person" liberated from the crippling influences of a servile tradition. (Zionism so often entailed militant secularism that it has been referred to in ultra-Orthodox circles as "the collective *yetzer harah* [evil urge] of the Jewish people.") Zionists expressly rejected the practices and beliefs of their mothers and fathers, going to extravagant lengths to make the implacable nature of their ideological insurrection manifest and palpable. What did survive this principled onslaught were only those elements of the tradition that could be recast into secular national symbols.

Until the 1960s, Jewish tradition as distinct from nationalized symbols was actively spurned by Israel's political elites. They saw it as part of an obsolete and enervated form of Jewish existence that was incompatible with the emancipated, sovereign Jewish present. This was the normative Zionist orthodoxy and it was broadly transmitted to the population at large. The majority of Israeli Jews, the new immigrants from North Africa in particular, continued to retain their fealty to tradition, but the negative attitude of Israel's cultural and political elite led many to question how long this fealty would endure.

The changes that altered Israeli society in the sixties and afterward, were, therefore, quite stunning.[13] From its uncertain position in cultural limbo, tradition became a legitimate, positive source for public and private values, warmly embraced by growing segments of Israeli society. This does not mean, of course, that Israeli Jews flocked to Orthodoxy. It does mean, however, that the classical Zionist vision of a revolutionary, ideologically principled secular Israeli culture, which rejects tradition except as a source for transvalued national symbols, is in full retreat. Even bastions of secularism such as the left-wing kibbutz movement have expressed regret over the excessively militant antitraditionalism that disfigured their ideological past. Kibbutz publications or kibbutz educational centers such as Oranim, today acknowledge that the previous animus against tradition was arrogant and self-destructive; it induced unnecessary alienation from the Jewish past, as well as a callous and dismissive attitude toward a reservoir of wisdom and meaning they might have easily tapped.

Overwhelmingly, Israeli Jews view their society and state as a perpetuation of, rather than as a rupture with, the traditional Jewish past. They tend to frame their present condition and their future aspirations in rhetoric and symbols drawn from the Jewish tradition. Efforts to formulate an alternative secular Judaism in conceptual, to say nothing of ritual terms has no attraction outside the ideological marginalia of Israeli society. To be sure, all would agree that Zionism transformed Jewish existence, but the great majority would insist, nevertheless, that it represents a natural extension, a logical closure, rather than a radical new beginning for Jewish history. Interestingly, when contemporary Israeli Jews speak of Israel as "Jewish" in character, they largely intend something considerably more substantive than a state in which Jews constitute the dominant majority. (Notably, while Herzl spoke of a state of the Jews, the currently favored term is a Jewish state.) Indeed, the pendulum seems to have swung so sharply in the other direction that surveys asking, "What does the word 'Zionism' mean for you?" consistently found that Israeli Jews in the mid-1990s associate the term with "the Land of Israel, Judaism, territories, settlements, settlers and knitted kippot." Zionism, once tantamount to revolutionary antitraditionalism, is now associated with the religious right.[14]

Levels of traditionalism among Israeli Jews are high not only when we consider the Zionist past; they stand out as well when contrasted with those of their American Jewish counterparts. A recent study of religious belief and practice in contemporary American society concludes that "secularization has progressed furthest among Americans of Jewish ancestry."[15] In 1991, the New York UJA-Federation conducted a survey of New York Jews that told of substantially higher levels of Jewish commitment and identity than those reported by the 1990 National Jewish Population Survey.[16] It is difficult to determine whether this is attributable to Jewish population density, to the higher proportion of Orthodox Jews in the New York area, or to a combination of these and other factors. Yet, whatever its source, it is quite clear that New York Jews are conspicuously more traditional and observant than their counterparts in other metropolitan locations in the United States. It is, therefore, quite instructive to compare the levels of traditionalism among Israeli Jews with those of the most committed and identified American Jewish community.

Even if we further restrict the New York sample to include only Jewish households in which both married partners report their religion of birth and upbringing, as well as their current religion as Jewish—that is, if we try to artificially create a sample that is demographically closer to the dominant Israeli pattern—important differences still remain. To be sure, with respect to some practices, the differences between the two groups are not very significant. Yet consider the following: While 48 percent of New York Jews report lighting Shabbat candles on Friday evening, 67 percent of the Israeli sample say they do so always or often—and an additional 7 percent say they do so sometimes. Twenty-eight percent of the New York Jewish sample report that they use separate dishes for meat and milk compared with 48 percent of the Israelis surveyed. Thirty-five percent of New York Jews relate that they attend some form of Purim celebration. The Israeli survey asked respondents whether celebrating Purim was an important element in feeling themselves part of the Jewish people and 73 percent reported that it was. Indeed, 45 percent reported listening to the reading of Megilat Esther (Book of Esther) always or frequently, while an additional 13 percent noted that they do so sometimes.

Another notable statistic relates to variations in religious behavior with respect to the respondent's age. Whereas in the United States and Western Europe the level of traditionalism correlates positively with age,[17] the Israeli survey reports little variation in observances for the different stages of life.

Israeli Traditionalism: Living in a Jewish Society

Waking up on Yom Kippur morning in Israel is remarkable for what is missing: One soon becomes aware of the total absence of familiar workaday sounds of cars and trucks, vacuum cleaners and whistling coffee pots, radios, and lawn mowers. An unaccustomed hush is palpable. *Nothing* moves on the roads, radios and televisions fall silent, everything shuts down. Knots of people—both those who are visibly religious as well a those whose non-observance is betrayed by a *kipah* sitting askew on the head or by a lace doily (rather than a hat) perched atop a fashionable coiffure—troop off to the synagogue, the former to pray all day, the latter to loiter in the synagogue's perimeter for lack of a better way of identifying with Yom Kippur's solemn mood.

Not only does a substantial majority (71%) of Israeli Jews report always fasting in the halachicly prescribed manner on Yom Kipper (10% sometimes fast, while 19% never fast),[18] there is virtual unanimity on the importance of preserving the day's uniqueness—whether as an explicitly religious holiday, as a day of national stock-taking, or simply as a day that Jews have observed from time immemorial. Whatever one's religious predilections, publicly transgressing this solemn mood is quite unheard of. So far as we can tell, there is no move afoot, not even from the most militantly secular circles, to challenge the practices that mark Yom Kippur observance. Although largely self-imposed rather than legally mandated, Yom Kippur observance in Israel is so deeply rooted and widely accepted that challenging it would be foolhardy, if not actually self-endangering.

Yom Kippur represents perhaps the most tangible and visible presence of Jewishness in everyday Israeli life. But there are dozens of other traditionally Jewish observances that dot the calendar and impose a densely Jewish character upon Israeli social life. Watching kindergarten and school-age children go to school on Purim, dressed up as King Ahasuerus or Queen Esther (although fairies, pirates, and Ninja Turtles are also well represented) makes the playful spirit of the holiday ubiquitous and unavoidable. The custom of *mishloach manot* (sending trays of food to other families to mark the failure of Haman's plot) is widespread and, as opposed to the United States, not limited to Orthodox neighborhoods. Television and radio programming mirrors the holiday's spirit, with masquerade parties galore—even with a public reading of *Megilat Ester* (the Scroll of Esther).

The approach of Passover is trumpeted in dozens of commercial ads recommending everything from brands of matzo to catering services for the seder meal. Preparations for the holiday are everywhere to be seen. Perhaps three-quarters of all Jewish households either always (near 60%) or sometimes (about 15%) change their utensils for Passover. Virtually all grocery stores and supermarkets reshelve their stock for Passover—with large sheets of paper covering all those products that are forbidden for Passover consumption. *Hametz* (leavened substances from bread to pasta to crackers) is unavailable for the eight days. (Those who insist on purchasing *hametz*—only 15% report always eating *hametz* on Passover—must go to Arab towns where it is available.) Model seders are held in both secular and religious schools and on television. Notably, those who report consistently not participating in Passover seders number a minuscule 6 percent of the population.

During the Hanukkah season, large menorahs adorn the tops of many public buildings, making it hard to turn in any direction without being reminded of the holiday's presence. Candle-lighting ceremonies are ubiquitous as is the public singing of the holiday's songs; Israeli television, for example, overflows with holiday music and prominently features the candle-lighting rite. Jelly doughnuts (along with potato latkes, the traditional Hanukkah culinary fare) are conspicuously available in every supermarket, kiosk, and cafeteria. It seems that all children turn into little Maccabees clutching school-made menorahs ingeniously put together out of readily available materials such as bottle caps and cardboard. Impressively, 91 percent of Israelis report always (72%) or sometimes (19%) lighting menorahs; only 9 percent consistently do not.

Beyond the specific festivals, all Jews in Israel live their lives in the context of the Jewish calendar. Sunday, and not Monday, is the first working day of the week, while Friday and Saturday are the days of weekend rest. Beginning on Thursday, Israelis part from each other with the customary blessing: "*Shabbat Shalom*" ("Sabbath peace"). School and business holidays are determined by the Jewish calendar: the autumn and spring vacations on Succot and Passover and, at times, a winter break on Hanukkah. The Christian holiday season at the end of December and New Year's Day are only marginally felt. In the religious community many will live exclusively within the ambit of the Jewish calendar—with little or no knowledge of the Western one. Most religious teenagers of our acquaintance are unable to recite the months of the Western calendar year in their proper order.

The accoutrements of Jewishness are everywhere in evidence. The flag, the national symbols, the anthem, the language, at times even the dress, all reverberate with Jewishness. On a more personal level, a full 98 percent of Israeli Jews have a mezuzah on their front door—including 92 percent of those who report that they are "non-observant." In addition, Israeli Jews are overwhelmingly committed to marking life-cycle events with Jewish ceremony. Religiously performed circumcision (*brit mila*) is observed by 92 percent of Israeli Jews. More than four-fifths (83%) celebrate bar mitzvahs with some form of Jewish ceremony. The numbers are higher still for those who feel that marriage (87%), burial, *shiva* (seven-day mourning for the dead), and kaddish for parents (88% to 91%) should be observed in a Jewish context. Many of those who define themselves as "totally non-observant" report wishing to observe these turning points with a Jewish ceremony. Only 4 to 7 percent speak of these ceremonies as "not at all important." All of this relates to the uncoerced predisposition of Israelis; it does not take into account the crucial fact that marriage, divorce, and burial, by law, must be performed within a religious context. Finally, it should be noted (against the background of intermarriage in the United States), that only one in every six (16%) Israeli Jewish parents would agree to their child's marriage to a non-Jew.

Kashrut is also an ever-present reality. All food served in public buildings (including schools, universities, medical facilities, and all government-related institutions) or in the Israeli army must comply with the Jewish dietary laws. (In practice, virtually all work places—even if they are privately owned—are kosher because of the overwhelming likelihood that Kashrut observers will be among the employees.) Whether as an employee or in the context of Israel's near-universal military service, the Jewish dietary laws are so dominant as to be simply unavoidable. Supermarkets and groceries are also kosher for the most part. To find a supermarket selling non-kosher products one needs to make a very special effort. And relatively few do—although many religious Jews distinguish between the acceptability of the different rabbinical authorities who certify a product's Kashrut. Almost all Israeli Jews (90%) observe some Kashrut regulations, at least some of the time. Two-thirds report they always eat kosher food at home. Because kosher food is so dominant in Israel—it constitutes a kind of national cuisine—it is important to note as well that roughly half the population also maintains separate utensils for meat and dairy foods as well as waiting the mandatory time interval between eating meat and dairy products.

The Israeli school system and the Israeli Army are important socializing vehicles, bringing home to all Israelis the Jewish significance of a Jewish state. Jewish youth in Israel may remember little from the hours spent studying Bible, Jewish history, and Jewish literature but they are likely to internalize notions of the precarious and vulnerable position of Jews and the momentous significance of a sovereign Jewish state after two millennia of wanderings, notions that have a high priority on the Israeli educational agenda. When they are ready to enter army service, this Jewish consciousness is, normally, deeply ingrained. Army service seals and concretizes this sense of belonging by having the young soldier (potentially at least) put himself in harm's way in order to protect the Jewish homeland. Recalled to service yearly as a reservist (many Israelis have fought in three or four wars), this sense of being personally implicated in the Jewish people's very struggle for survival creates bonds with Jewishness that are not easily sundered.

Another potent source of Jewish self-identification is the media. We have already called attention to the holiday-related programming of radio and television. Although the electronic and written media are, for the most part, entirely Western in technology and styles of delivery, there is a great deal of explicitly Jewish content that is regularly transmitted. Talk shows on Jewish subjects abound; Friday afternoon programming relating to the "weekly portion" (the section of Torah read in the synagogue) is standard; covering Jewish news from around the world constitutes a regular media feature; the "Jewish angle" on a surprisingly wide spectrum of topics receives a great deal of attention. For those who want their media more Jewish-centered still, there are radio channels that intersperse Jewish music with rabbinical homilies, Talmudic exposition, and religio-political talk. A spate of daily and weekly newspapers directed at Orthodox and *haredi* audiences provides religious news and opinion, halachic guidance on a variety of subjects, and ample information about religiously run commercial enterprises that cater to the special needs of the religious community.

There are also the memorable cameo illustrations that reflect the depth of Jewishness in Israel. For example, the classic children's tale *The Three Little Pigs* was translated into Hebrew as *The Three Little Goats*. The counterpart to the Red Cross in Israel is the Red Star of David. After basic training, Israeli army recruits are sworn in at the Wailing Wall carrying a Bible in one hand and a rifle in the other. One radio station has a countdown of the top 40 hasidic hit songs of the week. Getting directions in some parts of town will sound something like this: "Turn right at Rabbi Akiva Street, left on Maimonides, and continue straight past Warsaw Ghetto Uprising and Redemption Streets to—"

Most essentially, "living in a Jewish society" means internalizing the almost universally accepted axiom that Israel's existence derives its meaning and its justification from the Jewish historical and cultural context. It is the Jewish past that vindicates and authorizes the Jewish Israeli present. Hence, in defending a particular position in Israeli public life, one often finds oneself embroiled in all manner of long-standing Jewish controversies. Debates on public concerns are animated not only by specific judgments in regard to this or that issue; they are as likely as not to involve principled stands on the conception of Jewishness to which one is committed. And given the life-and-death realities in which Israel finds itself, the need to engage oneself in Jewish terms is intense and unremitting.

Moreover, given the fact that Israel is a tiny country with giant problems—problems with global importance entirely out of proportion to its size—it is not at all surprising that Israeli public concern rivets on local issues. Cosmopolitan tendencies—and they surely exist—are regularly overwhelmed by national crises, tragedies, moments of exultation, and war. Giving relatively scant attention to international problems, the Israeli media tends to limit its horizon to Middle Eastern and Jewish questions[19] or view international news through a local prism. The front page of *Yediot Aharonot*, Israel's largest selling daily newspaper, carried the picture of an African and an accompanying story headlined: "The Candidate for General

Secretary of the U.N. is married to a Swedish Woman, Niece of the Savior of Jewish Lives, Raul Wallenberg."[20] The outcome should be obvious: The regnant Judeo-centric perspective is only further entrenched.

With only a bit of overstatement one could make a case that secular Jews in Israel live in a more totally encompassing Jewish world than do even Orthodox Jews in the Diaspora. Orthodox Jews outside of Israel usually need to leave their exclusively Jewish surroundings to earn a living, to get from one place to another, to obtain a driving license or a passport. Radio, television, newspapers, and magazines do not reflect their communal concerns. For the most part, the issues that exercise the broader political community of which they are part are not Jewish issues and the political candidates for whom they vote are not Jewish candidates. When they pursue their communal interests, their claims must be presented in terms that address the concerns and sensitivities of their non-Jewish co-citizens. In Israel, by contrast, the total context is Jewish, the issues are Jewish, the personalities are Jewish; indeed, it is nearly impossible to escape the confines of a virtually omnipresent Jewishness.

Explaining Israeli Traditionalism: Gentile Hostility

The decline of traditional religion in advanced industrial societies has been reasonably attributed to the increasing sense of security and self-confidence enjoyed by most modern Western peoples. The need for the rigid and unconditional rules of traditional religions as well as for the formidable sanctions they could impose weaken dramatically when the sense of vulnerability no longer besets the mind. By contrast, when vulnerability does exist, especially when it is acute, a deep "need for a sense of security" develops and together with it a craving for absolute cultural standards.[21] Israel, we believe, is a special case: it is a "vulnerable" advanced industrial society.

Vulnerability is, of course, a matter of perception. Particularly in times of uneasy peace, the perception of a looming security threat is at least as important as its reality. It is perception that largely dictates policy, which in turn often interacts with reality in ways that reinforce the original perception. From the 1960s (and perhaps earlier still) until very recently, a broad consensus, which resonated with traditional Jewish motifs, provided a set of communal symbols, a common language of public discourse, and the sense of an integrated social order. For the vast majority of Israelis the central values of this consensus were: Jewish peoplehood and what has been called "the religion of security"[22] or, more conventionally, the "siege mentality."[23]

This threat-centered perspective persisted despite the entry of Israel into the club of advanced industrial nations.

When, as in the Israeli case, an acute security threat has become a permanent condition of life—especially when repeated outbreaks of hostility lend credence to these threats—the vulnerable party will crave for assurances that transcend the merely "rational and professional"; it will require a deeper sense of protection than what the Israeli Defense Forces, Israeli Intelligence, and the General Security Services can provide. Psychologically and symbolically, Israelis meet the challenge of persistent vulnerability through faith in the Almighty and a belief in the eternity of the Jewish people.[24] Indeed, in a survey conducted in 1986, there was found to be a demonstrably systematic relationship between the valuing of Jewish peoplehood and religious faith on the one side and perceptions of vulnerability on the other.[25]

Israeli Jews feel that many of the most important events in their lives are inextricable from their being Jewish and from their living in a Jewish state. Events of a personal nature, even milestone events in one's life, are often overwhelmed by intruding crises and security threats. Orienting oneself in an emergency-prone, crisis-ridden social environment requires an inordinate quantity of explanatory and interpretive constructs just so as to keep one's balance. The media attempts to do its part in this project of national orientation by regularly providing readers, listeners, and viewers with a great variety of commentators and "expert opinions." They purvey social scientific, rational analyses of perplexing realities, analyses that for some— especially the well educated—may well be satisfactory.

And yet, for the majority, some of whom are well educated, these explanations are thin and excessively cerebral; they fail to get at the source of underlying trepidation and confusion. This is not the kind of dissatisfaction that haunts all social scientific theories and explanations; nor is it related to the essential limitations of human reason. The weakness of these rational accounts is that they often fail to provide the individual person with the cognitive wherewithal to soothe existential anxieties, much less actually provide solace. Social science may explain the nature of terrorism or even why Israel is the target of indiscriminate violence but when a beloved family member or friend is crippled or killed, professional analyses are lifeless and unavailing. Moreover, the recognition that it just might as well have been me makes it difficult to escape the sense of how very vulnerable one in fact is.

The power of paradigmatic traditional Jewish explanations—what we have called "the ideology of affliction"—is, at moments like these, perhaps irresistible. Not only is one surrounded by rabbis, public figures, even politicians who interpret events through the prism of Jewish affliction, there is probably no other available means of coping with the agonies of bereavement. Linking oneself up with generations of Jewish sufferers who survived despite the nightmares of persecution affords at least a communal frame in which pain becomes meaningful rather than entirely random. At such moments Jewish self-identification, even belief, trust, and prayer are consolations that few will reject.

Building on this deeply embedded Jewish motif of a malevolent, menacing world, Israeli Jews embraced the notion "that the world was basically hostile and often antisemitic." This set the pattern for "the way the Israeli public viewed national security policy."[26] In a recent survey of Israeli public opinion, 71 percent responded that "all non-Jews" or "a substantial proportion" of them were antisemites.[27]

Even mainstream Zionist parties, it was found, analyze the conflict between Israel and the Arab world "in the spirit and often in the lexicon of the persecution suffered by Jews in most European countries and some of the countries of the Muslim world."[28] Briefly anticipating our next chapter, it is one of the distinguishing characteristics of those who are spoken of as the "post-Zionists" to insist that the Arab-Israeli conflict is properly understood as a straightforward territorial dispute, whereas the overwhelming majority of Israeli Jews see it as an ethno-religious struggle conceptualized in the traditional terms of oppressors and victims.

Despite the perceived antisemitic hostility of the Arab world and although Israeli Jews are prone to read impending threats into the proximate future, there is, nevertheless, a high degree of certainty that Israel will emerge victorious. Again and again Israeli Jews affirm: We "must trust in the guardian of Israel" and "the guardian of Israel will prevail." This belief in Israel's ultimate triumph "is related to religious belief, but the religious have no monopoly on it. It is to be found more often among those who support the right but supporters of the left also share the belief. . . . It permeates the society and legitimates behavior and policy."[29]

To be sure, Israeli Jews differ as to who or what is being referred to by the term "guardian." Many Israeli Jews assume it refers to the Israeli Defense Forces; others are certain it is a reference to the Almighty; still others think of the people of Israel or the state of Israel. It is not only that the usage "guardian of Israel" (*shomer yisrael* or *tzur yisrael*) resonates with religious significance (it is a synonym for God in traditional texts), but, as analysts have pointed out, the very belief that some redemptive entity must be trusted to prevail, is, at its heart, an extrarational belief. Whatever may happen, there is an often unspoken faith that Israel will in the end prevail just as it has always outlasted its enemies. Far from constituting an impediment to national consensus, the ability to read many diverse meanings into a touchstone term like guardian—all unified by their promise of deliverance—facilitates the development of a meaningful, common language of discourse.

The traditional religious paradigm of persecution and deliverance—including its profane national, military, and state-based varieties—is fundamental to the way a great majority of Israelis view their uncertain place in the Middle East. Security anxieties send them back to the tradition for comfort and assurance. The tradition, with its tendency to embellish upon Jewish tribulations, to portray the Jews as the "suffering servants of the Lord," confirms, in turn, the reality of their fears. If tradition fosters the expectation of Gentile hostility, security threats underwrite traditional expectations. A self-sustaining, mutually verifying "security-tradition loop" develops, and it deepens with each reciprocal confirmation. The indispensability of tradition to this cognitive construct supports and sustains the pattern of ritual behavior and religious belief that (among other things) distinguishes Israeli Jews from their co-religionists in the Diaspora.

For many Israeli Jews—those of Sephardic origin most especially—the tradition's image of inevitable Jewish victimization ("a lamb among seventy wolves") provides some basic explanation for Arab enmity toward Israel.[30] What is most intriguing about the persistence of this traditional outlook is the way it contradicts and undermines classic Zionism's most cherished tenet, to wit, Jewish suffering is a function of Jewish powerlessness and vulnerability in the Diaspora. Jews are hated and attacked (so the argument was made from Herzl onward) because they are defenseless and stateless guests in other people's lands. Were Jews to establish their own independent state, they would be transformed from a unique and problematic people into a "normal" one. In dealing with their non-Jewish neighbors they would, at last, become "normal actors."

This Zionist tenet is now the subject of deep controversy. One observer argues that the prospect of normalization divides Israeli Jews in a most basic way: They disagree as to "whether or not the Jewish people and its state are capable of being 'normal' and whether or not such a condition (if it is possible) is one that should be sought."[31]

For many, perhaps even a sizable majority, the very conception of a normalized Jewish existence is an intolerable affront to a people whose entire history bespeaks unparalleled uniqueness—whether in tragedy or in cultural distinction. Ironically, the period in which Zionism achieved its most impressive attainments nationally, materially, and militarily is also the period in which the revitalized traditional doctrine of Jewish precariousness—a doctrine that runs so deeply counter to the Zionist grain—made its most serious gains.

Developments since the signing of the first Oslo accord seem to have blurred this picture somewhat. The vision of a "new Middle East" in which

Israel is no longer alone and threatened has made small, tentative inroads in the minds of some, mostly left-wing Israeli Jews. We suspect that reservations about the traditional paradigm of Jewish-Gentile relations may well be growing; indeed, newly emerging attitudes could become crucial to the comprehension of future developments. What is certain, however, is that at least until very recently the traditional tale of oppression and deliverance was, for the lion's share of contemporary Israeli Jews, both alive and credible.

Threatened physical security, we have suggested, bolsters the need for absolute cultural norms. But there is a second aspect to this proposition that should be analyzed as well. The fear of hostile forces and of social breakdown also heightens the feeling that social solidarity is essential. Beyond the need for obligatory ordering principles lest society "tear itself apart,"[32] there is a concomitant drive toward dense social consolidation, toward organic rather than instrumental conceptions of social life. Hence, a religious norm like "honor thy father and mother" works to promote and maintain much-needed unity in perilous, menacing times. It flourishes especially when unmanageable realities require more than individual talents in order to be mastered, when networked familial support systems are indispensable to personal safety as well as to a sense of belonging and fellowship. Conversely, when advanced industrial societies provide alternate forms of security in the shape of affluence, stable democracies, and the welfare state, the need for familial hierarchy and for reciprocal responsibility becomes considerably less crucial.

Once again, Israel belongs to both categories simultaneously. Although it is a relatively affluent and stable democratic welfare state, its precarious security condition prevents the more private, individualist, and instrumental social attitudes from emerging. Broadly understood, familialism—the sense that Israeli society is an extended family animated by the principle that each person is his brother's keeper—is never far from the surface of social discourse. Even the Israeli army, not an institution in which we would normally expect to find familial virtues applauded, regards family ties as critical to maintaining troop morale; indeed, the sense of kinship and familial belonging is said to provide the individual soldier, no less than Israeli Jews from all walks of life, with a support system that effectively assuages their besetting fears.[33]

The energy focused on familialism, both in its immediate and its extended social sense, is further intensified because it is readily apparent that individuals—whether by themselves or even in league with each other—could not meet the challenge posed by the overwhelming numerical superiority and geographically enveloping presence of the Arab antagonist. Only genuine communal solidarity and fellowship is adequate to confront the looming dangers from without. Besides, the sense of being under fire is almost always directly attributed to the Jewish character of the state. It is "only because we are Jews" (so runs the familiar formula) that we are in this exceptionally vulnerable position. Hence, the strength to withstand must come from the collective resources of the Jewish people and the Jewish tradition.

The more ties of family and kinship are emphasized, the more Jewish identity and Jewish practice take on charged significance. If Israel is an extended family suffering and surviving for the sake of its cultural uniqueness, the Jewish identity for which these travails are undergone becomes, quite naturally, the central source of resolve, courage, and tenacity. Under these circumstances, it requires special fortitude—most Israeli Jews would dub it effrontery— to break ranks with the Jewish people or to make light of its traditions, observances, and rituals.

israeli jews

New Images

*T*he previous chapter ended on such a note of finality—the Jewishness of Israel seemed so manifest and deep-seated—that to begin so soon with counterarguments seems contrived, almost mean-spirited. But even a cursory familiarity with Israel's public life will have alerted the attentive reader to at least one conspicuous omission in our account, an omission that renders our conclusions more than a bit suspect. To put it in the coarsest of terms: If things are so good, why are they so bad? If there is such a wall-to-wall consensus on the Jewish character of Israel, if the vast majority of Israelis actively engage with the Jewish tradition in one way or another, why does the religious issue generate such rancor and enmity?

On its face, the Guttman Report presents a portrait of a broadly observant people who, even though they differ in degree of practice and belief, are united by their common commitment to Jewish identity and Jewish life. A continuum of observance appears to provide visible evidence of underlying accord, of basic unity. There is no data to support the popular journalistic stereotype of two rival communities—the one religious, the other secular— glaring at each other across an unbridgeable chasm. Using the Guttman Report as our guide, we would expect controversies related to the Jewish character of the state to be mild to moderate rather than spiteful to savage.

Why then is the quality of debate over the Jewish character of state so extraordinarily shrill? Why is compromise so difficult to come by? Why is the more or less traditional and centrist majority unable to mitigate the explosive tensions that regularly agitate Israeli politics? How are we to explain the fact that, despite all this palpable communality and unity, Israel may well be the Western state with the most bellicose and antagonistic religious-secular divide?

When Israelis are asked to describe the quality of relationship between the religious and the nonreligious communities, nearly three-quarters (74%) respond that they are "bad" or "rather bad."[1] More dramatic still, 47 percent of Israeli Jews, with varying degrees of certainty, believe that the Kulturkampf between secular and religious Jews will end in violent struggle or civil war.[2] The polls only confirm what is common knowledge, what Israelis take to be evident to the point of banality: Religious issues are profoundly divisive, indeed, they are probably at the heart of more social cleavage and polarization than any other issue on Israel's public agenda. The image of two nations that grow further and further apart—the one religious and insular, the other secular and cosmopolitan—is a staple of the written and electronic media. Notwithstanding the Guttman Report's evidence to the contrary, popular perceptions stubbornly cling to the image of a long-seething, variously contended Kulturkampf between warring communities. It is, we are told, a tale of two cities: On the one side there is Jerusalem with its growing *haredi* population, its fraught religious past and contemporary spiritual passions; on the other side, only forty miles distant but culturally of another universe, stands Tel Aviv, "the city that never stops," home to nightlife, restaurants, beaches, high fashion, business corporations, and Israel's "fast set."[3]

One seductive interpretation of the Guttman Institute data that would, ostensibly, account for the discrepancy between the widespread traditionalism it reports and the stridency of religious-secular discourse should be seriously and comprehensively considered. There is little doubt that the statistical evidence pointing to extensive Jewish observance is accurate; nonetheless, the conclusions drawn from the findings, it might be contended, miss their deeper significance and implications. The continuum of observance does not describe, as might be supposed, a basically fraternal community bound by a tradition that is widely, if variously, observed. On the contrary; it describes a people divided by the tradition itself, that is, two communities with essentially different conceptions of what the tradition and its observance signify. It is a case in which shared practices obscure deeper antagonisms.

For the devoutly Orthodox, Judaism and Jewishness are indistinguishable. The attempt to drive a wedge between Jewish culture and Jewish religion is both invidious and contrived. Jewish culture, they might say, relates to those practices that grow up in the interstices of halachic routine, that is, the informal and popular conventions that serve to flesh out the halachic life. To speak of these Jewish practices as if they possessed their own self-animating life source independent of their halachic derivation violates the integrality of a Torah-governed life. To observe tradition is not a matter of nostalgia or of cultural self-expression; it is, quite simply, taking upon oneself the yoke of Divine Will.

Moreover, distinguishing between Jewish religiosity and Jewish culture is intolerable because all manner of obnoxiously antireligious ideas can be paraded in ostensibly Jewish dress. Worse yet, it fosters the odious notion that there are Jewish alternatives to halachic Judaism. Better that Jewish pretenses be abandoned altogether than that they delude the ignorant into believing that there are different ways to lead a Jewish life.

From the non-Orthodox side, the argument continues, engagement with the tradition is based upon a radically different understanding of what partaking in customary Jewish observances entails. Traditional practices are ways of identifying with Jewish peoplehood and Jewish history. Divine categories are only an optional part of this cultural package. As such, engagement with the tradition is selective and nonobligating. Maintaining such a communal and creative relationship with the tradition is the modern Jew's entirely legitimate, cultural alternative to Orthodoxy. We might call this the weak case non-Orthodox position.

The strong case argument, by contrast, contends that the Jewish tradition is in need of a dramatic face-lift. The Orthodox have profoundly subverted the Jewish message by focusing exclusively on superannuated rituals and anachronistic prohibitions. A reappropriation and transvaluation of Jewish tradition, in which the dross of the old is replaced by a dynamic new message, is the order of the day. Whether the new content is said to be socialism, the just society, "a light unto the Gentiles," or to reflect the pursuit of an equitable solution to the Palestinian problem is, for our present purposes, immaterial. In each of these cases, engaging with the Jewish tradition entails struggling to liberate it from Orthodox domination.

At some blurred point on the continuum of observance presented by the Guttman Report, the transition from the Orthodox to the non-Orthodox takes place—a point that is occluded because it was the factual level of observance that was studied rather than the Orthodox or non-Orthodox identity of the observer. Although there may be only a few percentage points dividing the less observant Orthodox from the more observant non-Orthodox, the continuum is substantially ruptured at the point of their meeting— to say nothing about the divide with the strong case non-Orthodox.

Traditional observances mean different things on the two sides of the divide. Indeed, it is precisely the attempt of both to appropriate the same tradition that creates the intense friction that inflames Israel's religious-secular strife. The battle for hegemony rages over the same texts, the same symbols, the same ceremonies, with each side condemning the other's analogous practices as an abomination or an atavistic relic. For example, when members of a left-wing kibbutz and an ultra-Orthodox family each sit down to read the Passover Haggadah at the seder meal, the survey will reflect that both took part in a traditional practice. Clearly, this begs the question as to whether their respective seders have brought them closer to or driven them further away from each other. Conceivably, were there no continuum of observance but rather a sharp drop-off where Orthodoxy ends, tensions between the two communities might be more manageable. The argument we are pursuing concludes with a clear verdict: The Guttman data are both accurate in their portrait of Israelis as a moderately traditional people and, nevertheless, entirely consistent with the reality of intense religious-secular conflict.

Despite the admirable neatness with which this interpretation seems to resolve the incongruity between widespread observance and religious strife, we doubt its accuracy. To be sure, had these same numbers appeared in a survey taken, say, two generations earlier, in the fifties or even early sixties, explanations based upon two incompatible conceptions of Jewishness might well have been appropriate. In this early period of statehood, and even more so during the Yishuv (pre-state Jewish community in Palestine) period, there was indeed fierce competition between systematic and self-consciously Jewish worldviews. At the very least, two broad conceptions of Jewishness confronted each other: the traditionally Orthodox position (with its many variants), and the secular-socialist-*halutzic* (pioneering) doctrine (with its own variants). Both claimed to be the authentic representatives of the Jewish tradition and, in varying degrees of inflexibility, its exclusive embodiment.

Although the Orthodox worldview retained its doctrinal and communal integrity in the Yishuv and early state period, it was clearly not at the center of the Zionist movement. In its early "romantic" phase, Zionism was dominated by a secular, ideologically militant, and highly dynamic program, the central thrust of which was to unseat traditional religious conceptions of Jewishness and transvalue them into socio-political ideas that aimed at nothing less than "true socialism," "human renewal," and "Jewish rebirth." The idea of a secular alternative to religious Judaism was widespread, fervent, and credible. And until a few decades ago, defenders of this vision could still be heard making a spirited case for their dream.

The subsequent erosion and dramatic decline of this revolutionary faith do not detract from its erstwhile power and uniqueness. We are convinced that it was the single most arresting and creative modern attempt to refashion the Jewish heritage and provide it with fresh content. (Hence the undying enmity it earned from the religious community.[4]) There are, to be sure, a number of noble and stirring voices that continue to make the case for a nonreligious version of Jewishness,[5] but, it should be said (not without a sense of loss) that their visions are difficult to distinguish from the kind of "secular humanism with a social conscience" that is widely available in the modern world.

More important than the relative dearth of articulate spokesmen for Jewishly inspired secularism is the decline of a constituency that is moved by or interested in such messages. To put the point more subtly: Although large numbers of Israelis continue to be sympathetic to Jewishly couched images of the ethical life or of political justice, what stirs them is not the specific Jewish content that may be adduced but the Western liberal humanism that lies at its heart.

This is not said, of course, to register a criticism; it is merely to say that the era of highly energetic, specifically Jewish alternatives to the religious

version of tradition seems to have ended. Today, the religious version of
Jewishness is not met with articulate Jewishly based secular alternatives —
and, as we shall see, when such alternatives are presented, they often turn
out to be versions of secularism that come close to rejecting Jewishness
altogether. In a word, Jewish secularism as a systematic, fighting creed
appears to be largely an anachronism. One leading defender of radical secularism concedes the point outright. He claims that

> there are secular individuals, groups and even sub-cultures in Israel.
> Their daily behavior and their own identity is secular. There are
> even those who wage a cultural or religious war against this or that
> aspect of state efforts to impose this or that religious practice or
> *halachic* norm on the general public or on one segment of that pub-
> lic. But when the vast majority of Israeli Jews refer to their collective
> national identity, that identity is defined for the most part by con-
> cepts, values, symbols and collective memory that is anchored pri-
> marily in the Jewish religion. In other words, there are secular Jews
> in the world and in Israel, but there is grave doubt if there is such a
> thing as secular Judaism.[6]

With the decline of the secularist alternative, the religious world-view,
the status quo ante, rushed in to fill the void. Not that there was a surge of
belief or even a growth of identification with Orthodoxy; if anything the
numbers point in the other direction. The change that occurred was not
demographic so much as cognitive. Lacking competition, traditional religiosity, almost by default, reassumed its historical role as the legitimate
interpreter of things Jewish. It became increasingly difficult for many secular Israelis to resist the contention that the Orthodox are, in fact, the
authentic perpetuators of Jewish history.

For a majority of secular Israelis, secularism has ceased being a worldview; it has become a life-style, a preferred cultural ambience. Which is to
say that it is a personal predilection, it lacks in organization, and (for our
purposes most important) displays an unmistakable trace of defensiveness.
For many, it is grasped as a less demanding, less committed, more self-centered set of life activities than those imposed by the rigors of Orthodoxy.
We—the nontraditional seem to be saying—cannot accept the kind of life
that Orthodoxy ordains. But we recognize, nevertheless, that the Orthodox
retain a closer, more authentic relationship to Judaism. Of course, we feel
uncomfortable with much they do, and, yes, they can be trying, at times
even outrageously so. But they are our bond to the Jewish past and our guar-
antee of a Jewish future. We can continue living our lives as we prefer,

because we are certain that they will never abandon their Jewish faithful-ness.[7] Most important—here they are likely to shrug sheepishly—we have little to offer in the way of a viable *Jewish* alternative. As unflattering as it may be to their lives and identity, there is a grudging sense among many of the secular that the Orthodox bear the burden of a substantive, challenging doctrine (a "loaded wagon," in the common parlance) while they, unencum-bered and unchallenged, "travel light."

Notably, when the authors of the Oslo peace process spoke of a "new Middle East," popular reactions often ran along these same lines. The Labor Party vision of Middle Eastern peace promised economic coopera-tion, rising standards of living, open borders, and flourishing high-tech industries. But for a society weaned on epic historical missions, ideological fervor, and personal sacrifice, all of this had a somewhat empty, hedonistic ring to it. It may be that most Israelis, in their personal pursuits, desire nothing more than affluence, travel, and leisure, but for many these crea-turely pursuits are accompanied by a lingering sense of letdown, almost a bad conscience. They sense a moral void where once great missions flour-ished. It is into this void that the religious have entered. They present themselves as unabashed pursuers of great goals, as the only morally chal-lenged community in a self-centered society, as the only remaining Zion-ists; and for many in the nonreligious world, these claims appear to possess a certain prima facie credibility.

This kind of secular self-abnegation has been a constant source of frustra-tion among the more articulate representatives of secularism. One Knesset member (the Knesset is the Israeli legislature) assures the secular commu-nity that despite their often-heard dirges and defeatist rhetoric, their num-bers are actually growing; more shops, cafes, and restaurants are open on the Sabbath than ever before, the number of non-Orthodox marriages and nup-tial contracts has risen dramatically, and civil burial has been introduced. Yet for all this, he laments, the secularists remain weak-willed and apolo-getic. They are

> defeated by themselves, not by reality. Is the reason for this error
> that the secular still feel they are "an empty wagon," insufficiently
> "moved by values"? It seems so. Liberation from this complex is the
> stronghold that secularism still needs to conquer.[8]

Even more outspoken is a militantly secular columnist, Orit Schochat, who entitles an angry article: "Where Are the Secularists Hiding?"[9] The secular, she writes, seem to remorsefully concede that they are not "moved by values" in the way the religious are. She bemoans the sense of unease and inferiority they feel when confronting the religious community, as if their secular lives were less worthy, less principled, less honorable. They are "guilt-ridden because they do not fast on Yom Kippur, or put up a *succah*, or yearn for Hebron." This secular "surrender," she contends, is entirely self-imposed and voluntary. Gone are the days when David Ben-Gurion, a true secularist who was married in a civil ceremony, refused to wear a *kipah* even when he served as a witness under the bridal canopy. Today the secular are all too acquiescent; they act as if they need the inspiration of the religious to shore up their failing Jewish identity. Shochat concludes that only a proud and principled secularism, one that does not ignominiously capitulate before the Orthodox, is a secularism "worthy of its name."

The tendency to abstain from competition, in effect, to forfeit the field of Jewish identity to the Orthodox, has received interesting confirmation in recent Israeli voting patterns. When, beginning in 1984, Shas, a Sephardi ultra-Orthodox party, garnered a substantial number of votes from nonobservant Sephardic Jews, observers speculated that these voters were registering support for the proposition that Orthodoxy was the normative form of Jewishness, even if they did not live according to its precepts.[10] But, in the case of Shas, the argument was not conclusive; one could argue that it was the party's ethnic appeal that explained non-Orthodox support. This cannot be said about the dramatically improved showing of the National Religious Party—a party without any clear ethnic character—in the 1996 elections. Once again, substantial numbers of nonreligious Israelis of various ethnic origins cast their ballots for a party that did not represent their nonobservant life-styles.[11] It is hard to avoid the conclusion (which is substantiated by much anecdotal evidence) that for these voters, support for the NRP is tantamount to affirming the normative hegemony, the legitimate custodianship of Orthodoxy over Jewishness. Moreover, their vote appears to endorse the proposition that the need to shore up Israel's Jewish character—weakened and adulterated by the massive assault of Western culture—requires a return to the Orthodox agenda.

These voters can be spoken of as the religious community's fellow travelers. They epitomize how deeply the religious interpretation of Jewishness has sunk its roots into the nonreligious consciousness. In the absence of a credible Jewish alternative, Orthodoxy for them has become a kind of default position, a residual loyalty that is instinctively synthesized into (or compartmentalized alongside) their largely Western secular lives.

Not that they are likely to energetically defend residual Orthodoxy as a principled and articulate worldview. It is more accurately described as a cultural impulse of uncertain status or a nebulous historical reflex that passively adopts the status quo ante in the absence of other alternatives.[12]

Normally, they are neither sufficiently exercised by these inclinations nor interested enough in their implications to be distressed by the ostensible contradictions in which it involves them. (For example, they desist from going to synagogue but concede that were they to go to a synagogue it would surely be to an Orthodox one.[13]) Moreover, because of the patent incohesiveness of their position, they are content to let the Orthodox defend the faith while they go on with their secular lives. This is true of nonobservant NRP and Shas voters, but it is also quite relevant for the many who adopt vaguely traditional life patterns—many of whom, in terms of our earlier classification, would qualify as "weak case" secularists.

Obviously, there is a fundamental tension inherent in this curious blend of Orthodox axioms with secular behavior. The mantle of custodianship they bestow upon the Orthodox clashes, both cognitively and politically, with the lives they chose to lead. Not only are they convicted of inadequacy by their own beliefs, they are also forced into self-deprecatory and apologetic postures when confronting the impinging religious world. There is, after all, something demeaning in assigning legitimacy to those who abhor and denounce the life one chooses to lead.

To put it more concretely, for all of their acquiescence to the abstract legitimacy of religious Jewishness, they are not about to grant the Orthodox actual control over the political arena. Indeed, they continue to insist on their right to live their lives as they see fit. Attempts to interfere with their Western predilections and diversions through political prohibitions will be met with determined resistance, even with rage at the arrogance of those who presume to tell them what to do. In effect, there is little incompatibility between their residual Orthodoxy, on the one hand, and their spirited opposition to "religious coercion" on the other. In this light, the dilemma we posed at this chapter's outset ("if things are so good, why are they so bad?") may not be so difficult to resolve after all. At least part of the solution is to be found in the surprising ease with which vague traditionalism and a notional allegiance to the Orthodoxy can coexist practically with a steadfastly secular form of life. If we add to this already volatile mix the unconditional hostility provided by the militantly secular, our dilemma is very near solution.

For how long can such an intellectually incongruous and existentially improbable compound sustain itself? It is not our contention, of course, that bad logic self-destructs or that ideological incongruities ineluctably seek resolution. We know better. Still, it must be said that the seam that binds residual Orthodoxy with secular practice is under growing pressure. Beyond the intellectual dissonance and the political confrontations that fray the link between them, the surge of Western consumerism that has dramatically transformed Israel over the past decade places it in an increasingly untenable position—one that is already exacerbating both the dissonance and the confrontations. Secular life-styles and Orthodox norms grow ever more disparate. Opportunities afforded by affluence and cosmopolitanism render traditional prohibitions all the more constraining, onerous, and artificial. Entrance into the global market—whether as tourists, cable TV viewers, restaurant frequenters, weekend vacationers, or as businessmen and -women with international ties—carries with it an irresistible logic of its own.

To be sure, for many with triumphalist Orthodox convictions, the necessity for a decisive choice between Jewishness and Western secularism foreshadows an imminent large-scale return to Orthodoxy. Lacking their faith, we would humbly submit that this is not the most likely of outcomes. Assuredly, the committed Orthodox will find both the will and the creativity to forge forms of religious life that will easily survive the challenge. But for those whose residual Orthodoxy is based on a mix of nostalgia, inconsistent and often unexamined assumptions, and, not least, the practical absence of other Jewish alternatives, the prospects are quite different. As opposed to the consistent and firmly held commitments of *halutzic* Zionism in the past, the contemporary version of secular Jewishness gives clear signs of lacking emotional robustness and intellectual staying power. There is something essentially volatile and transitional in this kind of conditional, derivative Jewishness—certainly if the Western consumerist style continues to dominate, and most especially if the inconclusive openings toward peace in the Middle East are translated into reality-altering facts on the ground. This is a theme to which we shall return.

Not surprisingly, this acquiescent, self-abnegating relation to Orthodoxy has infuriated many principled and articulate secularists. Far more consistent and aggressively self-confident than the passive allies of the religious community, these secularists "without apology" reject the inferiority complex that has modern, liberal, pluralist humanism cowering in the shadows of Orthodoxy. Not only do they repudiate the demeaning fellow-traveler status to which muddled traditionalism demotes them, they insist that Judaism—or, for the more radical, Jewishness itself—be entirely banished from the public realm.

There are important gradations and shadings in these views, and, as is well known, the devil (!) is in the details. First, there is a large group (probably a solid majority in the secular community) of what might be called the secular accommodationists. Judaism and Jewishness, they insist, are not identical. While Jewishness should, undeniably, be cultivated and encouraged by a Jewish state, Judaism should not. A line of demarcation must be drawn (with as much clarity as such delicate exercises permit) between those elements of Jewish life that form the common cultural heritage of the Jewish people and those that are the confessional or theological concerns of particular groups. While the Orthodox would, needless to say, be free to continue with their beliefs and practices, there would be a strict prohibition against utilizing public power to promote narrowly religious objectives. Given the intimate interpenetrations of Jewish culture and faith, difficulties will no doubt arise in specifying the precise point at which the line of demarcation is to be drawn. Although problems of this kind are only to be expected, they do not involve us in insuperable difficulties. With wisdom and good will, a reasonably clear *modus vivendi* can be established.

For secularists of this accommodationist sort, there would be no problem in, say, requiring Bible instruction in public schools. The Bible, they would assert, is the charter document of the Jewish people and, as such, it should be the common possession of citizens of the Jewish state. Of course, this says nothing about how Bible should be approached: In the spirit of the pluralism they espouse, it could be legitimately taught as anything from Holy Writ to the Jewish counterpart to the *Iliad* and the *Odyssey*. For many of these moderate secularists, providing state-supported religious education or religious services for those who seek them would also be acceptable—just so long as they were available to those of all religious persuasions on an equal basis and were in no way binding on the secular. Because Israel's Jewish character is important to them, they have little sympathy for those who advocate de-Judaizing the state by abandoning all public expressions of Jewish particularity.[14] Obviously, they would have no problem whatever in retaining the Jewish accoutrements of statehood such as the flag, anthem, and national emblem. In a word, the state they envision would be Jewish, pluralist, civil, and secular.

What would be the Jewish content of such a state? Would it understand itself as presenting a Jewish alternative to Orthodoxy? If by the term "alternative" something analogous to the substance and system of secular Zionism is intended, the answer is clearly No. It is difficult to attribute to the accommodationists a unique, to say nothing of an ambitious ideological credo. Moreover, being ardently pluralist in character, we should not expect a definitive Jewish alternative. If, however, what is signified is a Jewishly framed and Jewishly conceived understanding of Israel and of themselves as integral parts of the saga of Jewish history, then the answer would have to be Yes.

It would not be difficult for the cynical to deconstruct their ideological value preferences, proving that they were little more than variants of liberal humanism adorned with Jewish peculiarities, but this would not daunt them. Jewish culture, they would retort, is alive and well where events and policies naturally reverberate within a Jewish context, where Jewish historical memories mix effortlessly with contemporary political discourse, where moral agents seek grounding for their deeds in the polymorphous Jewish tradition. Two generations ago, their grandparents of the *halutz* era thought of Zionism as a secular reinterpretation of the Jewish tradition intended to supersede Orthodoxy. Approaching the end of the twentieth century, Zionism's ambitions have been moderated considerably: It is now understood as a multifaceted Jewish cultural context, in which the tradition, variously understood, perpetuates itself by engaging with the challenges of the contemporary world.

That universal liberal and humanist themes thrive in this Zionist context is no badge of dishonor. On the contrary. Jewishness is not a museum of pure prototypes that disqualifies salutary influences from without. As a context of discourse rather than a militant ideology, Zionism is legitimately inclusive. To achieve a vibrant, Jewishly framed form of public discourse that is alive to the best in general human culture is as worthy a goal as contemporary Jews can pursue. After all, they might conclude, what are French or English culture at their best but a similar mix of the indigenous with the universally human?

As a Jewish survival strategy, accommodationist secularism has the clear advantage of framing Jewish existence in terms so ecumenical that few would be excluded. It would permit a host of survival strategies to operate concurrently without prejudicing the outcome of their mutual interactions or prejudging their individual efforts at success. Besides, it is the one strategy that makes an honest attempt to be true to both the Jewish and the generally human dimensions of modern Jewish existence. Do not all of these virtues combine to augur well for the Jewish future?

It is genuinely difficult to say. Of all the questions that have challenged our judgments and imaginations in the course of preparing this study, this is surely the most vexatious and elusive. Whatever the virtues of accommodationist pluralism (and we believe they are many), it is the secular strategy for Jewish survival per se that we are attempting to assess, and, hence, the claims made for its own viability are the proper focus of our analysis. Pluralism may allow a thousand Jewish flowers to bloom and some of them (not necessarily secular) may have remarkable qualities of hardiness. Our concern, however, is with the staying power of Jewish secularism itself, its ability to maintain itself in an aggressively intruding global village that puts Jewish particularity increasingly on the defensive.

How insistent this cultural assault on the indigenously Israeli and Jewish is can be evoked in a number of minor but symptomatic vignettes. There was a time when one did not need to be actually watching TV to hear the news. Israel had one TV channel and one news program. With everyone tuned in, the voice of the anchorman reverberated through the streets, from every porch and open window. (Indeed, in an era of inadequate and overloaded phone lines, the most promising time to place a call was a moment or two after the news broadcast had begun.) Today, even with two Israeli channels, fewer than 30 percent of the viewing audience watch the news on both channels combined—they are watching, via cable and satellite dish, shows from across the globe; a Spanish soap opera, the British soccer league, an American sitcom, news from CNN or the BBC. Dispersed and isolated, the shared TV experiences that created morning-after camaraderie and a single focus of perception are slowly fading into the past. And this does not begin to consider the borderless universe created by the e-mail and internet revolutions.

A stroll down a Tel Aviv street on a Friday evening is quite an eye-opener for those who recall these same streets two decades before. Discotheques and bars are omnipresent—so much so that drunken driving, previously not a problem among the traditionally abstemious Jewish people, has become a serious hazard. Sabbath closure of cafes and restaurants, once the general practice, has today become the exception to the rule. Kashrut-observing restaurants are harder and harder to find. (A recent search, conducted by a visiting Orthodox colleague, from Kikar Atarim to Mugrabi—the main promenade on the Tel Aviv's beachfront—did not turn up a single cafe or restaurant with an official certificate of Kashrut.) The immigration of ex-Soviet immigrants in the recent years has also meant the opening of about 600 pork-selling shops around Israel. The presence of guest workers from Thailand and Romania (unofficial estimates place their number at more than a quarter of a million) have altered the human horizon that was, at one time, almost uniformly Jewish. In line with dominant Western proclivities, individualist and careerist trends have intensified greatly and the readiness of the young to sacrifice their interests for the sake of the community is growing increasingly unusual. At the fringes, Christmas parties, replete with Santas and trees, have become quite the vogue.[15] (One cynic put it this way: If our problems are intractable, let us at least have a party.) Whether in terms of dress, daily habits, the music that is listened to, the food that is eaten, the TV programs that are watched, the leisure activities that are pursued, or the shopping malls that are frequented, it becomes more and more difficult to distinguish between the lives of many Israelis—especially those in the younger age cohorts—and their counterparts abroad. Certainly no less and probably more than the French and English, the indigenously Jewish and Israeli is retreating before a seeming irresistible wave of homogenized world culture.

Growing individualist careerism and dwindling commitments to national causes are perhaps nowhere better epitomized than in the sharp decline in motivation to serve in crack combat units in the Israeli army. Indeed, the kibbutz movement and the elite urban high schools—the social cohorts previously relied upon to provide the core cadre of fighter pilots, officers, and the various elite commando units—are now at the bottom of the list of volunteers. Insofar as their numbers are being replenished, it is, notably, from the national Orthodox youth, whose levels of volunteering have also fallen off, but to a lesser extent. This unprecedented phenomenon is so arresting that students of Israel's strategic position in the Middle East have begun to argue that it must be factored into the country's ability to maintain its security posture over time. Israeli society, one analyst wrote, "displays signs of fatigue and is more reluctant to pay the price for the protracted conflict with the Arabs."[16]

Two important caveats must be introduced here. First, our description is not intended as a disapproving critique or a piously nostalgic lament. It can be argued that the loss of provincialism, the entry into the larger cosmopolitan world, and the desire for a "normal" existence are entirely welcome developments. But our concern here is with the conditions for Jewish survival, and this, inevitably, disciplines our inquiry into narrower channels. Second, it is not the loss of social solidarity as such that is of interest here. We are concerned more specifically with the novel reality in which Jewish and Israeli sources are gradually ceasing to provide the essential values, personal models, and cultural goals for much of the Israeli citizenry. Moreover, so far as we can tell, the fashionable qualities associated with Western practices are distinctly more attractive than those of Jewish or Israeli origin among large parts of the secular youth. (For example, disco is far more popular than the traditional Israeli evenings of communal singing.) And so our question returns: Can Jewish secularism, with its openness to world culture, resist assimilation into the global village?

This is a speculative question, one that cannot be settled conclusively by simply compiling empirical data. One arresting method of advancing our inquiry—one that serves our purposes well—is to focus on that group of Israeli publicists, scholars, and ideologues who, to one degree or another, repudiate the Jewish character of Israel. Far from representing a problem for them, the de-Judaization of Israel lies at the heart of their program. Their views have received such rapt attention in the press and in countless journal reviews that it is difficult to escape the whirl of debate—the series of impassioned retorts and counter-retorts—that seem to confront readers wherever they turn. To be sure, this group of protagonists, who go under the catch-all and somewhat misleading label "post-Zionists,"[17] represent only a minuscule fraction of Israeli public opinion. (Recall that in the Guttman Report, 96 percent of Israeli Jews reported feeling that they "are part of the Jewish people throughout the world.") The post-Zionists are important to us not because they are poised to imminently capture the Israeli mainstream, but because they present, with verve and without apology, a position that many observers claim is already latent in Israeli society. Like many a radical avant-garde before them, the post-Zionists are said to be a portent of things to come. They have caught sight of what lies over the horizon and in their bold efforts to bring it home, they have stirred up an ideological hornet's nest. The denigration they suffer at the hands of the Zionist establishment, it is said, is a clear symptom that a dormant but highly sensitive nerve has been struck.

In what sense can the de-Judaization of Israel be a latent presence if the empirical findings of so much survey research make clear that Israelis understand themselves as steadfastly Jewish and Zionist in orientation? The explanation, some have urged, lies in the striking incongruity between, on the one hand, the Jewish and Zionist self-identifications Israelis report and, on the other, the lives they actually lead. Israel has, in large part, already become a post-Zionist state.[18] Even if the doctrine of post-Zionism is disdained in principle, the actual world many Israelis inhabit has long ago left recognizable Zionist substance behind. Authentically Zionist discourse is only rarely heard. When it is, it rings strangely outmoded and dowdy, perhaps even somewhat comic. The image of the *halutz* is only minimally more relevant to the Israeli teenager of the nineties than the western pioneers of the United States are to their American counterparts. Zionist youth movements—the erstwhile hothouses for ideological self-dedication—have turned into nondescript social clubs that are avoided by those young people concerned with cutting a dashing figure. (In the vernacular of the young, "Don't talk Zionism to me" translates as "Cut the high-falutin' rhetoric.") Hebrew is giving way to English in advertising promotions because the latter radiates a worldly aura that the former does not.

As a movement promoting collective national goals, Zionism has been overcome by the assertive individualism of the corporate ethos. Calls for personal sacrifice in the traditional Zionist style are rarely made and even less frequently answered. In short, Zionism has been practically relegated to the archive, the museum, to nostalgia. Some have already proposed alternate national missions: Israel, they say unabashedly, is to become the new Silicon Valley or the Hong Kong of the Middle East.

Post-Zionism as an idea system may, therefore, be understood as a radical extrapolation upon post-Zionism as a social reality, one that carries existing elements to their logical and psychological conclusions. If there is truth in this analysis, a careful study of post-Zionism's central tenets is likely to handsomely reward the effort. It promises to sharpen our ability to assess Israeli Jewish durability.[19]

Post-Zionism began initially as a scathingly revisionist history of Israel's War of Independence in 1948 (its practitioners are often referred to as the "new historians"[20]); it then spread to a disparaging reinterpretation of Zionist politics in the Yishuv era (including the allegedly self-centered reactions of the Zionist establishment to the European Holocaust); and, finally, it has become an all-out assault against the Jewish character of the state of Israel. Although the historical dimension of post-Zionism provides the academic muscle that powers the ideological punch, for our specific purposes it is post-Zionism as a fighting creed that is of immediate interest. Its core contentions have been summarized as the following: Zionism discharged a legitimate historical function in creating a Hebrew nation in the land of Israel. A half-century after the founding of the Jewish state, however, the imminent danger that faced Jews the world over is receding into the past. Zionism ought to follow suit. In its present form, that is, as the ideological justification for a narrowly national Jewish state, Zionism is little more than in-group narcissism that authorizes discrimination against Israel's non-Jewish citizens. Zionism is what stands between the insular, tribal Jewish state and its transformation into a state that can take its place among the enlightened communities of the world. "The time has come to transform Israel into a state like the properly constructed Western States: a state of all its citizens."[21]

Tom Segev, another prominent spokesman, identifies Zionism with Israel's security needs and concludes that it will wither away when peace finally arrives. For most Israelis, he admits, this prospect is not yet credible, but it is a matter of time, a question of when, not if. Zionism, he writes, is related to the

> war for the establishment of the State and the defense of the State— and I identify Zionism with its wars. When the wars will end, we will ask ourselves whether we wish to live without Zionism . . . . Except for a very small group, to which I also belong, most Israelis do not feel that the danger is over. We can write books and raise ideas, but the debate is still over the existential question—if we can already be Post-Zionists and play about with this idea, or whether it is still early.[22]

Much the same argument, presented with an American twist, assumes the following form:

As a measure of "affirmative action," Zionism was useful during the formative years. Today it has become redundant. There is a need to move ahead to a more Western, more pluralist, less ideological form of patriotism and citizenship. One looks with envy at the United States where patriotism is centered on the constitution; naturalization is defined politically and is based on law, not on history, race, religion, nationality or language.[23]

The main culprit in the Zionist drama is the Law of Return which grants "returning" Jews citizenship on request and, in addition, confers upon them privileged immigrant status. Not only does this open-door, preferential treatment of Jews add up to racist discrimination, the fact that Jewishness is defined in halachic, that is, religious terms, only adds insult to injury. The Law of Return perpetuates a spurious national bond between Israel and world Jewry; indeed, its true purpose is not the "ingathering of the exiles" but the strengthening of the Zionist state by importing a labor force and military reinforcements—to say nothing of providing the pretext for appealing to wealthy Jews in the West for contributions. What it does perpetuate, in fact, is the conflict with Israel's Arab neighbors who rightfully see the Law of Return as an imperialist stratagem to justify a "greater land of Israel" for a "greater Jewish people." The country that post-Zionists look forward to, therefore, is one entirely stripped of national Jewish distinctiveness: Jewish motifs in the national anthem and flag should be replaced by nationally neutral ones, just as the Afrikaner anthem was replaced after the fall of apartheid.

Not surprisingly, many post-Zionists applaud the advent of Westernism[24] and the erosion of Jewish particularism it brings in its wake. Respected journalist Gideon Samet, who is broadly sympathetic to post-Zionist themes, expressed satisfaction with the growing attenuation of Jewish identity. Finally, he asserted triumphantly (this was prior to the 1996 elections!), "we are ridding ourselves of that old bother; clarifying our national identity."

> In the past, so many efforts were made to examine what it is, what happened to it, how it was formed, whether it exists at all, and if it exists why isn't it visible . . . . It now appears that just as this old question threatened to bore us to death, it has begun to be resolved.

Symbolically, he contends, this resolution has its source in the Oslo peace agreements. The security paranoias of the right that shore up Jewish identity by alarmist cries of imminent catastrophe have lost both their credibility and their hold on the national imagination. In their place "normalization" is taking place, and this is an eminently healthy development. Commentators have

> noted the growing tendency to move from nationalist slogans to simple individualism . . . The lust for life . . . is not the self-destructive inclination of a declining nation, as the ideologists of the right see it . . . Madonna and Big Mac are only the outer periphery of a far-reaching process whose basis is not American influence but a growing tendency throughout the West, especially among its young people.

Like other Western youth, Israeli young people are naturally gravitating to these fresh tendencies; they are not aping the West, they are part of it. Their new forms of "cultural consumption and leisure activities have become supra-national. This is true of popular music, movies, trips abroad, dress and even the style of speech." Those who wring their hands over these changes are becoming increasingly anachronistic:

> Complaints against the destruction of myths is a slogan carried by the knights of the old identity. They have trouble with exposing the Israeli army to criticism. They have a bad time with the new historians. They see the seeds of destruction everywhere—in Madonna and in the opening to the outside world.[25]

But post-Zionism is not expressed only in overtly ideological forms. It has a sizable social and cultural periphery that supports it, without necessarily accepting its more radical assertions. Largely a phenomenon of the secular Ashkenazi, well-educated, upper class, it has made important inroads into elite academic, journalistic, and cultural circles. Moreover, post-Zionism has gained from the support of many otherwise ardent Zionists who favor specific elements of the post-Zionist program such as forwarding the peace process, protecting civil rights, fighting for equal rights for Arabs, and opposing religious exploitation of political power.

Israelis do not need to read the latest polls to be aware of the striking overlap of religious and hawk, secular and dove. The most visible and vehement spokespeople for the messianic Greater Israel movement are from the religious camp in the form of the politically aggressive settler's movement in Gaza and the West Bank or the mobilized, highly disciplined *haredi* community. The Baruch Goldstein massacre in Hebron and Yitzchak Rabin's assassination, both perpetrated by fundamentalist fanatics whose motives were expressly religious, have deepened and inflamed the religious-secular divide immeasurably. The electoral victories of the religious right in May of 1996 and the consequent stalling of the peace process have created a state of intense polarization that has few if any precedents in Israeli history.

In the eyes of many secular cosmopolitan Israeli Jews, their country is being hijacked by a band of crude obscurantists, relics from the Jewish past. Jewishness, so recently emancipated and brought into the enlightened ambit of Western history, has risen, in its most primitive form, out of the dark corners of history, to threaten them with a state of the Ayatollahs, if not actually with physical annihilation in an entirely avoidable war. For many, Jewishness per se has become tainted by the "messianic politics" and the "tribalist provincialism" of those who regularly speak in its name. Insofar as Jewish culture is equated with religion and religion remains a highly divisive issue, Jewish secularism faces a difficult uphill struggle. Not surprisingly, in this charged atmosphere the post-Zionist program of de-Judaizing the state of Israel gains a certain degree of attractiveness.

The depth and virulence of antireligious feeling that this confrontation has exposed will scarcely be comprehensible to American readers. (To be sure, the feeling is fully reciprocated by parts of the religious community, but this is not our subject.) This is not the mild kind of épater les bourgeois atheism one meets on secular American university campuses, nor even echoes of the more deeply rooted anticlericalism that may still be found in the Continental European tradition. It involves such a profound delegitimizing and demonizing of the religious that what in other contexts would be condemned as scurrilous antisemitic vulgarity passes here without remark. One graphic example of this genre will do. Tzitzim ("Tits"), a popular political cabaret, presents a scene in which an ultra-Orthodox man stands praying, his body gently swaying, his hands waving overhead beseeching heaven. A shapely women passes. The gentle swaying becomes jerky and libidinal, his hands are lowered into the folds of his black coat, and amidst cries of devotion and groans of ecstasy, the grisly scene comes to an end.

Israeli theater has been a leader in emphasizing secular-religious schisms. *Chametz*, honored as the best play of 1995, makes an overt plea for Israeli society to forget its past, ignore its pedestaled heroes, even forget the Holocaust and its victims, and to live as a normal society bereft of any Jewish attachments. The popular play *Fleischer* prompted great involvement on the part of the audience, who laughed and applauded at the antireligious jokes. One of the play's actors described his role as that of a catalyst for "venting all those expressions of anger that the secular have against the religious." Audience responses to the play's rancorous message were tested by questionnaires distributed at a number of performances. Most believed that the play provided a faithful representation of contemporary Israel. "Religious spectators sensed such hostility and even hatred directed toward them that they felt inclined to take off their skullcaps."[26]

Proposals, made only half-facetiously, to create two states for two peoples—the one secular, the other religious—have gained a certain currency in the press. One proposal argues that the differences between the religious right and the secular left about what Israel signifies, at the end of the twentieth century, are too deep to be plastered over:

> The controversy over peace is only one expression of a much deeper and truly more fateful divide. In essence, we have lost the principle common denominator for any society—a common language.[27]

A more colorful and savage variant on the same theme is presented by well-known novelist Yoram Kanyuk who reminds us that there is a Biblical precedent for two states: Judah and Israel. He tells the Orthodox that their

> religion has fossilized, become idolatrous. And when a religion that has become racist and political, confronts a democracy—the opposite of dogmatic, open and compromising—a barrier is erected, one that cannot be camouflaged by sweet talk . . . . If you wish to curse menstrual intercourse, do so in your state. With the money we save from not supporting your thousands of idlers [read: Yeshiva students] we will reduce income tax by two thirds and raise the salaries of school teachers. . . . If a woman is *halachicly* forbidden to you, do as you see fit. We will fuck just as much as we please . . . . We do not want Jewish values, because there are no such things; there are [only] universal values.[28]

And when antireligious sentiment goes this deep, the temptation to throw out the Jewish baby with the religious bath water becomes, for some at least, too powerful to resist.

Oddly, there is a striking symmetry here between the Orthodox and the post-Zionists. Both argue for the indistinguishability of Jewishness and Judaism. Whereas the Orthodox argument is entirely familiar, the post-Zionist position is quite novel. For them Jewishness as a nationality and Judaism as a religion form a unity—and they are both to be rejected. Having little concern with either and arguing moreover, that religion is the sole basis of Jewish nationality,[29] they are only too happy to grant custodianship over Jewishness to the religious. Echoing the religious position, they contend that there is no secular Jewish alternative to religiously based Jewishness. Secular Jewish culture is a contrived and flimsy construct, tending to either revert to its deeper religious and insular sources or dissipate itself naturally in the course of its exposures to the non-Jewish world. As such, the choices that face Israel are two and only two: Either a Jewish state in the fully religious sense, or a non-national, nonconfessional state of all its citizens. Clearly the prospect for secular Jewish survival in Israel depends on the fraudulence of this draconic choice.

The controversy over what a Jewish state entails is anything but new. It erupted among the state-founding elite, even in the company of the earliest Zionist ideologues. With the benefit of hindsight it is easy to see the confusion latent in their views. In the fashionable terminology of contemporary academia we might say that their vision of a Jewish state was constituted of both a text and a contradictory subtext. For most, the text was "to normalize and naturalize the Jewish people in the family of nations."[30] The subtext was, however, to create a Jewish state that bore the peculiar imprint of its Jewish composition and Judaic heritage. (Except for a tiny minority, this did not mean a religious state. Ben-Gurion was fond of repeating: "We are a state of law, not halacha.") For some, admittedly, the specifically Jewish vision was the text; but theirs was a minority position, outnumbered and outorganized by the "normalizers."

In practice, however, this relatively neat divide disappears. The two sides overlapped and the character of the Jewish state they envisioned turned out to be more complex than what their respective formulas would allow. Never was the issue presented as a Jewish state versus a Jewishly neutral state; rather, it was the degree to which the Jewish heritage—including the Jewish religion—was to be incorporated into the character of the state. It is of great significance that few if any were then concerned with the underlying contradiction between a Jewish state and a "normal" state. For all the heat it generates today, this was not an issue that exercised the creators of Zionism.

Nor should this be surprising. The era in which the Jewish national movement developed took for granted that nations, as well as the states bodying them forth, were associations that linked individuals sharing ethnic roots and a common past. Nation-states were precisely what this hyphenated unity implied: states representing distinct nations. The conspicuous exceptions to the rule such as the United States and the many multiethnic European states were glossed over. America was exempted because, despite its heterogeneous population, a common social vision was said to unify its people. Multiethnic societies such as that of the English, Scots, Welsh, and Irish were collapsed into one overarching ethnic unit and labeled British. Following these assumptions, a Jewish state intended as a homeland for all Jews would naturally bear the attributes of the Jewish people and the symbols of the Jewish heritage. Such a state would be both Jewish and "normal"—or, in other words, the latent tensions between a nationally Jewish and a "normal" state were entirely obscured.

How dramatically these assumptions have changed in the past half-century! Ethno-national states, and even those that are integrated around a shared vision of a society's ultimate purpose, have fallen into bad odor. In their place, an alternate, individualist-liberal-democratic conception has arisen. In this intellectually regnant image, the state does not possess a moral vocation; it is not in the business of embodying collective ethical purposes, national or otherwise. Indeed, the identification of the state with a specific ethnic group is understood to be fundamentally unacceptable. Even less palatable is a "confessional" state, one in which public power is in the service of a particular religious creed. The state legitimately represents citizens as autonomous individuals; its primary purpose is to service their interests and enforce the rules of the game by which they are to live.[31]

Virtually everywhere in the West the liberal democratic idea has replaced the older conception of the nation-state. If they were once allies in the struggle against aristocratic government, today the democratic urge in its liberal pluralist form increasingly undermines nationalist visions of the political community.[32] Liberal democracy has fared so well because it is the only regime that accords with the contemporary valuation of personal autonomy—the separateness of the individual as a moral agent—as the *ultimum desideratum*. Today, therefore, "normal" states avoid doing just what was once considered the central duty of nation-states: pursuing collective communitarian goals. They refrain from taking sides between the various ethnic communities that compose the polity. With this liberal democratic conception as the governing norm, it is clear that a democratic Jewish state becomes a contradiction in terms.

First and foremost, in such a state Israeli Arabs are unequal in a psychological if not actually in a legal sense. A "state of the Jewish people" does not belong to them—while it does belong to Jews living in Boston or Johannesburg. Moreover, the state departs from "normal" liberal democratic practice because it pursues national policies transcending the particular interests of its citizens as individuals. Although it is doubtful that there ever has been or even could be a state in which individuals constitute the sole unit of political concern, this does not alter the basic conclusion: Israel as the state of Jewish people has ceased to be "normal" at the end of the twentieth century.

Despite their numerical marginality, the post-Zionists are, curiously, today's most consistent protagonists of Israel as a "normal" state. The post-Zionist maxim, Israel as "a state of all its citizens," is the very heart of liberal democratic politics. Their program, so radical in the Israeli context, is eminently mainstream elsewhere in the West.[33] Here again, a secular Jewish culture that wishes to be both open to the Western world and, nevertheless, loyal to its particularist Jewish roots finds itself in an awkward position. An ethnically Jewish state runs increasingly athwart of the Western consensus. In many circles, terms like racism are common to the point of cliché. (Any Israeli academic visiting Western universities is entirely familiar with the problem.) Over time—as the older generation raised on images of the nation-state passes from the scene and as the intrusions of a homogenized global culture become more and more irresistible—the problem is bound to intensify. The secular Jewish framework of discourse will then confront the compound challenge of, first, preserving sufficient Jewish memory and content to sustain a recognizably Jewish form of cultural discourse, and, second, resisting the denationalizing thrust of the contagious liberal democratic worldview.

All of this, however, remains somewhat theoretical. Whatever the latent cultural pressures, Israel's security realities at present provide a semblance of national unity. For as long as communal physical security is threatened from without, group solidarity will tend to compensate for losses in cultural identity. (We suspect that there are already many Israelis with starkly compartmentalized worldviews: largely Westernized and urbane on the one hand, and yet combatively insular on the other.) National identity, whatever its cultural poverty, is easily expressed in terms of a common enemy. And the "ideology of affliction" can persist even in the absence of substantial Jewish literacy. The vision of a tiny people in a hostile sea threatened with extinction resonates with a paradigmatic sense of Jewish history and has enough Jewish content to deter the denationalizing thrust of the global village.

But what if the siege ends? We return to this question in our concluding chapter.

*I*t is not, of course, physical survival to which the chapter heading refers. Jewish physical survival in the United States seems assured. Our concern is with the survival of a community possessing recognizable Jewish cultural attributes. The loaded, question-begging term in this formulation is "recognizable." At what point do transformations and adaptations—natural life-sustaining processes undergone by all communities—so alter the basic structure and character of the Jewish cultural idiom that it becomes forced and trivial to speak of it as nonetheless "Jewish"? Any such proposed line of demarcation is, inevitably, somewhat arbitrary and conventional. Still, despite the difficulty and interpretive latitude involved in proposing such criteria, it is an inescapable part of our project. We cannot, after all, discuss the prospect for Jewish survival in America unless we first determine what counts as survival.

Two distinct questions are involved. The more mundane relates to those forms of Jewishness that gradually attenuate through lack of interest or involvement. Acquiescent assimilation into a dominant host culture to the point where little or nothing remains of one's original identity obviously constitutes a case of nonsurvival. There are, of course, many intermediate steps on the road to nonsurvival, and the point at which bare survival becomes nonsurvival is something that cannot be decided in advance or in principle. But it is a judgment that does not engage profound questions about whether this or that practice is properly classified as Jewish. Instead, in the case of gradual, passive assimilation where fewer and fewer Jewish elements survive, the sole question is whether what remains warrants the judgment that something at least minimally Jewish persists.

The only principled issue here is whether nominal Jewish self-identification in the absence of substantive forms of Jewish living is sufficient to justify the conclusion that Jewishness survives. This becomes an increasingly important question when being Jewish involves no stigma or injury and when, as in recent years, the denial of one's ethno-cultural antecedents suggests disreputable, "unauthentic" behavior. "Census Jews" who do not deny or reject their Jewish origins but do not incorporate Jewish perceptions, knowledge, loyalties, and practices into their lives are likely to become a growing presence on the "Jewish" American scene.

We are disposed to adopt stricter criteria than simple self-identification. First, because self-identification unsupported by Jewish practice is unlikely to sustain itself for very long. Intermarriage and the growing attenuation of Jewish identity will, especially among the younger generation, undermine even this ultraminimal form of Jewish designation. Moreover, unless Jewish survival is intended in a merely formal or technical sense, Jewishness must go beyond the nominal to the substantive; it must, as it always has, involve life-informing commitments and affiliations.

The second and more interesting question concerns those cases in which Jewishness does not so much fall into desuetude as evolve in unprecedented directions. In such cases, an innovative Jewish direction is undertaken, initially at least with zeal and passion; the Jewish heritage, judged to be miscarrying or atrophying, is injected with creative energies and reshaped in novel ways. Elements of the tradition that were previously latent or ignored are reclaimed and reworked into a fresh Jewish cultural idiom. There have been many such novel starts in modern Jewish history: the rise of pietist Hasidism, the exhortative Mussar movement, the literary, artistic, and philosophic revival of the *Haskalah*, and the (socialist) Zionist revolution, to mention only a few. There can be no doubt that in each of these cases, the sources of the transformative energies were Jewish in character. To be sure, these energies were awakened by contextual catalysts—cultural transformations are never ex nihilo in character—but few would wish to deny that they derived their inspiration and vitality from authentically Jewish sources.

(Clearly there are limiting cases: Some transformations, whatever their motives, depart too radically from the historical consensus to be counted "Jewish." Jews for Jesus, their protestations notwithstanding, would fall outside the Jewish category even were they to adopt Yiddish as their spoken language and to dance to Klezmer music. Here the Jewish heritage is unambiguous: Christians cannot be Jews. Similarly, Jews who would seek to utilize traditional cultural motifs to justify and sustain a drug culture or a criminal association or satan worship would be outside the pale. These activities run too profoundly against the grain of the Jewish heritage for them to be counted an authentically Jewish development.)

We might then formulate the criterion of Jewish survival through change as follows: Insofar as transformations express an active urge for Jewish renewal that derives from an energetic engagement with the Jewish heritage, we are justified in speaking of the resultant cultural phenomenon as belonging genuinely to the world of Jewishness. It is not, therefore, the radicalism of the innovation that constitutes the standard of judgment so much as its dynamic derivation from deep *Jewish* needs and its coming to be through active confrontation with Jewish sources. What is common to all the examples adduced above is the prevalence of ardor and commitment: In each case, the attempt to recast the Jewish experience in fresh terms derived from a spiritual and/or intellectual passion that moved many to great heights of creation and action. So that, for example, socialist Zionism in its heroic *halutzic* phase, despite its sharp departures from the Jewish status quo ante, must count as an exhilarating case of Jewish survival through adaptation and reconstruction. The quasi-messianic urge for the just, egalitarian society expressed in Biblical, prophetic categories represents an authentic variation on an age-old Jewish theme.

What can we say of the many transformations that are currently altering the American Jewish reality? Do they belong to the category of gradual attenuation through declining interest or to the innovative, transformative mode in which Jewish ideas and practices undergo creative extension and spirited revitalization? Indubitably, the most commanding transformations of recent decades such as the dwindling of Jewish literacy, the soaring rates of intermarriage, and the rush to disaffiliation belong to the former category. By no stretch of creative imagination can they be construed as an innovative mode of Jewish survival. Neither are we particularly sanguine about the capacity of moralism, universalism, personalism, and voluntarism to spark a survival-enhancing Jewish renewal. As we noted previously, the privatized-personalist style is, for the most part, unable to sustain communal cohesiveness or to advance the Jewish will to survive. And what is more, it appears to derive mainly from engagement with readily accessible American themes rather than from an energetic encounter with the Jewish heritage that is sparked by deep spiritual or intellectual needs.

We perceive only one broad-based, innovative, and passionate program (we discuss Orthodoxy separately below) that substantially tempers our despondent mood: the feminist movement in Jewish life. Much of it, especially in the least traditional circles, is essentially an effort to impose the feminist agenda on Jewish life rather than an attempt to explore the feminist potential within the Jewish tradition. Nevertheless, there are many Jewish feminists whose loyalties and commitments to Jewish continuity are unassailable. And their efforts fit precisely into the category of innovations that derive from an intense engagement with the tradition. The most striking examples of feminist innovation include the move to deepen the knowledge of Jewish tradition by encouraging the study of rabbinic and halachic texts by women, the introduction of women's prayer groups, and the initiation of new ceremonies and rituals for such occasions as the birth of a daughter and bat mitzvah.

But for all of its promise, we find it difficult to pin great hopes upon the feminist drive to restructure traditional Jewish priorities. Jewish feminism cannot stand alone. It can, perhaps, kindle a spark of innovation within an already animated Jewish culture. But it cannot be the engine of renewal. It is hard to see it flourishing unless it is part of an extensive and intensive reinvigoration of Jewish culture and identity. Jewish feminism's success depends upon the vitality of Jewishness generally.

It is patrilineal descent rather than Jewish feminism that is a more typical illustration of the metamorphosis that has overtaken American Judaism in recent decades. (We are not, of course, discussing the intrinsic merits of patrilineal descent, which is a separate question.) The decision to broaden the definition of "Jewish" to include children of Jewish fathers was taken by the Reform movement because widespread intermarriage made it a simple necessity. Denying the Jewishness of children of Jewish fathers would have meant denying the Jewishness of some of their most prominent and active congregants. Similarly, outreach programs to mixed Jewish-Christian couples followed the rising curve of intermarriage. Patrilinealism did not emerge from a principled confrontation with matrilineal descent, which was found to be Jewishly wanting. Neither were outreach programs moved by spiritual strivings or by ecumenical principles. Both were in the nature of rear-guard actions whose objective was stanching the dangerous demographic hemorrhage caused by intermarriage. It should come as no surprise that both of these practices were, after the fact, nominally rationalized in Jewish terms. But it would be quite contrived to count them as creative innovations deriving from a passionate encounter with the Jewish tradition.

Many American Jewish transformations of recent decades have been of this variety. Confronted by attenuation and disaffiliation, lay and religious leaders reacted with strategies of damage control, some well considered, others less so. It was hoped that by popularizing Jewish practices, relaxing religious rules, accommodating prevalent tastes, and broadening the definition of "Jewish," declining involvement would be reversed. On balance, this strategy has probably retarded the exit of even larger numbers of potential "defectors" but it has surely not created anything like a richly animated, culturally self-directed Jewish community with committed, mass-based support. There is, after all, a world of difference between creative innovation and reactive accommodation.

There have been, it must be said, sparks that might have kindled a Jewish revitalization—the *Havura* movement stands out—but, for the most part, they either have been extinguished over time by intellectual exhaustion, institutional cooptation, and the depredations of popular success or survive as eccentric and isolated phenomena. Still, we are beholden to record that there are today, here and there and with growing frequency, reports of Jewish cultural revitalization.[1]

In our view, the most important of these is the growth of serious study of Jewish texts.[2] The title of a recent article in the major Jewish weekly *For-*

ward says it all: "Next Revolution in American-Jewish Life Starts Here: Adult Education Classes in Torah Literacy Holds Key to Renaissance." The Reform movement has rededicated itself to adult Jewish education. One finds committed Jews in hundreds of communities throughout the United States. Many of them who were socialized in Conservative and Reform synagogues have retained their institutional loyalties, but their dedication to the larger concept of the Jewish people and more specifically to the state of Israel transcends their institutional loyalties. A recent study of the Conservative movement finds pockets of Conservative Jews in the under-forty-five age group preserving substantial ethnic, cultural, and religious vitality. More significant, they are reported to be more Jewishly committed and better Jewishly educated than their parents.[3] Whether these subcommunities of committed Jews can reverse the slow dissolution of the Jewish community is a question that only time can answer. But it must be understood that for these tendencies to successfully underwrite Jewish continuity, an ideological program justifying cohesive community structures and authorizing firm group boundaries would necessarily have to be adopted. But, we cannot refrain from asking, can such a relatively insular identity be comfortably internalized by Jews who otherwise tend to see themselves as champions of urbane, pluralist, and liberal worldviews?

These questions all lead us to a group about which we do not need to end with question marks, one that appears to be thriving by almost all standards of measurement other than numerical growth: the Orthodox. Although it is clear that Orthodox faith and practice are not viable options for the lion's share of American Jews, and although many American Jews think of the Orthodox as a quaint (if not actually embarrassing) cultural relic, we wish to submit that their current successes recommend them for serious study. It may well be that if American Jews are to survive in a Jewishly meaningful manner they ought to take a more careful look at Orthodox Judaism.

The Orthodox

The 1990 National Jewish Population Survey (NJPS) estimated that Orthodox Jews represent only 6 percent of the American Jewish population. This is probably an underestimate; 8 to 10 percent strikes us as a more reasonable figure.[4] But even using NJPS data, the Orthodox represent a quarter of those actively engaged in Jewish communal affairs.[5] A *New York Times* reporter for Jewish affairs claims that Orthodoxy has become a dominant presence within the organized Jewish community.[6] Although he probably exaggerates somewhat, it does reinforce our sense that Orthodox Jews wield far greater influence on the American Jewish scene than one could have anticipated from the NJPS estimate of their number.

What stands out sharply in the capacity of Orthodoxy to successfully socialize its younger generation and transmit intense dedication and commitment among its adherents is that it is not a function of an affliction or persecution mentality. Orthodoxy has flourished not because Gentile oppression encouraged communal segregation and a clinging to traditional beliefs. On the contrary, the ascendance of contemporary Orthodoxy coincides with the most promising and propitious period in all of American Jewish history. True, the image of "a people besieged" remains widespread among these very traditional Jews. After all, the ultra-Orthodox, who often set the tone for all of Orthodoxy, have little day-to-day experience with American pluralism or Christian acceptance. Nevertheless, it would be a mistake to attribute the Orthodox resurgence of recent decades to the persistence of a traditional adversity-centered worldview.

Why then did the resurgence take place only in the postwar decades? The question is a historically striking one: During the period when American Jews did, in fact, confront an episodically hostile, antisemitic environment, Orthodoxy declined precipitously. From the late nineteenth century to the early 1950s, Orthodoxy lost ground in every generation; its mainstays were the old, the poor, and the recently arrived immigrants—all categories soon to be superseded in one way or another. (One wit described it as the longest going-out-of-business sale in history.) Remarkably, just when antisemitism lost its sting and Jews successfully entered the American mainstream, Orthodoxy began its revival. And this revival gained strength parallel to the increasing acceptance, affluence, and power of American Jewry. It is difficult to conceive of a more forceful counterexample to the adversity thesis.

Clearly, we must look elsewhere for an explanation. One favorite of the sociologists and anthropologists relates the appeal of Orthodoxy to the cultural vertigo of the postmodernist age. Relativism, permissiveness, drugs, spiritual emptiness, the breakdown of the family, and rampant egoistic individualism contrast poorly with the secure, morally absolutist, and highly cohesive world of the Orthodox community. In this view, Orthodoxy is attractive to those who suffer the travails of modernity because it offers a solid Archimedean Point to those lost in the dislocations of culture and future shock. Doubtless, the sociologists well describe their own sense of modernist angst. And were they attracted to Orthodoxy (which they are not) it might be for reasons such as these. But the resurgence and growth of Orthodoxy derives neither its numbers nor its élan primarily from Jews who, fed up with secularism and suburbia, flocked to the yeshivas and began observing the religious commandments. Although one finds religious "penitents" (*hozrim be'tshuva*) in every Orthodox synagogue, the Orthodox world is not, for the most part, populated by refugees from the spiritual wastelands of modernity.

Another explanation deriving from similar quarters attributes Orthodoxy's gains to the current acceptability of ethnic self-expression in America. Multiculturalism legitimizes difference, Jewish difference included. It is no longer outré to dress in genuinely national costume. Hence, if saris and African robes are acceptable wear, why not long beards and black hats?

Once again, the explanation's terms of reference are all wrong. It is not liberal pluralist Jews who have forsaken the mainstream and are now donning caftans and growing ear-locks. These are not fleeing suburbanites who romanticize the shtetl and, vindicated by the multicultural vogue, now return to the Talmudic study hall in appropriate garb. The majority of Orthodox Jews are not the same people who frequent ashrams or experiment with Zen. Orthodoxy's renewed strength and multiplying cohorts are, for the most part, home-grown. Orthodox Jews are predominantly children of Orthodox Jews. In past generations many of them would have silently slipped away, perhaps even vocally renounced the world of their parents for more cosmopolitan quarters. Today they are staying. In fact, they are becoming increasingly devout and observant.

Consequently, explanations for Orthodoxy's revitalization must be sought within Orthodoxy itself. What was it then that kindled this New World reanimation of old-style Jewish piety? If there is a single coherent answer it must be sought among the post-World War II immigrants who arrived in the United States after the travails of the Holocaust. As opposed to the mostly poor, simple, and uneducated Jews who sought a new life on the American shores during the great waves of immigration a hundred years ago, the newcomers were often learned and deeply committed. And they were determined to rebuild the world that the European Holocaust had obliterated.

The Orthodoxy they confronted in America was not to their taste. It was bland and accommodationist with a tendency to confine religion to special times and places. There was a conformist, mimetic flavor to its observances, a shallowness to its religious aspirations, and, perhaps most critical of all, a disturbing ignorance pervasive among its adherents. The rabbinate—professional religious performers who conducted services, called out page numbers, and announced when to sit and when to stand—were ludicrous figures in their eyes. Orthodox institutions of learning lacked fire or real direction, and it was easy to see why they were abandoned by gifted young people. Orthodoxy was clinging passively to tradition without quite understanding why. American Orthodoxy could perhaps reproduce itself in the next generation but it certainly could not outdo itself. There was nothing challenging or imposing or inspiring about it. American Orthodoxy, one observer noted, could never produce the kind of figure (the reference is to Rabbi Abraham Isaac Kook) who feverishly paced the floors at night because he was "burning up with the love of God."

Although they cut odd figures on the American horizon, these uncompromising personalities from another world overtook the more decorous American rabbis and overwhelmed the established institutions. They began by teaching in the existing yeshivas, went on to found their own Talmudic academies, and gradually succeeded in capturing the imagination of a generation hungry for a spiritual challenge within the Jewish context. Four or five decades later a remarkable network of educational and religious institutions is testimony to the success of their efforts. Not only did they succeed in spreading their ardent message to an American-born generation that has taken over from the founders, they also altered the agenda and character of Orthodoxy. The swing to the right (both religiously and politically) that is so manifest in contemporary Orthodoxy cannot be understood without their electrifying influence.[7] The accommodating, low-key, compartmentalized Orthodoxy of yesteryear is today in full retreat.

What these "wild men" (one of the less offensive names given them by the temperate and acculturated Orthodox) contended was that accommodation to the American environment was not the strategy destined to win the hearts of the young. Accommodation was a classic slippery slope, and one could not construct a solid Jewish edifice while engaged in a balancing act. They proposed resisting American culture systematically, posing challenges that could be met only by dedication and sacrifice, calling for demanding life commitments rather than compromises or corner-cutting—above all, emphasizing the importance of life-long learning. Commitment to halacha, that is, to the written legal text as interpreted by outstanding scholars, needed to take the place of rabbinic homilies and pastoral counseling. Spiritual earnestness and religious passion needed to be heightened and deepened. In the end, they hoped to create a transplanted, Europeanized, ultra-Orthodox Judaism that would osmotically suffuse Orthodoxy as a whole—making itself felt even in those circles that resisted the more conspicuous and overt emblems of traditional Jewish dress and practice. If they could set the rhythm and pace, the others would fall into line. It cannot be doubted that their goals have been substantially attained.

The challenge they threw out to the young was to "dare to be better Jews than your parents." What, they asked, does the present insipid version of the Orthodox life offer you? A sheltered communal identification, a proper career, a reasonably comfortable life. No transcendence, no holiness, no fire.

Decency, perhaps, but no human distinction, no truly Torah-saturated lives, no surpassing religious challenges. Like the revolutionaries who ridiculed the complacent bourgeoisie, these religious revolutionaries ridiculed the *balebatim*, that is, the small-minded, pedestrian life of the respectable businessman. And their challenge fell on attentive ears.

Because the yeshiva environment is often quite remote even to many commited Conservative Jews, and because its success, as we shall contend, may hold lessons for non-Orthodox Jews as well, it is imperative to make a brief descriptive detour into the world of the yeshiva. Hopefully, our digression will help to convey some of the power and earnestness that energizes this resurgent community. Entering a traditional *bet midrash* (Talmudic study hall, the hub of the yeshiva) can be quite unsettling for those who come to the experience with Western expectations. Anticipating the hushed silence of a library, the uninitiated will be buffeted by the sheer volume of sound that echoes throughout the study hall. Apart from the din of discussion and argumentation, our visitor may be struck by the intensity and concentration—so different from the cool inexpressiveness of the academic library—that animates the various discussions among knots of students. For while restraint and dispassion are the hallmarks of Western learning, the Jewish tradition of scholarship is unbuttoned and uninhibited, engaged to the point of being physical, and deeply charged with nervous energy.

A lone student may be noticed pacing back and forth across the room, oblivious to his surroundings, his face knotted in thought. Occasionally he will gesticulate to himself as if in so doing he could grasp within his fingers the elusive idea he is chasing. He may stop momentarily, grab an available chair back with both hands, and begin to sway back and forth in the thrall of a sudden insight.

Our visitor may notice a pair of students, seated on opposite sides of a narrow table, studying with great animation. Their large Talmudic tractates open before them are pounded to underline a point as often as they are consulted to validate an interpretation. Their voice level will be unaccountably loud for the short space that separates them. Its register will be enthusiastic, urgent, and pleading by turns. Likely, their legs will be shimmying up and down under the table—a typical release of the great energies that are brought to the learning process. They will make full use of the space between them with their hands, each tracing the lines of his thoughts in the air: jabs and sweeping gestures to indicate the broad contours of argument, intensely executed small turns of the hand to convey subtlety and insight. When argumentation reaches its peak, one will likely grab the other's arm and hold it firmly to drive home a point.

This fusion of physical and mental energies extends to prayer as well. The traditional Jewish shul or *shtiebl* (as opposed to the more formal synagogues and temples) will strike our visitor as a rowdy and undisciplined place. And so it is. (*Shtiebl* frequenters would reject Western-style decorum as the kind of prim, inhibited behavior typical of those who are ill at ease with their religiosity.) A surprising amount of movement bordering on agitation will be our visitor's first impression. Few will be simply sitting in their seats and reciting the prayers silently. Prayer involves physical exertion, the translation of spiritual intent into kinetic energy. As spiritual intent grows more centered, physical movement becomes more strenuous. The body acts to focus spiritual concentration just as the spirit—far too intense to be confined to cognition alone—spills over into physical movement. "Let my very bones express" God's praise is the way the tradition puts it. Remarkably, the Baal Shem Tov (a great Jewish mystic and founder of Hasidism, 1700–1760) speaks of the swaying movement of prayer in explicitly sexual terms: One moves back and forth with growing intensity until, in a great searing moment, one unites with the spirit of God.

The transformative influence of the yeshiva has permeated most of the Orthodox world. It extends outward to suburbia, to the West Coast, to major cities and small outposts all over the American continent. And it continues to draw Orthodoxy rightward, both religiously and politically. It is this growing proliferation of yeshiva-based energy and the broad attractiveness of its spiritual ambience that is the decisive factor in Orthodoxy's dramatic comeback.

All this refers especially to the ultra-Orthodox—or, as we refer to them, the yeshiva world Orthodox. Clearly, it is less true of the modern Orthodox. Although the broadly defining characteristics of Orthodoxy are set by the yeshiva world, the modern Orthodox do manage to hold their own. More relaxed in their observances and more permissive in their interpretation of Jewish law, the modern Orthodox effect a form of selective and limited integration into the American mainstream. And with human nature being what it is, the "modern Orthodox" accommodationist style will, no doubt, continue to attract many followers.

Despite the current preeminence of the yeshiva world and the defensiveness of modern Orthodoxy, one does find, here and there, modern Orthodox rabbis and scholars who defy the prevailing paradigms of contemporary Orthodoxy. Sometimes they challenge yeshiva world Orthodoxy in the name of the tradition itself, or in the name of universal standards of justice (such as in the feminist case). At times the challenge is mounted in the name of simple common sense. Nor can we discount the organizational efforts made by the modern Orthodox elite to revive their flagging ranks.

Nevertheless, for the present at least, Orthodox standards continue to be set by the leaders of the yeshiva world.

The Lessons of Orthodoxy

Orthodoxy does not suit the analytic tastes or intellectual dispositions of most American Jews. First, the idea that the written Torah was actually dictated by God to Moses at Mount Sinai strains the credulity of current naturalist and rationalist persuasions. The belief that alongside the written Torah, the Jews at Sinai were instructed in the details of an Oral Law that was inscribed in the Talmud more than a thousand years later also runs profoundly against the grain of contemporary sensibilities. That this Jewish law as developed by the rabbis over the past millennium and a half (since the completion of the Talmud) is the logical extension of God-given law and, hence, Divinely sanctioned and Divinely mandated is even more implausible for the contemporary mind. (Why this should be so is, in itself, a commentary on current conceptions of reality.) What concerns us here is that for most educated Jews who reflect on the matter, the basic axioms of Orthodoxy are outlandish and inassimilable.

Second, the Orthodox system of detailed ritual practice is far too intrusive and arduous for the vast majority of Jews to incorporate into their lives. In the simplest terms: The halachic life interferes with the dominant ideals of individual autonomy and self-direction. Without the systematic inculcation of such observances in childhood, the many practices and prohibitions of Orthodoxy appear to be a routinized and enslaving codex of regulations rather than a world of spiritual expressiveness and personal self-realization.

Moreover, Jewish law aspires to control not only ritual practice but all aspects of human life. If, as normative Orthodoxy maintains, there are no areas outside the ken of Jewish law and halacha speaks to every problem an individual may confront, then by definition it includes everything from the most universal issues of public policy to the most private matters of individual life. Everything, that is, from issues such as the separation of church and state, and surrendering territory for peace, to intimate questions of sexual comportment and child raising. And since only those learned in the law are authorized to make halachic determinations, matters of public policy as well as intimate behavior are expropriated from popular and individual control to become the province of the rabbis. That this kind of expropriation transgresses the most basic of modern ethical axioms is too obvious a point to require further comment.[8]

Finally, Judaism, as interpreted by the rabbis, tends to provinciality, particularism, at times even to xenophobia. Harsh judgments about non-Jews are recurrent, as are references to Jewish superiority, and these are bound to offend those with modern liberal sensitivities. Furthermore, contemporary Orthodoxy imposes a demanding and constrained identity upon the individual person. It has little sympathy with the modern proclivity to applaud personal, idiosyncratic self-expression. Everything of value, it is often said in Orthodox circles, can and should be found in the Torah. "Turn it over [in your mind] and turn it over once again, for everything is in it."[9] Even those who cherish their Jewishness and honor their ties to the Jewish people also seek to express their unique selfhood in other ways as well—ways that have little or nothing to do with their Jewish identity. And there is little within Orthodoxy in its current dominant forms that lends support to such personalized extramural activities.

Clearly then, Orthodoxy is not the answer for the vast majority of American Jews. But this does not preclude the possibility that Orthodoxy does, nevertheless, provide potentially important lessons even for those who are not disposed to join its ranks. The important question, therefore, should be formulated as follows: What can non-Orthodox Jews, those concerned with developing new and viable forms of Jewish expression, learn from the Orthodox experience and its current success? What does contemporary Orthodoxy have to teach those who, in the light of growing disaffiliation and dissolution, seriously grapple with the insuffiency of available forms of Jewishness? We suggest three interrelated basic principles as answers.

First, any viable reconstruction of contemporary Jewishness should seriously consider Orthodoxy's emphasis on the intellectual challenge posed by the tradition and the life-long study necessary to meet it. Ironically, this central element in the Jewish status quo ante has fared extremely poorly in the modern world—even more poorly perhaps than ritual observance. (If, for example, Passover seders are conducted by a substantial percentage of American Jews, only a tiny fraction have any interest in delving below the surface of the bouncy melodies and charming rituals into the rich substratum of the Haggadah's meaning.) Study, to be sure, has continued in the form of graduate degrees and commitment to high culture. But Jewish study languishes grievously. The vast majority of American Jews, even those who do go through the passage rites of bar and bat mitzvah—are, in Jewish terms, rank illiterates.

Study of the sources is mandated not only because it is a condition for knowing what one's religious and ethical responsibilities are; study is understood to be a virtue in and of itself, perhaps even the highest virtue. Traditional texts emphasize that study does more than "inform" in the sense of providing information; it "informs" in the older, more basic sense of shaping and animating the consciousness of the one who studies. Study underwrites seriousness of purpose, thoughtfulness, and introspection. It promotes the adoption of a critical posture and the incorporation of high-minded standards into one's own life pursuits. To study regularly is to have available at all times a world that is not limited by the mundane constraints that daily entangle us all. To be learned in the Jewish tradition is, therefore, not merely to have encyclopedic information at one's disposal any more than it is to be simply clever or sharp-witted. Study's ultimate purpose is to create a specific kind of individual: One whose worldview and personal traits are mediated through the ennobling world of Jewish learning in which one is immersed.

Orthodoxy, then, adopts a strikingly distinct version of the virtuous life: the life devoted to study. Even those whose quotidian life pursuits render such single-minded devotion to learning impossible are nevertheless enjoined to set aside regular and specific times for the study of Torah. Although all of the modern person's life normally cannot be devoted to Jewish scholarship, study must be understood to be integral to Jewish identity— as integral as, say, contributions to Jewish charities or synagogue attendance.

Needless to say, the manner of study and the texts to be studied need not follow the Orthodox example. The best of modern scholarship and of contemporary thinking should obviously be made part of the educative process. Still, despite all the differences that a modern sensibility imposes, embracing the ideal of study alongside the more familiar Jewish ideals of philanthropy, social justice, and communal organization is, we submit, one critical ingredient in the renaissance of a vital Jewish culture.

Lest it be thought that we are speaking of rote learning, it is important to emphasize that Jewish scholarship has always held relentless questioning at a premium. (Not, to be sure, the kind of questioning that undermines faith or contests the basic framework of learned religious discourse. The paradigm is holy and unassailable.) The student who commands a vast recall of texts that can be recited verbatim (the *baki*) is valued considerably below the one whose analytic sharpness and restless challenging intelligence is the scourge of conventional thinking (the *harif*). If there is an unwritten goal toward which all the energies of traditional Jewish education, indeed all of Jewish communal life is bent, it is to produce the great critical intellectual. The cultivation of mental vigor, of intellectual intensity that often borders on the libidinal, is at the heart of the traditional Jewish enterprise. It is an odd thing to say about a traditional form of education, but its main purpose is to encourage independence of mind and audacious critical thinking. In this sense, at least, Jewish learning is entirely apposite to modern sensibilities.

A strong childhood memory intervenes here. One of us (B. Susser) was about ten years old and had just asked the Talmud teacher a question about the text we were studying. He stopped and thoughtfully reread the passage to himself. His face communicated perplexity and his hand stroked his beard methodically. After a few moments he stopped and simply beamed with the satisfaction of a father watching his child take its first steps. He asked me to come up to the front of the class, put his arm on my shoulder, and gave me a candy from the stash he kept in his drawer. I had stumped the teacher, and that was for him the deepest source of satisfaction.

Not only is critical thinking highly regarded, but the yeshiva world (like the modern world) does not posses any centralized hierarchical authority that might act as a final arbiter in matters of halacha and belief. Although there are revered authorities, there is no Authority. Authority is dispersed and points of view are diverse. And arguments, endless arguments. To study the classic rabbinic texts (Talmud and its myriad commentaries, the various codes of religious law, etc.) is to enter a vast battlefield of intellectual contention. In fact, many of the greatest Talmudic protagonists are known in pairs—Hillel and Shamai, Rava and Abaye, Rav and Shmuel, Resh Lakish and Rabbi Yochanan—because they contended with each other over a wide variety of issues and across many Talmudic tractates. There are very few pages of Talmudic text devoted to legal subjects that do not report some form of argument, to say nothing of a critical give and take of opposing ideas. Even the noisy exchanges of different points of view typical of the traditional Talmudic *bet midrash* call attention to its fundamentally dialectical character.

The yeshiva, with its unique ambience and self-referring intellectual assumptions, is clearly not an available option for most educated American Jews. But a similar dedication to study surely is. Turning the Jewish affinity for learning back on its own historical roots, appreciating Jewish literacy as the mandatory core of any viable Jewish identity, is arguably the most pressing item on the agenda of contemporary American Jewry.

A second element in Orthodox life that the non-Orthodox would do well to consider is its success in maintaining communal boundaries. Orthodoxy maintains its communal integrity by insisting on a series of practices—such as kashrut regulations and Sabbath observance—that selectively restrict extracommunal ties. But these conspicuous prohibitions and controls that set the outlying world at a distance are only a part of a broader Orthodox propensity to critically evaluate the surrounding, dominant culture rather than to simply accept it or adapt to it. From the perspective provided by (what it sees as) the Jewish tradition, Orthodoxy is in the constant business of critically evaluating, selectively rejecting, and accepting the fashions and values that are offered by the American host culture.

Jewish identity in the Orthodox ambit is contrasted with American identity. They are understood to be discordant identities and choices between them are deemed to be unavoidable. And in this regard at least, they are considerably more realistic than their more progressive co-religionists. Jewishness, the Orthodox insist, must constitute the lens through which American culture is evaluated, not vice versa: If rejecting an American cultural fashion occasions practical inconveniences for Orthodox citizens, principle, they insist, ought be chosen over practice.

To be sure, American Orthodox Jews have, in myriad ways, adapted to modernity. Nevertheless, they have continued to insist that modern culture pass the rigorous tests set by the traditional Jewish gatekeepers before it can be adopted. It is precisely because Orthodoxy sets itself over and against American culture in this way that it offers its adherents such a charged sense of moral community, a sense that the non-Orthodox, with their more sanguine assumptions about the Jewish American synthesis, for the most part do not share.

Community cohesiveness is clearly Orthodoxy's strong suit. Even when Orthodox Jews leave the densely concentrated neighborhoods of Brooklyn for suburbia or for cities and towns across the American continent, they sustain the cohesive insularity required for their religious life. The distinction between us and them, between the community and the outsider does not disappear upon arrival in suburbia. Because it is forbidden to drive automobiles on the Sabbath, they must have at least a handful of observant families in walking distance for a prayer quorum of ten men. Jewish schools also require a certain numerical critical mass to be maintained, as do kosher shopping, ritual baths, and burial societies. When traditional Jews are informed that one of their comrades will be spending time in an unfamiliar city, their first question will inevitably be: "Is there an Orthodox community there?" Without an active community to provide support for their social and religious lives, they cannot make such a place their home.

It is not easy to convey to those living in the borderless latitude of pluralist America just how profoundly self-enclosed the Orthodox world can at times be. Paradoxically, American pluralism provides the Orthodox with the liberty and legitimation to create their own unique cultural islands, even though these islanders have little or no use for the pluralist principle in their own religious credo. Because halachic Judaism—as opposed to the more abstract, faith-centered Christianity—imposes constant obligations concerning dress, speech, food, and so on, because it thoroughly organizes the waking hours, because it refuses to accept the notion that there are "free hours" not related to higher religious pursuits, Orthodox Jewish life evinces a dense life-ordering quality not often found outside its ranks. Little if anything escapes the special imprint of its all-embracing aspirations. And few will cultivate meaningful social relations outside its confines. Let it be said that the very language American-born Orthodox Jews speak to each other can at times be a virtually distinct communitarian dialect: a Yiddishized English peppered with Talmudisms, Biblical references, and Hebraic formulae largely inaccessible to speakers of standard English.

Parenthetically, it has been observed that American Jews have lost the immemorial Jewish ability to speak to each other in their own tongue and within their own cultural context—an ability that, in the past, allowed Jews to express themselves freely and without fear of reprisal. Today, others are always listening in over their shoulders. Because the writing and speech of non-Orthodox Jews are readily accessible to other Americans, they have been beholden to internalize the values of the majority lest they offend their compatriots. By contrast, the Orthodox retain the facility to speak into a closed communitarian space.

How can the non-Orthodox world incorporate this sense of communal cohesion without at the same time abandoning its cherished cosmopolitan character? This is perhaps the hardest question of all and we shall humbly refrain from offering specific or programmatic solutions. Still, there are a number of principles that should be enunciated. First, substantial Jewish literacy is surely a critical part of any possible answer. Second, the axiom that American and Jewish cultures march to different drummers (whatever their undoubted affinities and cross-fertilizations) must be deeply incorporated in the American Jewish consciousness. Even posing the problem in this way, that is, recognizing the potential disharmony between Jewishness and Americanism, is a great improvement over the very prevalent and highly facile assumption that the two constituent parts of American Jewish identity make for a perfect fit. With the problem posed in this way, it would at least be understood that difficult choices needed to be made.

Third, a discourse of difference needs to be legitimized in the non-Orthodox world. This could not be, of course, the same insularity-vindicating discourse as that of Orthodoxy. But it is imperative that the non-Orthodox Jewish leadership declare courageously to all who are still willing to listen that the ship is sinking and keeping it afloat will require radical remedial measures. Above all, it would require a different and more unambiguously critical approach to the sensitive question of intermarriage specifically and the dominant melting pot ideology more generally. The older, more sanguine strategy claiming that American Jews could preserve their social integrity despite overt disdain for clearly demarcated communal borders must be recognized as having failed the test of time.

Lastly, playing the numbers game, that is, judging the success of Jewish innovations by the number of people it brings into the synagogue, needs to be abandoned in favor of more qualitative measures of success. It may well be that the American Jewish community will dwindle over the course of the coming generations to a small part of its current numerical mass. This is saddening but not fatal. Jewish history is replete with communities shrinking down to a core of stalwarts that then regenerated both in creative energies as well as in numbers. This we believe ought to be the governing model rather than the continued insistence on counting noses. Criteria of Jewish success need, therefore, to be rethought so as to highlight learning, observance, and commitment—even if by fewer Jews—rather than sticking with the failing pursuit of popularity at any price.

Another strength of Orthodoxy that bears emulation by the non-Orthodox is its championing of Jewishness as a historical responsibility to be shouldered rather as a felicitous choice to be made. Clearly, non-Orthodox Jews will find it difficult to incorporate the Orthodox idiom of Divine command and unalterable fate, but there exists a mediate language between that of destiny on the one hand and that of free choice on the other: the language of responsibility and custodianship. The portrayal of Jewishness as a historical trust and a personal obligation needs to replace the prevalent justifications of the Jewish life as the most attractive option available on the market. Perhaps modernity has fatally undermined the language of destiny and command for most of us but we still are able to respond to the vision of ourselves as charged guardians and keepers. Refusing an immemorial trust rather than merely having made a personal decision to abandon the Jewish people is the forthright manner in which such things ought to be described.

Last, non-Orthodox leaders should not flinch from appealing for sacrifice and passion. Asking for little means getting less. It also means dousing the fire, devaluing the entire enterprise. Asking for sacrifice does not necessarily mean getting it, but it does mean conveying the sense that there is something vitally alive that is being proffered. So many non-Orthodox leaders seem to act on the assumption that they will offend against good taste if they demand, exhort, or appeal for fervor. Not surprisingly, passion is probably the last thing most non-Orthodox young people associate with Jewishness. When a rabbi speaks to a Bat or Bar Mitzvah before a hushed congregation and presents the young person with a siddur or *chumash* (Bible) asking "only" that s/he attend services occasionally and affiliate with a Jewish organization, an act of profound self-deflation, almost self-ridicule, has taken place.

If the Orthodox face the challenge of educating their young to religious passion without incurring extremism and zealotry in the bargain, the non-Orthodox confront the equal an opposite test: Can they educate to tolerance and broad-mindedness without, at the same time, surrendering the passionate heart of the matter?

nine
 a blueprint for jewish survival
Israel

*J*ewish survival in Israel is a compound question: First, the grave question of physical survival; second, the perplexing question of cultural survival. On the first question we shall remain silent, hoping only that good sense, open-mindedness, and humaneness triumph over bigotry, fanaticism, and national autism. It is the second question that concerns us here.

The Orthodox

Starting with what seems apparent, Orthodoxy in Israel will survive. Barring startling developments such as a sudden implosion of its dense social networks or a dramatic loss of its inner vitality—prospects that today seem highly remote—the Orthodox give every sign of entering the new millennium fortified by both cohesiveness and dedication. Indeed, for a number of weighty reasons, the prospects for Orthodox survival in Israel seem even more favorable than they do in the United States. First, the Orthodox receive substantial financial support from the Israeli state. Their religious institutions and educational networks enjoy far greater material largesse in Israel than do their Orthodox counterparts in America where a "wall of separation" segregates church from state. Religious elementary and secondary education in Israel, for example, is entirely state-supported. Second, as a multiparty parliamentary system in which the religious parties often exert decisive leverage over policy, the Israeli Orthodox community enjoys a substantial degree of protection for its interests, both material and symbolic. Even during the reign of "national unity" governments that were composed exclusively of the secular Labor and Likud parties, religious interests were not substantially impaired. The secular leadership voluntarily refrained from taking steps that would antagonize the religious parties, knowing full well that in the future they would become, once again, indispensable.

Demographically as well, the Israeli Orthodox are favorably poised. As opposed to the Orthodox and ultra-Orthodox in the United States who (notwithstanding their dramatic cultural resurgence) are doing no better than holding their own numerically, the Orthodox in Israel are growing both absolutely, and (despite the recent massive immigration from the former Soviet Union) they may even be increasing as a proportion of the Israeli population. The evidence on this last point is mixed. There are surely other reasons that account for the surge of Orthodox representation in the Israeli Knesset, but there can be little doubt that birth rates roughly double that of secular Israelis are an important contributory factor. Enhanced political leverage encourages the ultra-Orthodox to adopt a sometimes swaggering confidence in their future role in Israeli public life. Cities such as Jerusalem already give the appearance of becoming ultra-Orthodox strongholds.

There is also an inevitable advantage to Orthodoxy in a country that defines itself as Jewish. Until relatively recently Jewish *was* Orthodox. A country that bases its legitimacy on appeals to the Jewish past cannot avoid granting a certain legitimacy to those who represent continuity and persistence. It is not surprising to learn that in police actions against rioting ultra-Orthodox Jews, considerably less force is employed than against other kinds of rioters: "I can't club someone who looks like my grandfather" is the general drift of police explanations. Moreover, Israeli Orthodox are more insulated from secularizing Western influences than their American counterparts. Whereas the latter grudgingly permit higher and professional education for the sake of personal livelihood, the former categorically forbid any such Western exposure. Secular higher education has even become a troubling dilemma for the rabbinic leaders of the ostensibly "modern" religious Zionists.[1] As noted above, many national-religious Jews are entirely ignorant of elementary Western commonplaces such as the months of the calendar year. Because Hebrew, the language of the sacred religious texts, is the language of the land, there is also a greater ease of transition for those non-Orthodox "penitents" who are drawn to Orthodoxy. In a Jewish civilization, spiritual quests are more likely to lead the seeker in Jewish directions.

Neither are there any real religious alternatives to Orthodoxy in Israel. Conservative and Reform Judaism have failed to make serious inroads. Least of all have they served as a home for "penitents" seeking religious inspiration. The Orthodox are, therefore, without serious competition in appropriating Jewish religiosity and defining it in their own terms. Significantly, Conservative and Reform Judaism have two major constituencies in Israel: first, expatriate English-speaking *olim* and, second, secular Israelis whose antagonism to Orthodoxy leads them to utilize Conservative and Reform rabbis and facilities for life-cycle events such as bar and bat mitzvoth, weddings, and funerals. The latter are substantially less committed to Conservative and Reform Judaism than they are hostile to Orthodoxy. In any event, neither of these groups is sufficiently large or organized or influential to present the hegemonic Orthodox establishment with serious challenges. They are dependent upon protests and threats from their American counterparts to prevent passage of legislation detrimental to their interests. Nevertheless, they do have a potential for growth. Spirituality and the quest for the transcendent is hardly unknown in the contemporary world. For those who undertake such a quest, Orthodoxy may prove too intrusive into one's private life and too demanding at the ritual level—too far removed from all that contemporary individuals take for granted. In that case Conservative and Reform movements may offer an appealing alternative.

Furthermore, all is not sunny in the Orthodox camp. The ultra-Orthodox face a paradoxical problem: Their very cultural successes have created serious economic pressures that will, ostensibly, require painful social adjustments. Ultra-Orthodox ideology stresses life-long learning of the sacred texts as the highest, almost the exclusive virtue. Spending one's life studying (while receiving government and private stipends) as opposed to being gainfully employed has become the norm for a large segment of ultra-Orthodox men. This exacts a heavy economic price. The ultra-Orthodox stronghold of Bnei Brak, for example, has the lowest average family income in Israel. As the numbers of ultra-Orthodox grow, these economic pressures are intensifying—both internally and from a government that is increasingly loath to foot the bill. All this presages radical reorientations in ultra-Orthodox society. In the religious-Zionist camp, the peace process has severely challenged their regnant messianic assumptions, and the shock waves generated by these political changes may precipitate crisis and disorientation in that community as well. Furthermore, there is evidence of discontent in religious Zionist and modern Orthodox circles in Israel. Growing numbers of Orthodox intellectuals with a firm command of traditional text are challenging the very basis of rabbinical authority, in addition to regnant interpretations of the role of women or attitudes to non-Jews. Conflict between these intellectuals and the rabbinical establishment seems almost inevitable. But since our topic is survival rather than internal communal developments we shall leave these subjects without further comment.

But what of the Jewishness of non-Orthodox Israelis who constitute at least three-quarters of the Jewish population? Is there a future for secular Jewishness in Israel? And there is the inevitable companion question: What do we mean when we speak of "secular Jewishness"?

The Meaning of Secular Jewishness

Jewishness contains three analytically distinguishable components: ethnicity, culture, and religion. Although such distinctions belie the complex network of interrelations that, in practice, bind these three Jewish aspects together, we may, for the sake of more focused scrutiny, examine them individually. The ethnic component is perhaps simplest to describe. It involves the special family-like bond felt by Jews the world over. Sensing that they are of the same human stock and that they share the same forebears, Jews feel an affinity and concern for each other's welfare: a *Schicksalsgemeinschaft*, a sense of common destiny. Whether these ties are genuinely organic or merely mythical matters little. So long as Jews act "as if" the myth expresses their attachment to one another, the ethnic bond is alive and well.

Although we confront no difficulties in speaking casually of, say, American "culture," the term is one of the muddiest and most contested in the social scientific lexicon. But we shall invoke specificity of purpose to justify avoiding the definitional swamp. We content ourselves with discussing Jewish culture as a distinct pattern of living that includes the traditions, practices, habits, dispositions, norms, beliefs, and artistic and literary sensibilities that Jews transmit from generation to generation. To be sure, this pattern of living is neither monolithic nor static, but it does represent a large family of variants containing sufficient common elements to justify speaking analytically of "Jewish culture" in the singular.

Which brings us to the third component of Jewishness: Judaism or the Jewish religion. Although distinguishing between Jewish religion and Jewish culture does not offend our sense of linguistic propriety, in point of fact Judaism and Jewish culture are near-impossible to surgically sever. Three centuries ago, the distinction would have been utterly contrived and perverse. After all, today, like then, Jewish culture receives the bulk of its creative stimulants from Judaistic sources; in a very real sense, Jewish culture connotes those patterns of living that were forged by the Jewish people in practicing the Jewish faith. Precisely this is what makes the modern effort to distinguish between Jewishness in its religious significance and Jewishness in its cultural and ethnic sense such an intriguing project.

Secular Jewishness can mean a number of quite different things. First, it is sometimes spoken of—particularly by militantly anticlerical Israeli Jews—as a form of ethnic and cultural identity from which religious elements are entirely excised. Although this is theoretically conceivable, in practice it is highly improbable—perhaps even preposterous. If all elements with religious antecedents were removed from Jewish culture, what would remain? No holidays, no classical texts, no life-cycle events, indeed, no past. And by its very definition, culture involves an ongoing relation with its past. Transmittal and continuity are its life blood.[2] Radically quarantining religiously derived components outside Jewish culture would mean cutting Jewishness off from its own traditions, from its own historical identity.

With religious elements banished, Jewish culture would be an entirely present-centered, ahistorical, fabricated creation. Notwithstanding sloppy rhetoric to the contrary, we suspect that few truly intend this bowdlerized version of Jewishness when they speak of themselves as secular Jews. It is possible that some of the most radical *halutzim* had something like this in mind when they spoke of a "new Hebrew culture," but either their revolutionary ardor dimmed their historical judgment, or their experiment was doomed to failure *ab initio*, or both. There may also be, at the margins of those who champion what is called "humanistic Judaism," among whom are those who would entirely ban Judaistic elements from their practices and ceremonies, but again we are convinced that this is both intellectually ingenuous and practically untenable.[3]

A far more practical and, in our view, attractive understanding of secular Jewishness would retain the religious component but transvalue its theological character into cultural categories. Judaism would be affirmed as central to Jewish identity but the relationship to the Divine that the Jewish religion mandates would be converted into moral, aesthetic, and political imperatives, that is, transformed into life-organizing and life-enhancing ideals and standards. In this view, secular Jewishness self-consciously poses itself as an alternative to Orthodoxy. This was, in fact, the central project of the Enlightenment and of the nonreligious movements (such as Zionism) that derived from it.

To the extent that these attempts to constitute a secular form of Jewishness are historically self-conscious, they freely acknowledge that in the past Judaism, that is, the religious tradition, constituted the central if not actually the exclusive content of Jewish culture. They understand that it was precisely the atrophy of religion, its inability to effectively mobilize the Jewish people as it did in the past and its inability to offer meaningful solutions to contemporary challenges, that rendered a secularized version of Jewishness necessary. Efforts at nationalizing and secularizing Jewishness, therefore, are not so much attempts to annul and repudiate the Jewish religious past as they are efforts to carry on its familiar contours, patterns, and textures in a credibly contemporary idiom. Secular Jewishness is the continuation of Judaism by other (often very different) means.

Many were the efforts made during the Yishuv and early statehood years to create ceremonies, rituals, and symbols that drew upon traditional religious sources but were transfigured and reconstituted into national and cultural terms. Religious language that expresses the human existential and moral condition in picturesque and dramatic form was given characteristically secular intimations. Some of the most inventive of these efforts took place in the kibbutz movement—holiday ceremonials (the Passover seder being the most dramatic but by no means only example) were radically reconceived and rewritten. For the most part, however, these innovations failed to catch on and have, in any event, lost their vitality over the years.

Although this form of culturally redefined Jewishness is all too ready to acknowledge its debt to traditional Judaism, it is unwilling to abnegate itself before Orthodoxy's contemporary representatives. There is then an important distinction to be made between secular Jewishness a priori, which is a self-conscious ideological position, and the far more prevalent secular Jewishness a posteriori, which represents a passively accepted life-style. The former recoils at the Orthodox attempt to impose an exclusively religious significance upon Jewishness, while the latter, having no alternate agenda, lacks the cultural wherewithal to resist Orthodox claims.

What then are the prospects for secular Jewishness—whether as a doctrine or a life-style—surviving in Israel? This significant question breaks down into a number of subsidiary ones. First, we need to ask, How decisive is the role played by the official Jewishness of the Jewish state in preserving Jewish ethnic, cultural, and religious identity? At present and for the near future at least, Israel's Jewishness will be consolidated, even guaranteed by the authoritative association of Jewishness with the state. For the Orthodox, to be sure, state-sponsored Jewishness is so diluted and bastardized as to be barely recognizable; nevertheless, willy-nilly, citizens of Israel— including even Arabs to some degree—are subject to the hegemony of Jewish culture. This influence is often low-key and nonintrusive, but with the language and framework of public discourse reflecting Jewish concerns, with Jewish history and memories a constant presence, with Jewish symbols, myths, and holidays unavoidable, there is little reason to doubt its potent effect on prevailing attitudes and perceptions.

This link between the state of Israel and Jewishness is, however, under challenge from a number of directions. Hostility toward aggressive religious politicking, exacerbated by the clear (right-wing) correspondence between current religious and political allegiances, is creating a reservoir of resentment that threatens to discredit Jewishness along with overbearing clericalism. Moreover, the post-Zionists' demand that Israel divest itself of its national particularities and become a "state of all its citizens" has become a staple of the weekend literary supplements—its notoriety being somewhat diminished by its familiarity. Less ideologically systematic perhaps but with increasing articulateness and insistence, Israeli Arabs are pressing toward these same objectives. And for those who take their democratic institutions seriously, second-class citizenship is a difficult charge to live with. The increasingly audible voice of triumphant Western liberalism only validates and empowers these critiques. Should the various forces tending toward the dejudaization of Israel succeed in their efforts, were Israel to become an irreproachably liberal "state of all its citizens," how grievous a blow would this be to the survival of Israeli secular Jewishness?

A second, related question follows directly. Prevailing currents of modern Western intellectual, media, and consumerist culture are confronting Jewish distinctiveness—both in the United States and in Israel—with acute challenges. The value orientations attendant upon these cultural currents are osmotically incorporated by all but the most insulated and aggressively particularist. They are so invasive and insinuating that they tend to be adopted without even being recognized as part of a conscious process of decision. It is not too much to say that Israel's mass culture "came to be" rather than has been expressly chosen. By contrast, specifically Jewish values and orientations more and more require a conscious affirmation, an obligating, life-informing commitment. And all of this takes place, as discussed in Chapter 6, against the background of a peace process that may, over time, substantially lessen security threats and personal vulnerability. This then leads us back to our multifaceted query: With or without official state sanction, in face of the seemingly ineluctable incursions of Western culture, and in anticipation of the continued decline in security threats, can secular Jewishness survive in Israel? Responding to this compounded question requires a certain degree of indirection.

As dominant as they may be, the cultural products of the global village are rarely praised for their depth, originality, or authenticity. Israel's popular culture is no exception. Despite the life and death pressures and passions of Israeli public life, its prevailing cultural realities are, lamentably, no better than most. Broadly pessimistic conclusions seem to follow. Given that secular Jewishness operates largely within the confines of this globalized culture, it might be argued that the prospects for retaining Jewish distinctiveness over time are none too hopeful.

It is precisely the plausibility of this argument that makes it important to distinguish between our own individual reservations and anxieties about the quality of this culture, and the capacity of secular Jewishness to survive alongside it nonetheless. The merits of the Madonna-McDonald's civilization and the staying power of secular Jewishness are quite distinguishable issues. Peculiar though the relationship between them may sometimes turn out to be, popular culture and Jewish patterns of living show signs of being able to co-exist.

The Guttman Report,[4] whose findings are discussed in Chapter 6, provides strong evidence for the widespread persistence of Jewish commitments, and these commitments do not seem to have weakened over the course of the past two and half decades.[5] Its findings can be summarized as follows:[6] Religiously observant Israelis constitute about one-fifth of the population. The overwhelming majority of Israelis, by contrast, are not "religious" in the conventional, observance-centered meaning of the term.

Nevertheless, they do observe many traditional practices. Although these observances are only partially and selectively performed, the report's authors caution against dismissing them as random, subjective, and unsystematic. There is method here even if it is not the method of halacha. Observances cohere; they do add up to an intelligible pattern of Jewish behavior. Neither are these performances lacking in intent. They may lack the "proper" halachic intent, but they are motivated by a conscious commitment to Jewish continuity and, among sephardic Jews in particular, an attribution of magical quality to some rituals. But even the non-Sephardim are not without belief. Religious faith is widespread and there is, significantly, a substantial correlation between ritual performance and religious belief.

But perhaps the most telling evidence that secular Jewishness does indeed constitute a living and vital pattern of living is precisely the way it diverges from conventional religious belief. The majority of Israelis part company with the Orthodox-observant in the way they perceive their own Jewish practices. In their minds, that which they do does not derive from God's commandments at Sinai. The intent animating Jewish practices are not that of the pious believer but that of the ethnically loyal Jew. They are engaged in identifying with the Jewish people rather more than with approaching the Divine. The range of justifications for Jewish practices, as they might put it, is not limited to the theological. These secular Jews are aware of their "deviations" from halacha but, significantly, are unperturbed by them. Contrary to what is sometimes said—and we too, preliminarily, come close to such formulations in Chapter 7—Israeli secular Jews do not believe that it is mere laxity and negligence that account for their fitful observance. In their own perceptions, secular Jewish observances have an autonomous rationale of their own. Insofar as the underlying logic of their practices can be formulated, it would be roughly as follows: They understand themselves as participating in a patterned form of Jewish observance, which, to be sure, is not halacha but which they have transformed into the folkways of secular Jewishness.

Folkways are not ideological blueprints; they lack the discursive reasoning of intellectual systems. Hence, they fail to present rationally grounded alternatives to systematic creeds like Orthodoxy. Their justifications are more easily emoted than argued; they communicate and consolidate cultural identities rather than express worldviews. And lacking articulateness, they are often overlooked.

Secular Jewishness understood as a form of folkways was, in fact, missing from our discussion, in the earlier section of this chapter on the two varieties of secular Jewishness. Folkways are neither religion-rejecting (our first alternative) nor religion-transvaluing (our second alternative.) Indeed, folkways constitute a third, autonomous, and highly relevant conceptual tool with which to dissect and appraise Israeli secular Jewishness.

Folkways have been largely overlooked because, lacking articulate doctrines, they are unlikely to be expounded in print. And without systematic formulation, they fail to elicit the rejoinders and critiques that would render them and their underlying value assumptions visible on the Israeli cultural map. More important, Zionist history predisposes us to look elsewhere for secular Jewishness. Our preconceptions lead us to seek something analogous to the secular Hebrew culture of the Yishuv and early state periods, that is, we search for audacious, highly self-conscious, creative efforts to redesign Jewishness in toto. But contemporary secular Jewishness possesses a very different spirit. It is not that of the *halutz,* who with one hand on the plow and the other grasping a volume of poetry, was out to create the "new Hebrew person." The breeding grounds for today's secular Jewishness are not to be found among intellectual innovators such as Ahad Ha'am or religious seers such as Martin Buber. Its practitioners are more likely to be familiar with popular prayers, family-centered ceremonies, and seasonal holiday celebrations than with the classics of Western or, for that matter, Hebrew literature. Indeed, perhaps the central weakness of this form of secular Jewishness is its lack of a "high culture."

The secularism of contemporary secular Jews is not creative nor rebellious nor antireligious. Creativity entails intellectual engagement, rebelliousness a sense of principled repudiation, and antireligiousness an animus toward doctrines of transcendence. None of these is a relevant category. There is little concern here for the ultimate significance of what is being observed. What energizes these habitual, popular practices are social and communitarian objectives. As a system of community-sustaining folkways, those practices are adopted that amplify the sense of belonging and identity although superstition also plays a role.

Life-cycle events are emphasized for their solidarity-enhancing, kinship-supporting effects, whereas strict Sabbath observance is usually ignored. The laws of Kashrut are neither annulled on principled grounds nor are they preserved and endowed with dramatically new meaning. Loosely observed, they become the basis for a national cuisine. Holidays are neither rejected nor reconceived; they are selectively observed in the context of a communitarian national culture. Whatever the acknowledged religious sources of these practices, they are not observed in a conventionally religious context. In a word, folkways are not Orthodoxy manqué.

They do not contend with Orthodoxy for custodianship of Jewish religiosity because, strictly speaking, they are not presenting a *religious* alternative to it. Folkways are not a lesser form of religiosity. Nevertheless, because they seek to identify with the Jewish national past and to vindicate Jewish continuity, Orthodoxy retains a certain unchallenged eminence in their value preferences. In the end, then, secular Jewishness as folkways is rather more than a passively accepted life-style, the somewhat facile phrase we used in our preliminary discussions. It does, in a certain sense, present a national alternative to Orthodoxy, albeit a nonthreatening, spiritually mundane, and intellectually nebulous alternative—one whose central thrust is the vindication of Jewish identity through participating in its traditional communitarian practices.

Communitarianism is an especially powerful motif in Israeli public life—stronger, arguably, than in any other Western democracy. Being small in both size and population, personal friendships, associations, and acquaintances in Israel will often include sizable parts of the population. Few, certainly not within one's own social milieu, are more than an acquaintance's acquaintance away. The actor Chaim Topol famously quipped that he knows everyone his own age in Israel. (In this sense, Israeli Jews replicate the conditions of the *status quo ante* in the Diaspora and of contemporary world-wide Orthodoxy.) Moreover, communitarianism is reenforced by language. Hebrew, in world terms, is an exotic language. (The French say, *"C'est l'hebreu pour moi"* as English speakers might say, "It's Greek to me.") As a first language, it is exclusive to Israeli Jews. It is not difficult to imagine the communitarian effects of this singularity. Add to this the solidarity-heightening experiences of a tumultuous and tragic past, frequent wars, common vulnerability, universal army service—indeed the unremitting drama of everyday Israeli life—and the sense of communitarian fellowship becomes palpable.

Close-knit acquaintance circles, linguistic particularity, and unique experiential attachments mean that Israeli Jews are especially prone to social bonding. For all of their sometimes frenzied world-traveling and despite their abundant exposure to the international media, they tend to be drawn to one another. Although it would be difficult to document, we wish to state our conviction (born of decades of experience) that Israelis, more than any other people with whom we are familiar, feel most comfortable in each other's presence, seek each other's company, and, surely not least, exhibit a sense of mutual responsibility toward members of their own group. Interestingly, this in-group camaraderie is not exhausted by loyalty to the Israeli state or even to Israeli civil society (in fact that loyalty has significantly diminished in recent years); it constitutes a national instinct, a form of cultural huddling that jealously extends a protective covenant to each member of the group. To repeat, this is hardly "high" culture. At its worst, in fact, it can breed ugly forms of xenophobia. On the positive side, however, intense communitarianism gravitates naturally toward vital forms of cultural self-expression. As such it creates a firm foundation for the flourishing and survival of community-centered folkways. Let it be said as well that it provides the basis upon which a more ennobling Jewish culture can be constructed.

Indeed, there seem to be growing numbers of predominantly middle-class, Ashkenazi Israelis, firmly committed to their non-Orthodox Jewish identity, who seek to explore the meaning of classical texts from a secular perspective. They have contributed to the burgeoning phenomenon of informal study groups under non-Orthodox auspices. Some observers, sensing a cultural upheaval in the making, ask whether this might not portend a new, potentially transformative phase of Zionism.[7]

Neither are the community-consolidating threats to Israel's security likely to disappear anywhere in the vaguely foreseeable future. Even a successful peace process—a tangled issue in its own right—will not pacify the Middle East. First, because the Arab-Israeli conflict is only one of many national and political struggles that agitate the area; second, because revolutionary religious fundamentalism gives every sign of being a long-term hazard; and last, because the sources of Middle Eastern instability are considerably deeper and more basic than those involved in the struggle over Israel/Palestine.

At best, Israel will become a normal actor in the Middle East's turbulent politics, that is, it will become part of the familiar cycle of kissing and stabbing, of violence, betrayal, and conciliation that makes the Middle East such a favorite of the thriller writers. And as long as security threats loom, the Jewish tradition with its deeply entrenched "ideology of affliction" will remain the most credible and popularly available narrative depicting the destiny of Jews in a hostile world. Melancholy and discomfiting though it is, Jewish cultural survival in Israel may turn out to be more deeply indebted to Israel's neighbors than we would care to admit. Perhaps Moses, the great champion of Jewish perpetuity, knew just what he was doing when he led the Children of Israel to Canaan rather than Canada.

Folkways may sustain Jewishness, adversity may anchor it deeply in immemorial Jewish conceptions—but what if the post-Zionists allied with the Arab Israeli population succeed in severing Israel from its authoritative bond with Jewishness? Speculative and remote though the question may be, would this new Israel as the "state of all its citizens" spell the end of a secular Jewish civilization in the Holy Land?

What can we say about the practical consequences of dejudaizing Israel? It might well involve a ruinous setback for Jewish culture, because without state authority or the benefit of state largesse, Jewishness would be far more difficult to sustain. But an alternate scenario is also quite conceivable. To be sure, there would be a new nonsectarian national flag, anthem, and emblems, equality between Jews and Arabs in budgeting, employment, and public positions, the repeal of the Law of Return, Arabs conscripted into the army, and so on. But in the day-to-day conduct of social affairs, much of what is familiar today might well continue to prevail. Roughly 80 percent of the population would still be Jewish, Hebrew would retain its position as the lingua franca linking Jews and Arabs, Jewish holidays would continue to be celebrated in most parts of the country.

It is true that the cultural and geographical barriers separating Jews and Arabs might become somewhat more porous. This would be especially true if the population of foreign workers (unofficial estimates set their number at 300,000, of whom Romanians, Nigerians, Filipinos, and Thais are the most numerous) continues to grow and these workers marry, send their children to Israeli schools as they do in increasing numbers, but refuse, along with many of the new Russian immigrants, to identify themselves as Jews. But other things remaining equal, that is, so long as Arabs and Jews constitute the overwhelming bulk of the population, it is difficult to envision widespread intermarriage or even large-scale cultural mingling between the two peoples. After all, the current lack of cultural commerce between the two communities cannot be ascribed *tout court* to the state's official Jewish character. The two communities remain distinct and separate because they are culturally, ethnically, linguistically, religiously, even economically constituted out of very different materials. Altering the flag and anthem might, therefore, have little effect on this mostly voluntary segregation. Each community, it seems quite probable, would continue to prefer its own company and to require its own culturally distinct support system. It should not be forgotten that were a "state of all its citizens" to come into being, the very last motive to which it could be ascribed would be cultural affinities and intercommunal affections.

Neither is it easy to imagine—for linguistic reasons, if for no other—a single educational system for both Jews and Arabs. Indeed, it is entirely possible that a dejudaized state would continue to support religious education of all kinds (Jewish, Moslem, Druze, etc.) on the basis of equality. It has even been suggested, and not without ostensible justification, that a nonsectarian state that claimed to unite the two peoples would have the contrary effect of firming the borders between them. Each of them, fearing cultural erosion and ethnic assimilation, might well insist all the more jealously on its own national self-sufficiency.

Perhaps most important, there is no single historical narrative that both the Jewish and Arab communities could accept as their own, although we may be certain that a post-Zionist Israel would expend great efforts in inventing just such a common past. Nevertheless, each community would likely retain its own version of their charged, conflict-ridden past, its very different loyalties to peoples and states abroad, its own incompatible cultural heroes and villains. Even radical dejudaization is unlikely to make Jews and Arabs over into a third, ecumenical national category; neither Jews nor Arabs wish to be anything but Jews and Arabs. The American model of a melting pot creating a single pluralist society would not be relevant. It is foreign to both the Middle East in general and to the specific traditions of the two peoples in particular.

In practice, a dejudaized state would mean a binational one. Not, to be sure, binational in the way the Walloons and Flamands divide Belgium or the Czechs and Slovaks divided the former Czechoslovakia—numerical asymmetry in the Jewish-Arab case renders these analogies inappropriate. A Jewish-Arab binational state would remain overwhelmingly a state of Jews. A dominant culture and a minority culture would coexist without being converted into single ubiquitous national culture. The state rather than ethno-national identity would become the central, perhaps the exclusive object of joint (albeit reserved) loyalty. Of course, a "state of all its citizens" would remain neutral between its constitutive communities, and this would surely forbid many of the Zionist practices that are currently prevalent in the Jewish state. Nonetheless, the argument that a "state of all its citizens" would necessarily be fatal for the survival of secular Jewishness may be unwarranted. Whether such a loosely integrated state could survive in the turbulent Middle East is another question entirely.

None of this is to be taken as a circuitous argument for dejudaization. It comes to emphasize the power that massive numerical preponderance would confer upon the dominant national group even in a non-Zionist, binational state. In a word, the character of a "state of all its citizens" would nevertheless be determined by the overwhelming mass of its citizens. A very inexact but heuristically helpful analogy might be the United States as a Christian state. Although the American state certainly does not belong to the Christian majority, its Christian character is, in many ways, quite omnipresent. Christian holidays, symbols, rhetoric, images, and references dominate the public sphere—even if to a considerably lesser extent today than was the case a few decades ago. To adduce a single illustration: It was Billy Graham, the symbol of Christian missionary activity in the United States, who addressed the nation during Bill Clinton's second inaugural ceremony. (How ironic; were a rabbinical figure of similar stature and character to have been called upon to address a comparable Israeli event, it would have provoked a full-scale national scandal.) With Jewish propinquity and preponderance remaining intact, with Hebrew the dominant language, with

Jewish holidays and life-cycle observations omnipresent, a "state of all its citizens" might remain a Jewish state nonetheless.

But the steady de-Christianization of America—the success of a human-ist-liberal elite, abetted by the Supreme Court, in having its secular agenda for public life broadly accepted—points to other possible scenarios. In the Israeli context, were dejudaization voluntarily undertaken, it would already indicate a dramatic shift in popular allegiances and purposes. More than the mechanisms and effects of dejudaization itself, the very willingness to deju-daize would testify eloquently that a sea change had already taken place. Successful dejudaization would reflect a basic disavowal or a radical attenu-ation of Jewish identity. And were this willingness to divest the state of its Jewish character prevalent, much of what was said above about the vigor and staying power of Jewish culture might no longer hold true. So our ear-lier question returns: How likely is it that Israeli Jews will remain loyal to their Jewish identity and culture? And this earlier question brings us back to our earlier answer: Security anxieties and communitarian folkways are holding their own against the incursions of the global village.

For all of their staying power, however, habitual national folkways sup-ported by security threats do not represent an optimal Jewish scenario. They lack a "high" culture and a creatively self-conscious intellectual and spiri-tual character. They depend altogether too much upon external stimuli. And they can be made to support unthinking ingroup insularity. Given a precarious national reality, communal folkways are succeeding in preserv-ing Jewish identity. But it is surely not the strongest, richest, or most noble aspect of Jewish civilization. In many ways, in fact, it exhibits shallowness, habitual conformity, and muddled thinking. These qualities not only weaken it against the onslaught of global culture, they also entail that those seeking greater depth and meaning within Judaism will likely be drawn to the single broadly available Israeli alternative: Orthodoxy.

Because of the proximity and unavoidability of Orthodoxy in Israeli cul-ture, pondering how parts of it might be adapted and modified for secular purposes is probably an easier exercise than in the American reality where Orthodoxy is far removed from the mainstream. Especially salient is the proven ability of the Orthodox to generate passion and commitment to their cause, far more ardor, it needs to be conceded, than what the secular can usually muster in their favor. If secular Israeli society is to resist the worst of global culture and preserve a substantial Jewish character it will require enthusiastic dedication to alternative values. Rather than being automati-cally ratified as self-evident givens, these insistent cultural imports will need to be selectively assessed for suitability and quality. Although there are a number of incipient attempts to invest secular Jewishness with just such discrimination and energy, we cannot say that they have, at present, attained anything near a cultural critical mass.

A second ramification of this line of thinking suggests that secular Judaism, like Orthodoxy, must generate the "high" culture that it lacks and the cultural elite to body it forth. At present, the closest analogue to such an elite is the fellowship of contemporary Hebrew writers and academic publicists. But it remains an elite cut off from the folkways and communitarian traditionalism that animates the mass of Israeli Jews. How the bond between them might be secured is, presently, not at all clear.

conclusions

Our fascination with Orthodoxy as well as our mixed feelings toward it clearly have both biographical and intellectual sources. A curious form of attraction/repulsion governs our sensibilities.

On the one side, we cannot help but admire the steadfastness, the willingness to sacrifice, the depth of commitment, and the devotion to learning that animates its ranks. Moreover, the denseness and richness of Jewishness as it plays itself out in the Orthodox world has no parallel elsewhere.

Our reluctance (at times it rises to bona fide repugnance) is with the increasingly militant and aggressive ultra-Orthodox as well as with the politically uncompromising and messianic national-Zionist Israeli strain of Orthodoxy. The ultra-Orthodox intolerance of alternate expressions of Jewishness is matched only by their attempts (in Israel at least) to coerce the non-Orthodox to submit to their religious will. Ultra-Orthodoxy increasingly embraces outlandish superstition and, in its current triumphalist mood, does it with an "in your face" belligerence. Worse still, its practitioners tend to revel in those undeniably present dark sides of the tradition that celebrate Jewish self-aggrandizement and xenophobia.

Many of these same lamentable traits are becoming more and more evident in the religious-Zionist movement in Israel. Chauvinist xenophobia, raised to a particularly shrill pitch and invested with millennial theological consequences, is no longer an exceptional form of discourse in religious-Zionist circles. Those among them, and we suspect they are many, who hear these perverse declarations with personal misgivings, for the most part remain silent.

The age-old Jewish ability to distinguish sharply between the realities of power and the vision of messianic deliverance is, ironically, lost on those who, for the first time in two millennia, would wield sovereign Jewish power. The immemorial realism and shrewdness that sustained the Jewish people during centuries of exile, wisdom carried by the least prescient backbencher in the traditional *shtiebl*, is absent in these self-proclaimed "liberated" Jews—whose liberation, it seems, is mainly from common prudence. And all this does not begin to assess the deep moral disfiguring that comes with overt, often religiously sanctioned, racism toward Arabs.

Modern Orthodoxy in both Israel and America attempts to hold the line against these destructive tendencies but without notable success. Winds of change have been blowing recently, though it is too early to tell what effect they will have. A small albeit growing segment of Orthodox Jews seems to be impatient with the strictures of the rabbinic leadership and even with the right-wing politics of the National Religious Party. This group does not find secular Israeli culture a viable alternative. Without specific spiritual leadership they have nonetheless created a modern Orthodox subculture that not only provides for the social needs of its followers (including their own stand-up comics, musical groups, and even discos), but a literature including a children's literature that is geared to their particular sensitivities. A most important development is the increase in the number of modern Orthodox academics with good Talmudic backgrounds who have found university positions in such fields as philosophy, law, sociology, and history and who utilize the tools of their disciplines to analyze the Jewish tradition and Jewish practice. In recent books such as *Authority and Autonomy in Jewish Tradition*[1] these tools are brought to bear and dramatic suggestions are made concerning the autonomy of the individual and the propriety of rabbinic interference in many aspects of contemporary political life. Feminism among the Israeli Orthodox is another development that signals possibilities for changes in how Jewish law and the Jewish tradition are to be interpreted. The fact that some younger rabbis have associated themselves with these orientations reinforces our sense that Israeli Orthodoxy is not as stagnant as many have suspected.

However, these developments, as we noted, are rather recent. Modern Orthodoxy usually finds itself fighting rear-guard actions against a preponderant and implacable foe. Their efforts to adapt Jewish tradition to contemporary needs have, for the most part, gone awry—or at least remained limited in scope—because the authority of the yeshiva Talmudists and legalists (*poskim*) is dauntingly difficult to challenge in the contemporary Orthodox milieu.

Our reservations regarding Orthodoxy notwithstanding, we must acknowledge and learn from its strengths. One lesson, which perhaps encompasses all the others, stands out. As simple and patently obvious as it may seem, it must be repeated, emphasized, and deeply incorporated into the contemporary Jewish consciousness. Modern existence, for all of its attractiveness, affluence, and ease, does not necessarily fit the patterns, rhythms, and values of a viable Jewish life. There is no seamless fit between living as a Jew and affirming the values of modern or postmodern liberal Western society. More often perhaps than we would like to acknowledge, a steep price needs to be paid for survival.

Jewish continuity in the Diaspora and a Jewish renaissance in Israel require a constant weighing and measuring: Which of modernity's fashions, values, and assumptions can harmonize with a Jewish life, and which cannot? The cost may come in convenience and creature comforts; it may demand an unconventional departure from the mainstream's consensus and behavior. But the most critical part of these constant evaluations lies in the essential recognition that, at times, that which is good and beautiful in modernity may well endanger Jewish survival. Only in our fantasies are all desirable objectives compatible. All things are not simultaneously possible. This, for our time, is the entire Torah while standing on one foot.

In some such cases, we may, in the end, resolve to side with modernity over Jewishness. And Jewishness may survive, nevertheless. But unless it is squarely recognized that the future of the Jewish people lies in the complex balances we strike, that in this weighing and measuring we cannot possibly have all we might want, little chance for long-term Jewish survival remains.

The Adversity Thesis Reconsidered

Whatever the merits of contemporary Orthodoxy may be, its current resurgence in both Israel and the United States has clearly been accomplished without the galvanizing effects of adversity; indeed, it coexists with growing confidence, affluence, influence, and unprecedented freedom. What underwrites the Orthodox revival is the power of a religious idea, the spiritual demands it makes, and the human fulfillment that it ostensibly offers its enthusiasts. Our conclusion, therefore, needs only to be stated: Jewish survival and flourishing do not depend on adversity-inspired solidarity. They can be independently sustained by the positive forces of learning, belief, and cultural vitality.

What then is the place of adversity in the preservation of the Jewish people? It has been too intimately associated with Jewish consciousness, too often expressly invoked, to be set aside as inconsequential. One response, one about which we harbor reservations, runs as follows. Two factors preserve Jewishness: cultural richness and adversity. Together they create a formidable will to live and provide abundant motivation for the sharp demarcation of Jewish communal boundaries. Nevertheless, either of them by itself is sufficient to create the communal solidarity necessary to prevent assimilation.

The contemporary revival of Orthodoxy, for example, is based on cultural flowering and owes little or none of its success to adversity. By contrast, in the far more prevalent historical instances when catastrophe decimated the community, "the ideology of affliction" served to preserve the sense of Jewish unity and uniqueness. Adversity worked even when cultural vitality was overwhelmed by circumstances. Since large doses of both cultural richness and adversity were normally present in the pre-Enlightenment era, it is easy to account for the remarkable saga of Jewish stamina and continuity. In our era, by contrast, since both cultural literacy and adversity have substantially declined, the Jewish prospect seems bleak.

But this formulaic hypothesis is too simple because it overlooks the insufficiency of adversity as an autonomous explanation for Jewish survival. Cultural disruption caused by calamity, it was proposed, did not result in defections from the Jewish community because adversity had a galvanizing, solidarity-enhancing effect. This seems inadequate. It was not adversity itself that kept Jews together but the ability, in times of adversity, to embrace and reaffirm their cultural/religious traditions, to interpret adversity in continuity-vindicating ways. Jews survived because adversity rendered their Jewishness the only source of solace and meaning in an otherwise cheerless world.

In itself, adversity is only adversity. There is no intellectual or moral compulsion resident in the brute fact of adversity. Uninterpreted, it leads to no survivalist imperative. To be grasped as a credible justification for preserving Jewishness, adversity needs to be mediated through categories that give it Jewishly meaningful consequences. Suffering needs to be appropriated by and construed within a viable Jewish worldview.

To be sure, adversity is always a potent catalyst. But it is far from a simple, autonomous stimulus that evokes a predictable response. The same calamitous experience can trigger antithetical reactions depending on how it is decoded. Adversity may send powerful charges of solidarity through Jewish consciousness, heightening the forces of unity and, simultaneously, sharply demarcating communal borders. It may stimulate profound identification with the tradition in the name of which one suffers. It may be perceived as part of God's design or as the inevitable fate of righteous Jews. It can even be interpreted, as many revolutionary Jews did at the beginning of the century, in Promethean terms: It is the price Jews pay for bringing the light of progress to a tarrying world. In a word, for adversity to have a continuity-enhancing effect, sufferers must interpret their travail in the light of a Jewish mission or message with which they identify.

Prior to the Enlightenment, when the Jewish world was the sole and mandatory reference point for virtually all Jews, adversity echoed within a closed Jewish chamber. It resonated within the ambit of Jewish historical self-understanding and was naturally shunted through the familiar grooves of "the ideology of affliction." Hence, when Jews were beset by their foes, their sense of a common faith and fate was inevitably heightened. In the present, when the Jewish context is neither mandatory nor exclusive, adversity can echo off any number of ideological surfaces—each with its own peculiar kind of reverberation and impact.

When Jewish suffering befalls a Jewishly lapsed sensibility, dramatically different kinds of reactions are possible, ranging from survivalist steadfastness to the resolution to put as much distance between oneself and the cause of one's suffering as possible. Some beset individuals may be driven to reexamine their ties to the national/religious identity that until very recently held very little significance for them. In cases such as these, adversity may be the stimulant for Jewish revival, although we would venture the guess that this is a minority reaction.

But adversity may well intensify their sense that Jewishness is a unfortunate accident of birth, an identity imposed by conventions not of their own making. If it is only the irrational forces of circumstance that hold them to this life-threatening and irrelevant tribal affiliation, they must do all they can to be free of it. When, in addition, there is an attractive ideology of humanist universalism available to them, that is, when a seamless human community invites them to join its ranks, the repudiation of Jewish affiliations is likely to become all the more forceful and principled.

It is, therefore, by no means the case that adversity necessarily entails the heightening of Jewish solidarity. Suffice it to say that in the Weimar Republic, in the shadow of Hitler, more than one-third of German Jews were intermarrying. Despite the palpable menace of antisemitism—signs of which were everywhere—assimilation continued apace. In addition, as one of the most cosmopolitan, progressive cultures of the twentieth century, Weimar Germany offered a standing invitation for Jews to shed their particularity and join the mainstream. For many disaffected Jews the threat of adversity coupled with the promise of acceptance was translated into redoubled efforts to disappear into the woodwork of an all-embracing German culture. Adversity, in this case, may well have hastened assimilation.

Neither does the persecution of Jews in the Soviet Union appear to have triggered any notable return to Jewishness. Bereft of Jewish education and culture, Soviet Jews, for the most part, slid into Jewish oblivion. Despite growing suppression and mistreatment, intermarriage rates soared, Yiddish was replaced by Russian, great centers of Jewish learning vanished, and a community of some three million Jews was on the verge of extinction. Vague nostalgia and very quiescent national memories were all that survived. (Notably, if anything sparked a revival it was not adversity but rather Israel's spectacular victory in the 1967 Six-Day War that evoked a positive Jewish identification.) Lacking a Jewish frame through which adversity could be harnessed to Jewish survival, Jewishness all but expired.

Nor is the experience of the Holocaust substantially different. The destruction of European Jewry—far and away the most harrowing form of adversity the Jews have ever suffered—did not spark revivals of Jewish commitment. No significant return to Jewish identity, learning, belief, or practice followed the full disclosure of the Holocaust's horrors.

Although we are unaware of any relevant empirical data that quantifies personal reactions to one's Jewishness immediately in the wake of the Holocaust experience,[2] there is ample experiential and anecdotal evidence that reactions varied widely: At the one pole, the Holocaust was understood to be Divine retribution on the grandest scale; at the other, it was perceived to be the most decisive argument imaginable for nihilism. Some drew from it the need to reaffirm their Jewish heritage. For others, Jewishness was a plague to be cursed and abandoned. Overwhelmed by the sheer enormity of the disaster and at least somewhat estranged from traditional Jewish self-understanding, perhaps the greater part of the surviving Jewish people despaired of finding any meaning in this, the Jewish nightmare incarnate.

Although there were celebrated cases of committed Jews who abandoned their commitment and, on the other side, of lapsed Jews who dramatically returned to their Jewish roots, these are, in all likelihood, exceptions. For the most part, reactions followed assumptions. Committed and believing Jews assimilated the Holocaust into their worldview; for them, adversity, comprehended in traditional Jewish terms, fostered Jewish continuity. It may have even deepened their ethnic loyalty and religious faith. Estranged Jews, on the other hand, drew their own ineluctable conclusions: Some chose the silent, informal, pragmatic path of assimilation, others explicitly espoused universalist worldviews. Perhaps the greatest number settled precariously on the Jewish fence—too implicated in the Jewish world to leave but too traumatized by its suffering to stay.[3]

Notably, the single explicit attempt in recent years to justify Jewish survival in adversity-centered terms has had little or no impact. In 1978, Emile Fackenheim wrote that the Holocaust had added a 614th commandment: Deny Hitler a posthumous victory. Do not assimilate![4] But—as has become clear over the ensuing years—defiance, in itself, is not a program. Without a substantive Jewish reason for resisting the assimilatory impulse, even the Holocaust is impotent. Defiance, even when mixed with guilt, has no content: It can perhaps justify momentary stands of pique or irrational bursts of recalcitrance but it cannot underwrite Jewish survival.

If, as has been remarked, modernity means the movement from destiny to choice, then adversity too has become modernized: It has gained its own interpretive latitude. It no longer cuts only one way. The era when adversity instinctively quickened the Jewish sense of identity and fostered continuity is over. After the fall, even adversity cannot put the Jews back together again. Together with the monopoly of Jewish tradition over Jewish consciousness, this survivalist impulse has retreated into smaller and smaller

socio-religious enclaves. The adversity-centered worldview, although preserving a certain latent, inertial momentum like a low flame that will occasionally flare-up, is losing its hold apace. In the absence of a governing
Jewish sensibility, adversity is what you make of it.

If very large segments of American Jewry suffer from advanced disaffection, it is ultimately because Jewish learning and Jewish sensibilities have
lost their hold upon them. Without internal, positive motivation to vindicate Jewish communal distinctness, the force of American pluralist universalism is probably overwhelming and irresistible. The lack of adversity may,
perhaps, render it easier to exit the Jewish fold without embarrassment or
distress, but the lack of adversity is not, per se, the grounds for the mass exit
of recent decades.

If, on the other hand, American Orthodoxy survives and prospers it is
because the message of learning, halachic rigor, and religious challenge exert
a powerful effect upon its followers. To be sure, the age-old vision of the
Jews as a beset and afflicted people continues to suffuse the Orthodox imagination but, in itself, this is certainly not the cause of Orthodox endurance.
It involves little risk to predict that were this to change—as it seems to be
in the course of doing—it would not significantly affect their cultural vitality and communal insularity.

The essential guarantor of contemporary Jewish survival is not to be
found outside the Jewish world. It is what Jews think rather than what
Gentiles do that is decisive. If the will to live rooted in a commitment to
Jewish ideas, values, and practices perishes, nothing can—perhaps nothing
should—retard the natural death of the Jewish people.

Do we then end our study with this disheartening assessment? Were the
subject of Jewish survival not so dear to our hearts, we would probably need
to end on this dour and stoic note. Like Bernard Wasserstein, whose book
Vanishing Diaspora[5] studies the survival prospects for European Jewry, we
would come to what appears to be the beckoning conclusion: The Orthodox
and various other pockets of commited Jews will continue to flourish, but
the remainder of American Jewry is in a destructive, probably fatal down-
ward spiral. We might also conclude that contemporary Israeli culture with
its largely shallow and nonchalant folkways is all that a secular Jewish culture can aspire to. This bleak mood, after all, would seem to flow from all
that we have said to this point.

We bridle at such conclusions. First, because the disappearance of liberal
American Jewishness is a loss to which we find it difficult to reconcile ourselves, and second, because we believe in the possibility of a Jewish renaissance in both Israel and the United States, one that is authentically rooted

in the tradition, incorporates Orthodox energy and dedication, but is not Orthodox. This belief derives not only from the fact that without such a renaissance we are bereft of a Jewish home. It is also a matter of our abiding confidence in Judaism's immemorial capacity for renewal and change.

We hesitate to be categorically pessimistic for substantive social scientific reasons as well. The predictive power of social science depends on all other things remaining equal. Which is, of course, precisely what never happens. Major changes in the climate of Western values, for example, may transform the entire equation of Jewish survival. Above all, the very imminence of Jewish extinction, the recognition that the Jewish end-game is being played out, may have its own potentially transforming consequences. As opposed to Europe where dissolution was quick and apparently irreversible, American Jewish attenuation and the uninspired qualities of secular Jewish life in Israel are part of long and gradual developments, which provides both American and Israeli Jewry with the opportunity to assess and react to its own distress. So we still dare to believe that they will courageously appraise their jeopardized condition and react with the necessary remedial measures.

Orthodoxy and national folkways share an important trait: Both base themselves firmly on the premodern concern with a constraining destiny rather than upon the modern obsession with autonomous choice. In neither case is transmittal from generation to generation understood as an open question freely decided upon by individuals who attain maturity. Jewishness is not like the career or spouse one chooses; it is a tradition into which one is born, a destiny thrust upon one by God, history, or ineluctable communal bonds. To reject it is to be deemed a turncoat by one's comrades.

Orthodoxy, of course, does not regard itself as one alternative among many. In the Orthodox view, Jews are bound by halacha whether they choose to accept its authority or not. Although it cannot be denied that choices do, in fact, take place (especially at Orthodoxy's liberal margins), these are alien to the spirit that animates the Orthodox worldview and to the principles that control Orthodox education. The Israelites at Sinai proclaim "*Na'aseh Ve'nishma*" ("We shall do and we shall hear"), and for the Orthodox this is the proper sequence of religious practice. Doing precedes understanding, accepting precedes choosing.

National folkways are the dynamic, operative aspect of national consciousness. They are not chosen any more than one's own national consciousness is selected out of an assortment of available national options. These are primordial attachments grounded in the feels and textures of childhood experience. Precisely this accounts for their unreflective, instinctive character.

Both these forms of Jewish attachment are adept at demarcating communal boundaries and legitimizing them. Orthodoxy by intense communal solidarity and strict religious prohibitions, Jewish national folkways in Israel by numerical preponderance and cultural isolation in an adversity-ridden reality. The source of their common survival is, doubtless, to be found here. It is surely no coincidence that the two most robust forms of Jewish survival at the end of the twentieth century are not choice-centered. Neither is it happenstance that those forms of Jewish identity in which destiny has been supplanted by the autonomous choosing individual find themselves in such difficult straits.

We need to add emphatically that national insularity has no appeal for us. Boundaries and walls, for all their effectiveness in preserving Jewishness, are not pleasing options. Indeed, we freely concede that national segregation is a substantial price to pay even for something so valuable as Jewish survival. Precisely for this reason it is of paramount importance to recognize the current Jewish dilemma for just what it is: a growing inability to sustain Jewish commitments without the boundary-imposing force of tight-knit communal cohesiveness. Making light of this distressing impasse—claiming that there is little strain between communal identities and cosmopolitan loyalties, contending that we can freely enjoy the best of both worlds—appears to us a particularly self-indulgent form of wishful thinking. It is sad indeed that at this critical historical juncture, the alternatives between which we are forced to choose are not much to our taste.

Our time has known a number of striking instances in which Jewish commitments have burgeoned and thrived without resting either on Orthodox insularity or on a ritualized sense of national belonging. Labor Zionism in the Yishuv period, Bundism in Eastern Europe, and nineteenth-century *Haskalah*-centered cultural nationalism are some of the more significant. But none of these enjoyed more than short-term success. Each, for its own reasons, quickly succumbed after a period of great distinction. Perhaps the weightiest of all questions, therefore, comes down to this: Are these failures endemic to the enterprise? Can a literate, inspired, and attractive form of Jewishness that is neither combatively Orthodox nor communally exclusivist escape the fate that has overtaken all the others? Are there forms of sustainable Jewishness gestating in history that can rest more on choice than on destiny, more on well-considered commitment than on historical habit, more on learning and creativity than on in-group complicity? We wish to express our sincerest hope that there are.

notes

Notes to Chapter 3

1. See Yirmiyahu Yovel, *Spinoza and Other Heretics: The Marrono of Reason* (Princeton, N.J.: Princeton Univ. Press, 1989).

2. *Tractatus Theologico-Politicus*, trans. Samuel Shirley (E. J. Leiden: E. J. Brill, 1989), 99.

3. Steven Zipperstein, *The Jews of Odessa: A Cultural History, 1794–1881* (Stanford: Stanford Univ. Press, 1986).

4. George Friedman, *The End of the Jewish People?* (New York: Doubleday, 1967). This is an English translation of the original French edition published in 1965.

5. Sara Bershtel and Allen Graubard, *Saving Remnants: Feeling Jewish in America* (New York: Free Press, 1992).

6. Jonathan Sacks, *Will We Have Jewish Grandchildren?: Jewish Continuity and How to Achieve It* (Ilford, Essex: Valentine Mitchel, 1994).

7. Cited in Lucy Dawidowicz, ed., *The Golden Tradition* (New York: Holt, Rinehart and Winston, 1967), 95.

8. Keli Yaqar (Ephraim of Luntshits, late 16th to early 17th-century Poland), *Exodus*, 37.

9. Jane Gerber, "Antisemitism and the Muslim World," in David Berger, ed., *History and Hate: The Dimension of Antisemitism* (Philadelphia: Jewish Publication Society, 1986), 74.

10. Salo W. Baron's work contains a systematic critique of this view. See, e.g., his *History and Jewish Historians* (Philadelphia: Jewish Publication Society of America, 1964).

11. See M. J. Rosman, "Jewish Perceptions of Insecurity and Powerlessness in 16th–18th Century Poland," *Polin* 1 (1986): 19–27.

12. See Seymour M. Lipset, ed., *American Pluralism and the Jewish Community* (New Brunswick, N.J.: Transaction Publishers, 1990), 18. Among others, Lipset cites Lucy Dawidowicz, *On Equal Terms: Jews in America 1881–1981* (New York: Holt, Rinehart and Winston, 1982), 131–32. Two-thirds disagreed with the position that virtually all positions are open to U.S. Jews.

13. Steven M. Cohen, *The Political Attitudes of American Jews, 1988: A National Survey in Comparative Perspective* (New York: American Jewish Committee, 1989). Cited by Lipset, ed., *American Pluralism*, 22.

14. See, for example, Jerome Chanes, "Antisemitism and Jewish Security in America Today: Interpreting the Data. Why Can't Jews Take 'Yes' for an

Answer?," in *Antisemitism in America Today* (New York: Birch Lane Press, 1995), 3–30.

15. See Lipset, ed., *American Pluralism*, 22.

16. Appears in her semi-autobiographical book: *Fear of Fifty* (New York: Harper Collins, 1994).

17. Ibid., 79.

18. Isaac Bashevis Singer, *The Slave* (New York: Farrar, Straus and Giroux, 1979), 108.

19. Judges, II, 11–14.

20. Judges, II, 20–23, and III, 1–6.

21. See, e.g., Ben Halpern, "Reactions to Antisemitism in Modern Jewish History," in Jehuda Reinharz, ed., *Living with Antisemitism* (Hanover, N.H.: Univ. Press of New England, 1987).

22. Jacob Katz, "The Historical Image of Rabbi Zvi Hirsch Kalischer," *Jewish Nationalism: Essays and Studies* (in Hebrew) (Jerusalem: Zionist Library of the World Zionist Organization, 1979), 285–307.

23. Ben Halpern, "Reactions," 3–15.

Notes to Chapter 4

1. Barry Rubin, *Assimilation and Its Discontents* (New York: Times Books, 1995), 252.

2. Sara Bershtel and Allen Graubard, *Saving Remnants: Feeling Jewish in America* (New York: Free Press, 1992), 22.

3. See Irving Howe, *Land of Our Fathers: The Journey of the East European Jews to America and the Life They Found and Made* (New York: Simon and Schuster, 1976).

4. See Arthur Hertzberg, *The Jews in America. Four Centuries of an Uneasy Encounter: A History* (New York: Simon and Schuster, 1989), 152–95.

5. For one of the most distressingly memorable depictions, see Henry Roth, *Call It Sleep* (1934; New York: Avon Books, 1964).

6. See Deborah Dash Moore, *At Home in America* (New York: Columbia Univ. Press, 1981).

7. See the very important essay by Ben Halpern, "America Is Different," *The American Jew* (New York: Theodor Herzl Foundation, 1956), reprinted in Marshall Sklare, ed., *The Jews: Social Patterns of an American Group* (New York: Free Press, 1958), 23–39.

8. See Charles Silberman, *A Certain People: American Jews and Their Lives Today* (New York: Summit Books, 1986), for a variety of statistical and anecdotal evidence.

9. For a review of these practices, see Charles Stember, ed., *Jews in the Mind of America* (New York: Basic Books, 1966), and Silberman, *A Certain People*.

10. See Leonard Dinnerstein, *Antisemitism in America* (New York: Oxford University Press, 1994), and David A. Gerber, ed., *Antisemitism in American History* (Urbana and Chicago: Univ. of Illinois Press, 1986). For survey data and analysis since the prewar era, see Harold Quinley and Charles Glock, *Antisemitism in America* (New York: Free Press, 1979). Much statistical material is collected in Herbert Stember et al., *Jews in the Mind of America* (New York: Basic Books, 1966).

11. See Silberman, *A Certain People*, for a stunning catalogue of American Jewish achievement.

12. As reported by Alan Ryan in *New York Review of Books*, Nov. 17, 1994, p. 8 n. 2.

13. Leonard Fein, *Where Are We?: The Inner Life of American Jews* (New York: Harper and Row, 1988), 8.

14. See David Schoem's very sobering "Learning to Be a Part-Time Jew," in Walter P. Zenner, ed., *Persistence and Flexibility: Anthropological Perspectives on the American Jewish Experience* (Albany: State Univ. of New York Press, 1988), 96–116.

15. See Deborah Dash Moore, *To the Golden Cities: Pursuing the American Jewish Dream in Miami and L.A.* (New York: Free Press, 1994).

16. The survey was conducted by Steven M. Cohen. It is described with greater detail in Charles S. Liebman and Steven M. Cohen, *Two Worlds of Judaism: The Israeli and American Experiences* (New Haven: Yale Univ. Press, 1990), chap. 3.

17. Most of these studies were conducted by Steven M. Cohen for the American Jewish Committee or are cited by him in his report of these studies. Two such studies are: "Unity and Polarization in Judaism Today: The Attitudes of American and Israeli Jews" and "The Political Attitudes of American Jews, 1988: A National Survey in Comparative Perspective." Both of these reports were published by the American Jewish Committee in 1988.

18. Rashi, Genesis 23:4.

19. See Tractate *Avodah Zarah* 27A and 29A.

20. The Lubavicher Rebbe is cited as having observed (early fall 1976) in regard to peace talks in the Middle East: "Jewish lives are put in danger because of reliance on the Goy's promises, despite its being very clear what kind of trustworthiness he has . . . . " See *Ha'Aretz*, April 20, 1996, p. A2.

21. *Midrash Raba* chapter 32:5 relating to Parshat Emor (Leviticus).

22. Bershtel and Graubard, *Saving Remnants*, 79–80.

23. Ibid., 80.

24. Arthur Hertzberg, "How Jews Use Antisemitism," in Jerome Chanes, ed., *Antisemitism in America Today* (New York: Birch Lane Press, 1995), 337–47.

25. Ibid., 342.

26. Bershtel and Graubard, *Saving Remnants*, 119.

27. Ibid., 118.

28. Michael Lerner, *Jewish Renewal: A Path to Healing and Transformation* (1944; HarperPerennial edition, 1995), 202.

29. James Young, *The Texture of Memory* (New Haven: Yale Univ. Press, 1993), 348.

30. Ibid., 348–49.

31. Ibid., 347.

32. Sidney Bolkosky, Betty Rotberg Ellias, and David Harris, *Life Unworthy of Life: A Holocaust Curriculum* (Farmington Hills, Mich.: Center for the Study of the Child, 1987), 176.

33. Jonathan Woocher, *Sacred Survival: The Civil Religion of American Jews* (Bloomington: Indiana Univ. Press, 1986), 77.

34. Silberman, *A Certain People*, 185.

35. Nathan Glazer, *American Judaism* (Chicago: Univ. of Chicago Press, 1957), cited by ibid., 204.

36. Young, *Texture of Memory*, 348.

37. Marshall Sklare and Joseph Greenblum, *Jewish Identity on the Suburban Frontier* (New York: Basic Books, 1967). The book appeared almost a decade after the research was done.

38. Ibid., 7.

39. The report, originally published in *Midstream*, was reprinted in a collection of Sklare's essays under the title *Observing America's Jews* (Hanover: Univ. Press of New England, 1993), 107–27.

40. Ibid., 110.

41. Arthur Hertzberg, "Israel and American Jewry," *Commentary* 44 (Aug. 1967): 69.

42. Ibid., See also Sklare, *Observing American Jews*, 115.

43. Ibid., 113.

44. Ibid., 115.

45. Ibid., 116.

46. Ibid., 117.

47. Ibid.

48. Hertzberg, "Israel and American Jewry," 72.

49. Sklare, *Observing American Jews*, 126–27.

50. Steven M. Cohen, "Israel in the Jewish Identity of American Jews: A Study in Dualities and Contrasts," in David Gordis and Yoav Ben-Horin, eds., *Jewish Identity in America* (Los Angeles: Univ. of Judaism, 1991), 128.

51. Ibid.

Notes to Chapter 5

Epigraph: Cited by Sara Bershtel and Allen Graubard from an interview with an anonymous American Jew in their *Saving Remnants: Feeling Jewish in America* (New York: Free Press, 1992), 43.

1. See, e.g., Jacob Neusner, *Strangers at Home: "The Holocaust," Zionism, and American Judaism* (Chicago: Univ. of Chicago Press, 1981).

2. *Portnoy's Complaint* (New York: Bantam Books, 1972), 84.

3. We, of course, mean this term in its American rather than in the very different Israeli or European sense. Liberalism here entails a commitment to social justice, to human rights, and to the welfare of the disadvantaged.

4. Steven M. Cohen and Charles S. Liebman, "American Jewish Liberalism: Unraveling the Strands," *Public Opinion Quarterly*, 61 (Fall, 1997), 405–430.

5. John Dos Passos, *Airways, Inc.* (New York: Macaulay, 1928), 53–54. The following monologue emphasizes how close reformist-radical attitudes and Jewishness are often perceived to be:

"The fact that we were Jewish Communists was not accidental; somehow it all fit together. Being a Communist and being a Jew were part of the same ineffable thing. The connection wasn't something we thought about at the time, it was just a given. My own kids have the same feeling. My sons believed that there are Jews and there are Republicans; those are the two groups in the world. When they first encountered Jews they considered reactionary, they were shocked. They didn't quite know how to deal with it."

Mickey Flacks speaking in Bershtel and Graubard, *Saving Remnants*, 242.

6. Cited by Henry Lewis Gates from a letter sent to him, *New York Times*, April 14, 1993, OP-ED page.

7. For an analysis of the data, see Steven M. Cohen, *The Dimensions of American Jewish Liberalism* (New York: American Jewish Committee, 1989).

8. Leonard Fein is an important spokesman for this position. See his *Where Are We? The Inner Life of American Jews* (New York: Harper and Row, 1988), esp. chap. 11, "Politics as a Vocation." See also his pamphlet, *Smashing Idols and Other Prescriptions for Jewish Continuity* (New York: Nathan Cummings Foundation, 1994). In the introduction, Rachel Cowan, director of the Foundation's Jewish Life program, notes that " . . . with Fein we believe that the vitality of the American Jewish community in the coming decades depends on an enhanced commitment to social justice . . . . "

9. Chaim Waxman, *Jewish Baby Boomers* (Albany: State Univ. of New York Press, 1998).

10. An interesting historical parallel to this phenomenon can be found in the historical reception of John Locke's celebrated *Letter on Toleration*. It remains one of the central sources for toleration and mutual respect in the liberal tradition, even though Locke acknowledged the justice of restricting the liberty of Catholics and atheists. These restrictions do not diminish our debt to Locke. We tend to accept the principles he enunciates and attribute the shortcomings to the effects of time and place.

11. Charles S. Liebman and Steven M. Cohen, "Jewish Liberalism Revisited," *Commentary* 102 (Nov. 1996): 51–53. The data are based on Steven M. Cohen and Charles S. Liebman, "American Jewish Liberalism: Unraveling the Strands," *Public Opinion Quarterly* 61 (Fall: 1997), 405–430.

12. The retreat from organizational affiliations and collective activities is not peculiar to American Jewry. It has been the subject of a great deal of well-known research. See Robert Bellah et al., *Habits of the Heart: Individualism and Commitment in American Life* (New York: Harper and Row, 1985). See also Robert Putnam's *Making Democracy Work: Civic Traditions in Modern Italy* (Princeton, N.J.: Princeton Univ. Press, 1993) and especially his much-discussed "Bowling Alone: America's Declining Social Capital," *Journal of Democracy* (Jan. 1995).

13. On the lower levels of participation by younger Jews, see Chaim Waxman, "Religious and Ethnic Patterns of American Jewish Baby Boomers," *Journal for the Scientific Study of Religion* 33 (March 1994): 74–80.

14. See Bernard Reisman, *The Chavurah: A Contemporary Jewish Experience* (New York: Union of American Hebrew Congregations, 1977), and Riv-Ellen Prell, *Prayer and Community: The Havura Movement in American Judaism* (Detroit: Wayne State Univ. Press, 1989). An excellent case study of one havura is Chava Weisler, *Making Judaism Meaningful: Ambivalence and Tradition in a Havura Community* (New York: AMS Press, 1989).

15. Michael Lerner, *Jewish Renewal: A Path to Healing and Transformation* (New York: G. P. Putnam, 1994).

16. These characteristics were first suggested in Charles S. Liebman and Steven M. Cohen, *Two Worlds of Judaism: The Jewish Experience in Israel and the United States* (New Haven: Yale Univ. Press, 1990).

17. See Bershtel and Graubard, *Saving Remnants*, 231.

18. *Supplementary Prayer Book: Guardian of Israel* (1986).

19. James S. Hirsch, "An Exodus from Tradition," *Wall Street Journal*, April 5, 1996, p. 8A, cited in Sylvia Barack Fishman, *Negotiating Both Sides of the Hyphen: Coalescence, Compartmentalization and American-Jewish Values* (Cincinnati: Judaic Studies Program, Univ. of Cincinnati, 1996), 21.

20. Cited in Charles Liebman, *Deceptive Images: Towards a Redefinition of American Judaism* (New Brunswick: Transaction Books, 1988), 83.

21. *Connecticut Jewish Ledger*, July 31, 1986, p. 2.

22. Rabbi Barry Friedman as cited in Bershtel and Graubard, *Saving Remnants*, 146–49.

23. Marshall Sklare and Joseph Greenblum, *Jewish Identity on the Suburban Frontier* (New York: Basic Books, 1967), 89.

24. The study from which this material has been drawn has not yet been published. We are indebted to Steven M. Cohen for the information. A summary report of the study is found in Jack Wertheimer, *Conservative Synagogues and Their Members: Highlights of the North American Survey of 1995–1996* (New York: Jewish Theological Seminary, 1996).

25. Fishman, *Negotiating Both Sides*, 40.

26. See Bershtel and Graubard, *Saving Remnants*, 225–26.

27. Ibid., 224.

28. Ibid., 234–35.

29. Probably the best place to explore the character of the personalist Jewish revival in its more restrained and mainstream form is the very popular best-seller, *The Jewish Catalogue*, compiled and edited by Richard Siegel, Michael Strassfield, and Sharon Strassfield (Philadelphia: Jewish Publication Society of America, 1975).

30. Sklare and Goldblum, *Jewish Identity*, 48.

31. For a summary of the data see Barry Kosmin et al., *Highlights of the CJF 1990 National Jewish Population Survey* (New York: Council of Jewish Federations, 1991).

32. The information was obtained in private communication. The study, by Bruce Phillips, commissioned by the Wilstein Institute for Jewish Policy Analysis, is as yet unpublished.

33. Mary Waters, *Ethnic Options: Choosing Identities in America* (Berkeley: Univ. of California Press, 1990).

34. Leonard Fein, *Where Are We: The Inner Life of American Jews* (New York: Harper and Row, 1988), 26.

35. Ibid., 27–28.

36. Jeffrey Dekro, "Prayer and Anger," *Response*, no. 46 (Spring 1984): 73.

37. Temple Beth Ami (n.d.).

38. Calvin Goldscheider and Alan Zuckerman, *The Transformation of the Jews* (Chicago: Univ. of Chicago Press, 1984).

39. Steven Cohen, *Unity and Polarization in Judaism Today: The Attitudes of American and Israeli Jews* (New York: American Jewish Committee, 1988).

40. Egon Mayer and Amy Avgar, *Conversations among Intermarried Jews* (New York: American Jewish Committee, 1987), 9.

41. Amy Richards, "I Wish to be a Jew. My Husband Doesn't," *Sh'ma* 17, no. 326 (1987): 41.

42. Anne Anderson, "My Support Is Real—So Are My Memories," *Sh'ma* 17, no. 326 (1987): 42–43.

43. Ibid., 43.

44. Ibid., 44.

45. Sharon Haber, "Gaining a Faith but Not Losing a Family," *Sh'ma* 17, no. 327 (1987): 51.

46. *Commentary* 84 (Sept. 1987): 78.

47. In one of her most successful stories, *Are You There God? It's Me, Margaret* (New York: Dell, 1970), Judy Blume, the best-selling writer of children's books, recounts the tale of young Margaret, growing up in a mixed Jewish-Christian family, beset by doubts as to where she belongs religiously. The personalist themes, borderless identities, and undifferentiated "spirituality" we have been discussing come through clearly in her final summation written for her teacher, a summation that serves quite well as a youthful credo for our times:

> I have conducted a year-long experiment in religion. I have not come to any conclusions about what religion I want to be when I grow up—if I want to be any special religion at all. I have read three books on the subject. They are: *Modern Judaism, A History of Christianity*, and *Catholicism—Past and Present*. I went to church services at the First Presbyterian Church of Farbrook. I went to the United Methodist Church of Farbrook on Christmas Eve. I attended Temple Israel of New York City on Rosh Hashannah, which is a Jewish holiday. I went to Confession at Saint Bartholomew Church, but I had to leave the Confessional because I didn't know what to say. I have not tried being a Buddist or a Moslem because I don't know any people of these religions. I have not really enjoyed my religious experiments very much and I don't think I'll make up my mind one way or the other for a long time. I don't think a person can decide to be a certain religion just like that. It's like having to choose your own name. You think about it a long time and then you keep changing your mind. . . .

48. The volume is described in the Jewish Telegraphic Agency bulletin, "Community News Reporter," Aug. 21, 1996, p. 3.

49. See, for example, Bernard Lazerwitz, "Jewish-Christian Marriages and Conversions, 1971 to 1990," *Sociology of Religion* 56 (Winter 1995): 433–43.

50. See, for example, the brochure *Gateways* referred to above. Rabbi Amy Walker Katz writes in a recent issue of *Sh'ma* (Jan. 5, 1996, p. 6):

> When I was a rabbinical school student at the Jewish Theological Seminary of America, I was certain about my position on intermarriage. I strongly believed that intermarriage was detrimental to the continuity of the American Jewish community and needed to be discouraged. It seemed obvious to me that intermarried couples should not be made to feel welcome in synagogue because to do so tacitly condones intermarriage. . . .

> After my ordination in 1992 . . . my interaction with some of the intermarried couples in the synagogue forced me to reconsider my views about the manner in which intermarried couples ought to be treated in the synagogue.

Notes to Chapter 6

1. Only those with a very limited sense of Israeli reality can suggest, as Norman Cantor did in *The Sacred Chain: The History of the Jews* (New York: Harper Collins, 1994), that Israeli Jews will soon fade into a new "Near-Eastern Arab culture" (425).

2. This view is expressly articulated in some important texts in the Jewish liturgy. For example, one of the central Hanukkah prayers, which describes the Jewish victory over the Syrian Greeks, says that God "delivered the strong into the hands of the weak, the many into the hands of the few, the defiled into the hands of the pure, the evil into the hands of the just, the insolent into the hands of those who occupy themselves with Your Torah. . . . "

3. For example, the Haredi member of Knesset, Rabbi Ravitz, as reported in *Ha'Aretz*, July 14, 1996, p. 1.

4. Benny Eilon on July 11, 1996 on channel 1 of Israeli TV, in the context of a program entitled "Two Brothers."

5. Dr. Yair Hirshfeld, as reported in *Ha'Aretz*, July 31, 1996, p. 1.

6. A notable case of contemporary Israeli issues being debated in Jewish historical terms is the controversy over the status of Bar Kochba, the zealous leader of the insurrection against Rome in the second century C.E. Yehoshafat Harkabi saw Bar Kochba's vehement and uncompromising commitment to Jewish independence from Rome (rather than adopting a moderate policy of prudence, compromise, and realism) as leading the Jewish people to tragedy and exile—with overt parallels to the contemporary zealots whose all-or-nothing messianic style of "settlement" politics was leading Israel to a contemporary calamity. Harkabi's argument was criticized in the press by a number of right-wing writers who defended Bar Kochba as an authentic Jewish hero and, concurrently, justified the politics of the settlers. See Yehoshafat Harkabi, *Facing Reality: Lessons from Jeremiah, the Destruction of the Second Temple and Bar Kochva's Rebellion*, with comments by Avigdor Lewontin and Michael Rosenak (Jerusalem: Van Leer Jerusalem Foundation, 1981).

7. See the discussion of the Guttman Report in this chapter.

8. There are even substantial Jewish elements in Israel's foreign policy, for example, the sense of responsibility for Diaspora Jewish communities in distress. See Shmuel Sandler, "Is There a Jewish Foreign Policy?," *Jewish Journal of Sociology* 29 (Dec. 1987): 115–21.

9. See Chapter 5 above.

10. However, there is some evidence of growing dissatisfaction among well-educated, middle-class Orthodox women. This has already resulted in changed attitudes, a changed rhetoric, and even some changes in practice.

11. The current exodus of Jews from the former Soviet Union represents a third wave. They too have not undergone this liberal-pluralist-individualist transformation, although their connection with things Jewish, after decades of Soviet rule, is quite tenuous.

12. It was authored by Shlomit Levy, Hanna Levinsohn, and Elihu Katz and published as *Beliefs, Observances and Social Interaction among Israeli Jews* (Jerusalem, 1993). A concise summary of the findings was concurrently published under the same title. The study was commissioned and funded by the Avi Chai Foundation. Henceforth it will be referred to as the Guttman Report. The results of the report are analyzed in Charles Liebman and Elihu Katz, eds., *The Jewishness of Israelis: Responses to the Guttman Report* (Ithaca: State Univ. of New York Press, 1997). Another large-scale, even more recent survey is Yaacov Ezrachi and Reuven Gal, *The World-Views and Positions of High-School Students in Regard to Social Issues, Security and Peace* (in Hebrew), 2 vols. (Zichron Yaacov: Carmel Institute for Social Research, 1995).

13. See Charles Liebman, "Tradition, Judaism and Jewish Religion in Contemporary Israeli Society," in Jack Wertheimer, ed., *The Uses of Tradition* (Cambridge: Harvard Univ. Press, 1992), 411-28, and Charles Liebman and Steven Cohen, *Two Worlds of Judaism: The Jewish Experience in Israel and the United States* (New Haven: Yale Univ. Press, 1991).

14. Reported in *Ha'Aretz*, April 29, 1996, p. B2. In considering its campaign strategy for the 1996 election, the National Religious Party contemplated using the slogan: "Zionism without Cynicism." In surveys it conducted, cynical forms of Zionism were associated with being Ashkenazi and intelligent.

15. Barry Kosmin and Seymour Lachman, *One Nation Under God: Religion in Contemporary American Society* (New York: Random House, 1993), 121.

16. Bethamie Horowitz, "Jewishness in New York: Exception or Rule?," paper delivered at the conference on National and Cultural Variations in Jewish Identity and Their Implications for Jewish Education, Jerusalem, January 1994. The Orthodox represent 15 percent of the New York sample, roughly equivalent to the 14 percent of the Guttman Institute sample who report they are "strictly observant." Nevertheless, it is less than the 23 percent of the Guttman sample who characterized themselves as "religious." Still, if we add Conservative Jews who substantially adhere to religious law (about a quarter of New York's Conservative Jews) we arrive at a comparable figure. The New York report was published under the title *The 1991 New York Jewish Population Study* by Bethamie Horowitz (New York: United Jewish Appeal—Federation of Jewish Philanthropies of New York, 1993).

17. Ronald Ingelhart, *Culture Shifts in Advanced Industrial Societies* (Princeton: Princeton Univ. Press, 1990), 187.

18. Guttman Report, 40.

19. Even a relatively cosmopolitan newspaper such as *Ha'Aretz* devotes no more than a very small fraction of its pages (less than a tenth, we would guess) to world issues that do not have a Middle Eastern or a Jewish connection.

20. *Yediot Aharonot*, Nov. 22, 1996, p. 1.

21. See Ingelhart, *Culture Shifts*, 177–78.

22. Asher Arian, Ilan Talmud, and Tamar Hermann, *National Security and Public Opinion in Israel* (Boulder, Colo.: Westview Press, published for the Jaffee Center for Strategic Studies, Tel Aviv University, 1988).

23. Daniel Bar-Tal and Dikla Antebi, "Siege Mentality in Israel," *International Journal of Intercultural Relations* 16 (1992): 251–75. Also by Bar-Tal and Antebi, "Beliefs About Negative Intentions of the World: A Study of the Israeli Siege Mentality," *Political Psychology* 13, no. 4 (1992): 633–45.

24. See Arian et al., *National Security*, 48.

25. Ibid.

26. Ibid., 80.

27. The study by Shlomit Levy was commissioned by the Vidal Sassoon Center for the Study of Antisemitism of Tel Aviv University and reported in Eliyahu Salpeter, "The Whole World Is Still Against Us," *Ha'Aretz*, Dec. 25, 1996, p. 1B.

28. Arian et al., *National Security*, 46.

29. Ibid., 84.

29. Ibid.

30. See Charles Liebman, *Attitudes Toward Jewish-Gentile Relations in the Jewish Tradition and Contemporary Israel* (Occasional Papers, Kaplan Center, University of Cape Town, 1984).

31. Myron Aronoff, "The Origins of Israeli Political Culture," in Ehud Sprinzak and Larry Diamond, eds., *Israeli Democracy under Stress* (Boulder, Colo.: Lynne Rienner, 1993), 58.

32. Ibid., 178.

33. See Elihu Katz, Yaacov Trope, and Hadassah Haas, "Integration in Army and Nation: An Essay in Institutional Permeability," in Eric Cohen, Moshe Lissak, and Uri Almagor, eds., *Comparative Social Dynamics: Essays in Honor of S. N. Eisenstadt* (Boulder; Colo.: Westview Press, 1985), 315–33.

Notes to Chapter 7

1. Poll reported in *Ma'ariv*, Aug. 12, 1996, p. B2.

2. As reported by the Geocartographic Institute (a polling company), Dec. 2, 1996.

3. See, for example, *Ha'Aretz*, Nov. 22, 1996, p. D1. Even the most perfunctory review will establish that the image of two cultures pervades the religious press as well.

4. Although parts of the ultra-Orthodox community share dovish ideas with the Labor Party, their natural affinity is with the right because it never attempted to supplant Jewish tradition with alternative content.

5. See, for example, Amos Oz's magisterial lecture, presented at Bar Ilan University, Nov. 17, 1996. Summaries were printed in *Ma'ariv*, Nov. 18, 1996, p. 6, and *Hatzophe*, Nov. 26, 1996, p. 4. The full text of the lecture has yet to be published.

6. Baruch Kimmerling, "Religion, Nationalism and Democracy in Israel" (in Hebrew), *Zmanim*, nos. 50–51, thirteen (Winter 1994): 129.

7. This is an old theme in Zionist literature. C. N. Bialik, modern Hebrew's poet laureate, wrote in one of his most celebrated poems, *Hamatmid* (The Diligent One), that whatever we, the worldly and wayward, may do, it is the diligent one, sitting day and night before the tractate of Talmud, who is the secret of Jewish survival.

8. Dedi Zucker in *Ha'Aretz* weekend magazine, Nov. 22, 1996, p. 11.

9. Orit Shochat, *Ha'Aretz*, Nov. 15, 1996, p. B1.

10. See, for example, Eliezer Don-Yehiya, "Religion and Ethnicity in Israeli Politics: The Religious Parties and the Elections to the 12th Knesset" (in Hebrew), *State, Government and International Relations* 32 (Spring 1990): 11–54.

11. Some preliminary figures and analysis are available in Shevach Weiss, *Analysis of the Election Results to the 14th Knesset and for the Prime Minister: 1996* (Labor Party, 1996), 99–117.

12. It should be made clear that this rather nonchalant approach toward Orthodox hegemony over Jewish identity in no way reflects a similar attitude toward Jewish self-identification itself. Jewishness as a category of self-identification consistently scores in the 90+% range. Very notably, in a 1996 survey by Professor Sammy Smooha, 58% of Israeli Jews would prefer a Jewish state that was not democratic to a democratic state that was not Jewish. Reported in *Ha'Aretz*, Dec. 4, 1996, p. 9A.

13. In this regard, the authors recall a lecture given by Jerusalem's mayor, Ehud Olmert, at a conference (Dec. 1993) on the findings of the Guttman Report. Olmert, a secular, cosmopolitan figure with distinctly bon vivant tastes, described a visit to New York in which his hosts took him to the very formal and stately Reform synagogue, Temple Emmanuel. Olmert, expressing the relief of one who can relax in the company of a sympathetic Israeli audience, described his intense unease with the churchy atmosphere, the darkened sanctuary, the ethereally chanting choir. If I'm not going to go to a synagogue, he cracked, it will be an Orthodox one.

14. See the interview with Amos Oz, "I Would Switch My Political Alliance from the 'Hellinizing' Left to a Spiritual Alliance with Religious Zionism," *Hatzophe*, March 8, 1996, p. 7.

15. See "It's Beginning to Look a Lot Like . . . ," *Jerusalem Post Magazine*, Dec. 23, 1994, pp. 12–15.

16. Efraim Inbar, "Contours of Israel's New Strategic Thinking," *Political Science Quarterly* 111, no. 1 (1996): 56. The former Chief of Staff, General Ehud Barak, echoes this message. Weariness, cynicism, and the demythologizing of Zionism create "a perception as well as a reality of weakness."

17. There is, as of this writing, no scholarly book or article that treats post-Zionism and its critics in a systematic manner, although a number of such studies are in preparation. A compendium of scholarly articles on the whole gamut of topics related to post-Zionism, including literature, history, sociology, politics, and Jewish thought, is available in Pinhas Ginossar and Avi Bareli, eds., *Zionism: A Contemporary Controversy: Research Trends and Ideological Approaches* (in Hebrew) (Sede Boquer: Ben-Gurion Research Center, Ben-Gurion Univ. of the Negev Press, 1996). The discussion of post-Zionism assumed popular dimensions in the summer of 1994 with the publication by the Israeli writer Aharon Meged of "The Suicide Wish of the Israeli," *Ha'Aretz*, June 10, 1994 and in English "Self-Hatred in the Jewish State," *Avar ve'Atid: A Journal of Jewish Education, Culture and Discourse* 2 (Sept. 1995): 36–40. Post-Zionists replied with vigor in the weeks that followed (one of the articles by Benny Morris, "My Response to Aharon Meged," was translated into English in ibid., pp. 41–44). These were answered no less vigorously by their critics. The sense that denuding Israel of its Jewish character is the primary item on the post-Zionist agenda was articulated by the distinguished historian of modern Israel, Anita Shapiro, in an interview with her in *Yediot Aharonot*'s literary supplement (Dec. 23, 1994). Post-Zionist thought is to be found in the pages of two Hebrew language journals, *Teoria U'Bikoret* (Theory and Criticism), published by the Van Leer Institute and, more selectively, in the pages of *Zmanim* (Times), a publication of Tel Aviv University's School of History. Many of the editorial and feature writers of *Ha'Aretz*, Israel's most prestigious daily newspaper, are sympathetic to post-Zionist themes. See, for example, Orit Schochat, "Who Is a Post-Zionist?" (Sept. 1, 1995). Post-Zionists are best known as historical revisionists—one phrase (attributed to Benny Morris) that catches their mood is "The state of Israeli was born in sin." There have been a number of articles replying to post-Zionists. Shabtai Teveth has been especially active in this regard and mention should be made of his reply to the post-Zionist attacks on Zionist behavior during the Holocaust in his recent volume, *Ben-Gurion and the Holocaust* (New York: Harcourt Brace, 1996). Many though not all of the contributors to a volume by Uri Ram, ed., *Israeli Society: Critical Perspectives* (in Hebrew) (Tel

Aviv: Breirot, 1993), are broadly post-Zionist in approach. For a critical evaluation of their work in sociology, see Moshe Lissak, "Notes on the Debate
between 'Critical' and 'Establishment' Sociology in Israel," *Israel Studies Bulletin* 11, no. 1 (Fall 1995), and " 'Critical' Sociology and 'Establishment' Sociology in the Israeli Academic Community: Ideological Struggles or Academic
Discourse?," *Israel Studies* 1 (Spring 1996): 247–94. A sizable proportion of the
articles on politics that appeared in the first three annuals, *Critical Essays on
Israeli Social Issues and Scholarship: Books on Israel*, 3 vols., are written from a
post-Zionist perspective.

18. Stuart Schoffman writes in the *Jerusalem Report*: "The Jewish World
According to 'Country Gimel' [a posh health and sports club in the upscale Tel
Aviv suburb of Ramat Aviv Gimel] is the *reductio ad absurdum* of Zionist spiri-
tual *yerida* [lit: 'going down' or leaving Israel]. Emigration and assimilation right
here at home, without the airfare or the guilt." Cited by Frederick Krantz in
"The Impact of the Peace Process on Israel-Diaspora Relations," *The Jewish
World in Turmoil* (Jerusalem: World Zionist Organization "Seminars on Zionist
Thought," papers delivered at the Second Pan-American Academic Conference
held in Rio de Janeiro, Brazil, 1995), 12–25.

19. There are, of course, intermediate positions of many shades between
accommodationist secularism and post-Zionism. We refrain from exploring
them because they add little to our argument.

20. For accuracy's sake it should be noted that not all "new historians" are
also post-Zionists. This is especially true of Benny Morris, the ground-breaking
historian of the War of Independence.

21. See Boas Evron, "Medina Ke'hilchata" (in Hebrew), *Eeton* 77, no. 196
(May 1996): 20–21.

22. *Ha'Aretz* conducted a symposium under the title "Zionism, Post-Zionism and Anti-Zionism" that was translated into English and reprinted in
Newsletter no. 21 (March 1996) of the "Seminars on Zionist Thought" published by the World Zionist Organization. The quote from the journalist and
author Tom Segev is on 11–12.

23. Amos Elon, "Israel and the End of Zionism," *New York Review of Books*
43 (Dec. 19, 1966): 27–28.

24. Many but certainly not all. Some argue that the intrusive vulgarity and
conformism of the "Madonna-McDonalds" culture has decimated the remains
of a self-confident and autonomous secular Jewish culture in Israel and has con-
ferred legitimacy on the various religious groups who attempt to fill the void.
See, for example, Doron Rosenbloom, "Now Hurry and Put on a Yarmulke,"
Ha'Aretz, Dec. 13, 1996, p. B1.

25. Gideon Samet, "The Nation Goes Up a Grade," *Ha'Aretz*, July 28, 1995,
p. 1B.

26. Dan Urian, "The Stereotype of the Religious Jew in Israeli Theater," *Assaph C*, no. 10 (1994): 131–54.

27. Gadi Yatziv, "Separation, Not Unity," *Ha'Aretz*, Oct. 30, 1996, p. B2.

28. Yoram Kanyuk, "Let's Divide," *Ha'Aretz*, Nov. 12, 1996, p. B2.

29. "When we search for a national attribute that is common to all Jews, in the East and the West, in India and Ethiopia, as in Germany and Sweden, we find nothing except for a common religion. Apart from religion, they are as different from each other as an Ethiopian Christian from an English Christian. Therefore, when the state defines itself as Jewish and the question 'Who is a Jew' is posed in order to establish the eligibility [of individuals] for the positive discrimination the state endows upon its Jewish citizens, there is no definition acceptable to all apart from the Jewish definition." Evron, "Medina Ke'hilchata," 21.

30. Boas Evron, *Jewish State or Israeli Nation?* (Bloomington: Indiana Univ. Press, 1995), 202.

31. One interesting formulation is that of Robert Bellah, "Religion and the Legitimation of the American Republic," in Robert Bellah and Phillip Hammond, eds., *Varieties of Civil Religion* (New York: Harper and Row, 1980), 9. The point and its application to Israeli society is discussed in Charles S. Liebman and Eliezer Don Yehiya, "The Dilemma of Reconciling Traditional Culture and Political Needs: Civil Religion in Israel," *Comparative Politics* (Oct. 1983): 53–66.

32. See Bernard Susser and Eliezer Don Yehiya, "Israel and the Decline of the Nation-State in the West," *Modern Judaism* (May 1994): 187–202.

33. Prior to the post-Zionists, opposition to Zionism was almost invariably of diversely Marxist origin. Today, with the discrediting of Marxist thought, the inspiration for such opposition derives from liberal and post-Modernist radical ideas.

Notes to Chapter 8

1. One finds periodic references to interest in adult Jewish education, the revival of Klezmer music, the adoption of some form or another of Jewish ritual, and so on in publications such as the monthly *Moment Magazine* and in local Jewish weeklies, especially around the High Holiday period. The most systematic survey of American Jewish life that interprets all these signs as evidence of a renewal of Jewish life remains Charles Silberman's *A Certain People: Jews in America* (New York: Summit, 1985). Significantly, however, Silberman, in public lectures, has retracted his previously optimistic vision of the future of American Jewish life. On the other hand, there is no denying that some synagogues have succeeded in attracting growing numbers of members and evoking enthusiasm with regard to their modified and energetic services. (Lively guitar music

and congregational singing is often an important component.) In some cases, New York's congregation B'nai Jeshurun is the outstanding example, it is said that one must arrive from a half an hour to an hour before Friday night services in order to find a seat. However, what strikes us is that for many newly energized Jews, their Jewishness tends to slight the boundary-vindicating, pluralism-limiting themes that are imperative for Jewish survival.

2. *Forward*, Sept. 19, 1997, pp. 1, 4.

3. The preliminary findings are reported in Jack Wertheimer, *Conservative Synagogues and Their Members: Highlights of the North American Survey of 1995–96* (New York: Jewish Theological Seminary of America, 1996), and Jack Wertheimer, ed., *Jewish Identity and Religious Commitment: The North American Study of Conservative Synagogues and Their Members, 1995–1996* (New York: Jewish Theological Seminary of America, 1997).

4. According to the 1990 National Jewish Population Survey, the number of Jews who define themselves as Orthodox has declined as a percentage of the total Jewish population. The details are reported in Bernard Lazerwitz, J. Alan Winter, Arnold Dashefsky, and Ephraim Tabory, *Jewish Choices: American Jewish Denominationalism* (Albany: State Univ. of New York Press, 1998). But by every measure of communal vitality they are clearly on a steep upswing. Indeed, it is not too much to speak of their present mind-set as "triumphalist." The absence of numerical growth may be related to the fact that standards of Orthodoxy have become increasingly rigorous. Jews who heretofore defined themselves as Orthodox may no longer do so. This provides at least a partial explanation for denominational switching among American Jews. The movement from Orthodox to the less rigorous Conservative movement is very evident, according to the Jewish populations survey. On the other hand, "denominational switchers tend to be less Jewishly involved than are those who stay in the denomination in which they were reared" (89). When we couple the fact that the Orthodox seem increasingly successful in socializing their youngsters to their own norms, and they now have a far greater percentage of children 17 years or younger than do the Conservatives (p. 60), the latter the most aging of the Jewish denominational movements, even the numerical growth of Orthodoxy seems assured.

5. Jack Wertheimer, Charles Liebman, and Steven Cohen, "How to Save American Jews," *Commentary* 101 (Jan. 1996): 47–51.

6. J. J. Goldberg, *Jewish Power: Inside the American Jewish Establishment* (New York: Addison-Wesley, 1996).

7. For a discussion of the change they wrought, see Haym Soloveichik "Rupture and Reconstruction: The Transformation of Contemporary Orthodoxy," *Tradition* 28, no. 4, 1994, 64–121 and "Migration Acculturation, and the New Role of Text in the Haredi World," Martin Marty and R. Scott Appleby (eds.),

Accounting for Fundamentalism, The Dynamic Character of Movements (Chicago: Univ. of Chicago Press, The Fundamentalism Project, vol. 4, 1994), 197–235. The article was reproduced in an expanded version in pp. 64–121.

8. It should be noted nevertheless that there have been a number recent efforts within the Orthodox camp to interpret the Jewish tradition in more latitudinarian terms. The most intellectually serious of these efforts include the work of David Hartman, Moses Halbertal, and additional fellows of the Hartman Institute in Jerusalem, Gerald Blidstein of Ben-Gurion University, and Avi Sagi of Bar-Ilan University. But they are clearly a small minority within the Orthodox world.

9. *Pirke Avot*, 5: 22.

Notes to Chapter 9

1. On the comparison between U.S. and Israeli ultra-Orthodox, see, for example, Amnon Levy, "Anglo-Saxon Haredim," in Charles Liebman, ed., *Religious and Secular: Conflict and Accommodation Between Jews in Israel* (Jerusalem: Keter, 1990), 1–20. On the opposition of many religious Zionists to the antimodern, antisecular education stance of the religious-Zionist rabbis, see Yair Sheleg, "The New 'Holy Revolution' " (in Hebrew), *Gilyon*, Shevat, 1997, pp. 4–7.

2. "The secret of the vitality of culture is its historical continuation and continuity. Culture develops in organic forms from its sources, and the national self exists by preserving the continuity of national consciousness from generation to generation." Eliezer Schweid, *The Idea of Judaism as a Culture* (in Hebrew) (Tel Aviv: Am Oved, 1995), 174.

3. The opinion and controversies of this group are recorded in the journal *Yahadut Chofshit*, a publication of the Secular Israeli Movement for a Humanistic Judaism (Tnuah Hilonit Yisraelit L'Yahadut Humanistit).

4. Shlomit Levy, Hanna Levinsohn, and Elihu Katz, *Beliefs, Observances and Social Interaction Among Israeli Jews* (Jerusalem: Louis Guttman Israel Institute of Applied Social Research, 1993).

5. Peri Kedem, "Dimensions of Jewish Religiosity in Israel," in Zvi Sobel and Benjamin Beit-Hallahmi, eds., *Tradition, Innovation, Conflict: Jewishness and Judaism in Contemporary Israel* (Albany: State Univ. of New York Press, 1991), 251–77.

6. See Elihu Katz, "Behavioral and Phenomenological Jewishness," in Charles Liebman and Elihu Katz, eds., *The Jewishness of Israelis: Responses to the Guttman Report* (Albany: State Univ. of New York Press, 1997).

7. Yossi Klein Halevi, "Zionism, Phase II," *Jerusalem Report* 7, no. 17 (Dec. 26, 1996): 12–18. During the High Holiday season, Israel's major newspapers

carried full-page ads exhorting readers to accept and support what it spoke of as "a Jewish secular faith." It argued that the growing dominance of the Orthodox meant "less faith and more ritual, less Torah and more commandments, less morality and more Halakha, less Judaism and more religion." See, for example, *Yediot Ahronot*, Oct. 10, 1997, p. 18.

Notes to Chapter 10

1. Avi Sagi and Zeev Safrai, eds., *Between Authority and Autonomy in Jewish Tradition* (in Hebrew) (Tel Aviv: HaKibbutz HaMeuchad, 1997)

2. For a recent study, see William Helmreich, *Against All Odds: Holocaust Survivors and the Successful Lives They Made in America* (New York: Free Press, 1992).

3. For a moving literary exposition of these choices, see Chaim Grade's story, "My Quarrel with Hirsh Rezeiner," in Irving Howe and Eliezer Greenberg, eds., *A Treasury of Yiddish Stories* (New York: Schocken, 1958). It has been made into a film of exceptional power entitled *The Quarrel*.

4. See Emile Fackenheim, *The Jewish Return into History: Reflections in the Age of Auschwitz and a New Jerusalem* (New York: Schocken, 1978).

5. Bernard Wasserstein, *Vanishing Diaspora: The Jews in Europe Since 1945* (Cambridge, Mass.: Harvard Univ. Press, 1996).

A NOTE ON THE TYPE

This book was set in Trump Mediäval.

Trump Mediäval was designed by Georg Trump and
first issued in 1954 by the Weber Foundry in
Stuttgart, Germany.

Book design by Jeff Hoffman